D1065308

I'LL BE HERE IN THE MORNING

John and Robin Dickson Series in Texas Music

SPONSORED BY THE
CENTER FOR TEXAS MUSIC HISTORY
Texas State University–San Marcos
Gary Hartman, General Editor

A list of titles in this series appears at the back of the book.

I'LL BE HERE IN THE MORNING

THE SONGWRITING LEGACY OF TOWNES VAN ZANDT

BRIAN T. ATKINSON

Texas A&M University Press   College Station

This paper meets the requirements of
ANSI/NISO, Z39.48-1992 (Permanence of Paper).
Binding materials have been chosen for durability.

Library of Congress Cataloging-in-Publication Data

Atkinson, Brian T.
    I'll be here in the morning : the songwriting legacy of Townes Van
Zandt / Brian T. Atkinson. — 1st ed.
        p. cm. — (John and Robin Dickson series in Texas music)
    Includes selected discography.
    ISBN-13: 978-1-60344-526-9 (cloth : alk. paper)
    ISBN-10: 1-60344-526-9 (cloth : alk. paper)
    ISBN-13: 978-1-60344-527-6 (e-book)
    ISBN-10: 1-60344-527-7 (e-book)
    1. Van Zandt, Townes.   2. Van Zandt, Townes—Influence.
3. Country musicians—Texas—Biography.   4. Lyricists—Texas—
Biography.   5. Musicians—United States—20th century—
Interviews.   6. Country music—History and criticism.
I. Title.   II. Series: John and Robin Dickson series in
Texas music.
ML420.V248A85   2011
782.421642092—dc22
2011016691

All photos by author unless credited otherwise.
On the cover: Townes Van Zandt, Nijmegen, Holland, Novembr 13, 1996.
Courtesy Paul Needham, www.mohawkvisuals.com
Title Page: Art by Sean P. Tracey, Mosquito Studios; image courtesy Graham Leader

DEDICATED TO MY FATHER,
TED ATKINSON,
THE FINEST KIND

We don't care about material stuff. We want to hear the guitar ring one note correctly and your voice ring the same note correctly with the proper meaning correctly for that instant. Travel 5,000 miles all over and lose jackets and end up . . . looking like me, but if you hit that note, it goes around the world and maybe—this is not bragging but it's hopeful, kind of prayerful—maybe somehow [it will] connect up with a baby in England or Ireland or Ethiopia and somehow make a shade of difference. Plus, it keeps us off the streets.

—Townes Van Zandt, 1995

CONTENTS

FOREWORD

"COWBOY" JACK CLEMENT

I met Townes around 1966.[1] I wanted to help a friend of mine who worked for RCA make some money on the side, so I paid for a trip down to Houston and went to see a guy who owned the studio there. He kept talking about this guy named Townes Van Zandt. He played us some tapes, and we thought they were really good. We wound up signing Townes to a contract.

Townes was fun to work with, but he didn't think much of the recording process. He just wanted to have some action going. His weren't ordinary songs that people were singing. I knew they wouldn't be easy to get recorded, but I knew they had merit. *At My Window* was my favorite album, probably his most successful record and the best that I did with him. We did that here in the studio in my house. That picture of Townes at the window was taken in my kitchen. He was more mature by then, and we got along good.

Townes was a good guy. People loved him and still do. He wasn't morbid all the time. He had a great sense of humor. He wasn't like everybody else, and I like that. I always try to be different. Townes didn't have to try. He just was.

He has gotten a lot of respect along the way. I think his career will grow, even though he's passed away. Enough of his songs got out that he's pretty well known by now, and I think his legacy will endure. Endurance is important. Townes kept writing and believed in himself, believed that they were good songs. They were. He had faith. He never had a great amount of success, but his songs are still there. People remember them.

January 2011

FOREWORD

HAROLD F. EGGERS JR.

I met Townes in 1967, the year my brother Kevin signed him to his label, Poppy Records. We worked together over a span of twenty years. I started off as his road manager in 1976 and eventually became his manager, agent, and business partner. My music education was in the school of Townes, through the eyes and thoughts of this extremely intense and overwhelming spirit who was obsessed and consumed with songwriting, performing, and traveling.

Townes believed that you can't sing the blues unless you've lived them, and he lived them to the extremes and beyond. As Steve Earle has said, Townes would go to the depths of darkness where we were all afraid to go, and then he'd come back and tell us about them. Townes lived his songs right to the end. That may be what killed him.

The highway was Townes's home. "Normal" would be the last way of describing our travels, but I got used to the extreme craziness that Townes brought along with him. We zigzagged across North America and Europe, talking about his life, his songwriting, and all the highs and lows that haunted him daily. I feel very privileged that he chose me to work and travel with him, but the truth is that he always did what he wanted to do. I just held on for dear life as the years and miles flew by. It was always about where we were off to now. It was the going, not the getting there. That was part of the beauty and mystique of touring and working with this maddening and troubled artist.

Every show was different because Townes's extreme moods changed from day to day. I started recording his shows from the very beginning and continued throughout the entire time that I worked with him. We would listen to the recordings as we traveled, and his favorites were the darkest. I never got used to the intensity of his shows. His words and music rattled me every time. Townes's music and lyrics still run through my mind every day, even now. You can feel lines like "sorrow and solitude, these are the precious things" right to the bone.

I like the title *I'll Be Here in the Morning* for this book. A line from that Townes song—"There's no prettier sight than looking back on a town you left behind"—reminds me that we were always here and gone and on the road to the next show. In mid-1996, Townes recorded a duet of "I'll Be Here in the Morning" with Barb Donovan, who through opening many shows for Townes earned the distinction of being his favorite female singer-songwriter. While we were touring overseas later in that year, the German *Rolling Stone* magazine approached Townes for a unique recording to include on a CD with the publication. Townes suggested their duet. That compilation, *Rare Trax*, which included songs by major artists such as Sting and Sheryl Crow, was released the day that Townes died.

I think Townes would have felt honored by this book, with so many peers and younger artists recognizing him as a great songwriter. At the same time, he would say that there are many more important people to write a book about. He was very humble, shy, and unassuming. The international press called Townes one of our greatest songwriters and a living legend, but he always said a legend is someone who's dead. Townes was at peace just knowing that his words and music will go on forever.

February 2011

PREFACE

Oh, Loretta, she's my barroom girl, wears them sevens on her sleeve
Dances like a diamond shines, tells me lies I love to believe
—TVZ, *"Loretta," from* Flyin' Shoes

The tall, sleepy-eyed young man pulling drafts stepped out from behind the bar later that evening. He quietly took the stage. Cracked a corny joke. After all, we were in Galveston, Texas, raising glasses at the Old Quarter's sixth annual Townes Van Zandt Wake on New Year's Day 2003. Then, as I wrote for *No Depression* magazine, Hayes Carll coaxed Van Zandt's "Greensboro Woman" as breathlessly as the songwriter himself and journeyed even deeper into the heart of "Loretta." "In his fistful-of-*Exile* stomp through the ode to a barroom girl who 'dances like a diamond shines,'" the review said, "Carll summoned not only Van Zandt's ghost to the stage, but the spirits of Gram Parsons and Keith Richards as well."[1] Carll's poised and poignant delivery cannot be overstated.

As the fresh-faced songwriter resumed serving drinks, glimpses of his craft emerged. Carll mindfully stuffed bills in the till, but his peripheral glances froze snapshots real and imagined: strangers laughing too loudly, salty sea hands squaring off outside, locals swapping bring-your-own bottles. Five years later, the Houston-area native would release those hardscrabble vignettes on his breakthrough album *Trouble in Mind.* "Some will go to heaven / Some will never leave," he sings, "Pills in the tip jar, blood on the strings / Oh lord, I never thought I'd see these things."[2]

This book was born well after midnight that night when Carll pressed his debut album *Flowers and Liquor* (2002) into my palm as the Old Quarter's creaky front door closed behind us. As a measure of thanks for the unforgettable way he spun those tunes that New Year's Day and what his

(L-R) Rex "Wrecks" Bell, Hayes Carll. Old Quarter Acoustic Café, Galveston, TX, January 1, 2003

own music has meant to me since—effectively corralling the legends and spirits in this book as key instigators to move from Denver to Austin in early 2007—I would like to give the guy I called a "hotshot songwriter" the first words on Townes Van Zandt.[3]

"Townes ruined me and saved me at the same time," Carll says today. "I don't think there's anyone who's ever done or ever will do what he did, and as a young writer trying to figure out your own voice and how you're going to express yourself, it's sort of devastating and inspirational and painful and beautiful, all the emotions he was able to make you feel that no one else could. As a writer, you realize on some level that you're never going to be able to connect or channel that way. Ultimately, I realized that I couldn't do what he did.

"With Townes it was particularly tough, because you realize that on some level it feels like everything else is very trivial. I think probably Guy Clark feels that way. I can't imagine if [Townes was] your best friend and onetime pupil. Guy Clark's one of the greatest of all time, [but] Townes could write in ways that no one else could. I don't even know that I would want to. It's a heavy burden.

"I spent so many nights playing Townes's songs at the Old Quarter. [Owner] Rex [Bell]'s New Year's Day wake is an interesting gathering. You have this collection of people that could not be more different, everyone from suburbanite yuppie kids who are aspiring singer-songwriters to old prostitutes who were friends with Townes to old drug addicts who knew him in the day to legitimate, successful singer-songwriters to accountants from North Dakota. The Old Quarter only holds seventy people, but it's this collection of people who are there for one reason and from all walks of life.

"I never knew him. For me, it was just trying to interpret his songs. Rex in some ways is a channel for that. He is a direct connection to Townes, and he keeps that alive for many people, whether through the club and the memorabilia and the ability to sing a song or through the stories. For me, it was just hanging out with a guy who'd hung out with a guy. I mean, I love Rex, and he was a great friend and mentor to me, but there was always something about the fact that this was a guy who used to run with a guy who created this stuff. It was always kind of magical.

"I remember one time playing 'Flyin' Shoes' at the Old Quarter. I was twenty-two, and there was a woman at the bar who was probably fifty years old. After I got off stage, she said, 'Oh, that was cute.' You know, that was not what I was going for. I was trying to stir souls with the depth of this thing, but I hadn't lived it, and I didn't know what the fuck I was doing. I was trying to connect on a level that I wasn't ready to connect on. There's pain and life experience in Townes's music that you can't fake or even learn."[4]

Thanks to Sam Halpert for his book *Raymond Carver, An Oral Biography* (Iowa City: University of Iowa Press, 1995), Kathleen Hudson for the collection *Telling Stories, Writing Songs: An Album of Texas Songwriters* (Austin: The University of Texas Press, 2001), and George Plimpton for his oral biography *Truman Capote: In Which Various Friends, Enemies, Acquaintances and Detractors Recall His Turbulent Career* (New York: Anchor Books, 1997). Each served as theoretical guideposts. I wanted songwriters to tell Townes's story as they saw it, and my initial idea was to write nothing beyond the main introduction. However, the material clearly needed contextualization. I added chapter introductions to provide background and tie together the stories. Otherwise, the extent of my fingerprints on primary source material is minimal. I occasionally cut and pasted sections of an interview to improve flow. I edited out peripheral words and phrases when necessary (such as, if an interviewee said, "You know," or "I mean" repeatedly). I cut redundancies. If the interviewee simply left out a word (say, when citing a lyric), I added it. As can be assumed, I never deliberately changed words said by an interviewee except to correct factual errors or add clarity. Those passages are bracketed.

Of course, this book truly began one frigid Iowa City, Iowa, morning—if memory serves, the very month that Townes Van Zandt died—when a friend handed me a copy of Steve Earle's album *Train A Comin'* with no introduction or promise, unwittingly opening a new world. "They found her down beneath the stairs / That led to Gypsy Sally's," Earle sang at close. "In her hand when she died / Was a note that cried / Fare thee well, Tecumseh Valley."[5] Never had a melody carried more weight. Never has folk music—any music—sounded the same again.

Very special thanks to Tamara Saviano for creating this opportunity and many others, to John and Robin Dickson Series in Texas Music editor Dr. Gary Hartman for his advice, guidance, and patience throughout the writing process, and to Thom Lemmons and Texas A&M University Press for making this idea a reality. I am grateful to *Austin American-Statesman* editor Sharon Chapman for all the work and thoughtful management, to *Lone Star Music* magazine editor Richard Skanse for use of his interviews with artists involved in the *Poet: A Tribute to Townes Van Zandt* album, to the photograhers who contributed their work, and to songwriters David Broza, Shawn Camp, Linda Lowe, and Terri Hendrix for going extra miles. Thanks also to the Cactus Café and Waterloo Records for so many unforgettable afternoons and evenings.

Hayes Carll, Austin
City Limits Music
Festival, Austin,
September 18, 2011

Needless to say, great gratitude goes to all the songwriters who gener-
ously offered their time to talk about Townes Van Zandt and his impact
on their lives and music. Several singers and songwriters I wished to
interview remained unavailable despite numerous requests, but these
artists frequently approached interviews with eagerness that eclipsed
my own. Ultimately, this book would not have been possible without my
personal advisory board: my mother Ruthanne Atkinson and better half
Stephanie Sunshine, as well as Janet Berger, Rick Cranford, Mike Grimes,
Kate Hubbard, Jennifer Traina McAndrew, Kaye Mitchell, Margaret Ryan,
Troy Schoenfelder, Dr. Bruce Siders, Jason Stone, Cooper Sunshine, Sean
Tracey, Marianna Whitney, and Jodee Wright. Thanks for listening.

Brian T. Atkinson
Austin, Texas

I'LL BE HERE IN THE MORNING

INTRODUCTION

Townes Van Zandt simply never fit this earthly world.[1] After all, the Fort Worth native, a cult figure at best outside the Texas and Tennessee music communities during his lifetime, knew his time here would be short. "I don't envision a very long life for myself," a youthful Van Zandt says early in Margaret Brown's 2005 documentary Be Here To Love Me. "Like, I think my life will run out before my work does, you know? I've designed it that way." The "electric cowboy" lived fast and wrote faster, even as his blueprint devolved into alcoholism and drug addiction's slow suicide.[2]

Townes Van Zandt, born in Fort Worth, Texas, on March 7, 1944, baited his demons for fifty-two years, a journey further darkened by severe manic depression and electroshock therapy, before dying at his Smyrna, Tennessee, home on January 1, 1997.[3] Along the way, he became one of the modern era's most elegant lyricists. Consider the opening lines of "Quicksilver Daydreams of Maria": "Well, the diamond fades quickly when matched to the face of Maria / All the harps they sound empty when she lifts her lips to the sky / The brown of her skin makes her hair seem a soft golden rainfall / That spills from the mountains to the bottomless depths of her eyes." Every word frames his desire's beauty. His poetic skills eventually earned Townes Van Zandt the admiration of millions, including his own musical peers. "As far as I was concerned, he was the best songwriter that ever lived," legendary tunesmith Billy Joe Shaver says of Van Zandt, "and that's it."[4]

Van Zandt believed his craft demanded high sacrifice. "You have to blow off your family," he said. "You have to blow off comfort. You have to blow off money. You have to blow off your ego. You have to blow off everything except your guitar."[5] Many music critics agree that at least two dozen of his songs—including "For the Sake of the Song," "If I Needed You," "Waitin' Around to Die," "Snowin' on Raton," "Marie," and "Flyin' Shoes"—justify his claim. Others cite high-water marks such as "Pancho and Lefty," "To Live's To Fly," "Tecumseh Valley," "Lungs," "The Highway Kind," and "Rex's Blues" as unparalleled lyrical masterworks. Remarkably, Van Zandt composed his most timeless lyrics before age thirty.[6] "When I heard 'Marie,' I thought that was one of the greatest tunes ever written," says country music legend Willie Nelson, who recorded that song on the album *Poet: A Tribute to Townes Van Zandt* (2001). "You could tell exactly who Townes was by what he wrote. I think I knew him before I met him, just by listening to his songs."[7]

Townes Van Zandt disciples have labeled him a poet and prophet for four decades, but the songwriter's own reckless and reclusive behavior stifled widespread notoriety.[8] Living in shacks without indoor plumbing and performing fall-down (or fall-asleep-onstage) drunk concerts at the University of Texas' Cactus Café in Austin and elsewhere fueled his myth as a brilliant but tragic figure. His was art ripe for posthumous renaissance.

Recent history has obliged. Van Zandt has gained broader respect and appreciation in the years since his death, and biographers John Kruth (*To Live's To Fly: The Ballad of the Late, Great Townes Van Zandt*, Da Capo Press, 2007) and Robert Earl Hardy (*A Deeper Blue: The Life and Music of Townes Van Zandt*, University of North Texas Press, 2008) have chronicled his life in detail. Songwriting pupil Steve Earle, who refutes theories that his tutor was ahead of (or simply beyond) his time, cracked *Billboard*'s Top 20 in May 2009 with his Grammy-winning tribute album, *Townes*. Earle says, "I don't think [Townes] was a misunderstood genius. He shot himself in the foot constantly."[9]

Most critics agree that the troubled troubadour produced his finest recorded work in Houston in July 1973. Taped over a consecutive seven-night stand at Rex Bell and Dale Soffar's original Magnolia City club, *Live at the Old Quarter* (1977) showcases Townes Van Zandt's raw narratives, solo and acoustic, before a rare full house and delivered in peak form. "I used to go see him at the Old Quarter when I was a kid," says Jesse Dayton, a current Texas roadhouse staple. "I'd be the only one in there with the wait staff. It'd be like seeing Bob Dylan and Hank Williams all rolled into one—if he wasn't drunk, of course.

"Townes went from moaning these country blues to having this re-ally smart folk sensibility without ever seeming like less of a hillbilly," Dayton continues. "To me, 'Tecumseh Valley' is the saddest song I've ever heard. I intentionally don't listen to that song because it makes me bawl like a baby. Townes had an intellectual side to his music that wasn't something he was copying. I mean, Dylan has come out and said that 'Pancho and Lefty' is the best song ever written."[10] Like his childhood hero, Hank Williams, Van Zandt died on New Year's Day. He rests in Fort Worth's Dido Cemetery.

"Townes was covered with more grace than about any human being that I've ever had the privilege of knowing," says singer-songwriter Michelle Shocked, who crossed paths with Van Zandt at the Kerrville Folk Festival. "The gifts that he had and the inspiration he gave and received were truly spiritual gifts. Was he worthy of them? Did he de-serve them? Did he earn them? Did he treat them well? No. But he was a manifestation of grace to all of us. This very weak human vessel carried the weight of these incredible gifts of grace so admirably. God doesn't choose the strong and the noble to do the work. He chooses the weak and foolish, so the wise things of the world confound us."[11]

Townes Van Zandt often mentored and learned from other song-writers, shared stories, and relied on peers and followers alike to temporarily ground his self-destructive behavior. The following are selected interviews with contemporaries who fortify his legend and younger devotees more focused on deconstructing its creative core. As the interviews reveal, Van Zandt was a thoughtful and creative songwriter, but a complex individual whose near-mythic status is rooted in both fact and fiction. Each artist interviewed has drawn significant inspiration from Van Zandt's unflinching dedication to the art of songwriting and the music he produced. "Perhaps the twenty-first century musicians will sit and chat about the troubled times of Bob Dylan, the heartaches of Hank Williams and Don Gibson, the imagination of Paul McCartney and John Lennon," the late songwriter Mickey Newbury once wrote. "These were men that opened doors. John Townes Van Zandt was one that walked through."[12]

(L-R) Townes Van Zandt, Vince Bell. The Cactus Café, Austin, TX, 1996. Courtesy Sarah Wrightson

PRELUDE
VINCE BELL

The wicked king of clubs awoke, it was to his queen he turned
His lips were laughing as they spoke, his eyes like bullets burned
—TVZ, "Mr. Mudd and Mr. Gold," from *High, Low and In Between*

Vince Bell, born September 16, 1951, in Dallas, Texas, is one of several Texas artists who learned about songwriting from Townes Van Zandt in the 1970s. While Bell has not achieved widespread commercial success in his own right, many musicians including Nanci Griffith ("Woman of the Phoenix") and Lyle Lovett ("Sun and Moon and Stars") have recorded his songs. Bell's memoirs *Sixtyeight Twentyeight* and *One Man's Music* chronicle his personal and professional recovery after a near-fatal car accident on December 21, 1982, following a recording session with Stevie Ray Vaughan in Austin, Texas. The *Austin*

American-Statesman's early edition that morning erroneously reported that Bell had died in the accident.[1]

"Townes Van Zandt was filling houses in Texas," says Bell, who included a version of Van Zandt's "Mr. Mudd and Mr. Gold" on his album *Recado* (2007), "when most of the rest of us were nailing the quarter we made in tips to the backstage wall. Townes and I met right off the bat at Sand Mountain Coffeehouse in Houston in 1971. He probably taught me how to play an A-minor chord in the back room. When he wanted to be, Townes was powerful with a lyric and a guitar. He was the most convincing of us all for many moons. There was a time when we all learned most everything from him and Guy Clark. In the early days, Townes made the utterly simple elevating. He was fearless. 'Mr. Mudd and Mr. Gold' is my favorite in the fleet of Van Zandt, a poet's poem. It's an excellent talking blues that Steve Earle and I will probably do until we drop. Because of Townes, we songwriters have turned what began as a pop song on an AM radio station into some of the relevant literature of our time. He would have liked that."[2]

GUY CLARK

It's goodbye to all my friends; it's time to go again
Think of all the poetry and the picking down the line
—TVZ, "To Live's To Fly," from *High, Low and In Between*

Guy Clark's autumnal renaissance arcs further toward his folk-singer roots with every measure. The legendary songwriter's earthy Grammy-nominated album *Somedays the Song Writes You* (2009), which includes a version of Townes Van Zandt's "If I Needed You," liberates unforeseen introspection ("Somedays You Write the Song") and trademark narratives ("Hemingway's Whiskey") with minimalist production. Clark confirms a frequently told story about the popular Van Zandt song: "Townes was living with Susanna and me in the early 1970s. One morning, he woke up and picked up a guitar and laid a piece of paper on his leg and proceeded to sing ['If I Needed You']. I went, 'Wow, where'd you come up with that?' He said, 'I dreamed it last night. I dreamed the whole song, the melody and everything, rolled over and wrote it down, and went back to sleep.'"[1]

Van Zandt met his closest friend Guy Clark, who was born November 6, 1941, in Monahans, Texas, while both were working the Houston folk club circuit in the mid-1960s.[2] Clark soon joined the Peace Corps and later moved between Houston, San Francisco, and Southern California, where he built Dobros at the Dopyera brothers' Long Beach guitar factory. In 1971, Clark signed a songwriting contract with RCA's Sunbury Music and moved to Nashville, Tennessee, with his wife, Susanna Clark, an artist and successful songwriter in her own right ("I'll Be Your San Antone Rose," "Easy from Now On," and "Come from the Heart," among others). An accomplished luthier, Clark has continued to build guitars in his home workshop for the past four decades.[3]

Townes Van Zandt, who served as best man at Guy and Susanna Clark's wedding on songwriter Mickey Newbury's houseboat in early 1972, sporadically lived with the couple for extended periods throughout the 1970s. "Townes and I had a bottle of vodka [at the wedding] and got as shitfaced as we could till we got back to the dock," Clark says. "We got back in the car and went back to our house, and he was there for eight months. We were as close as you could get, closer than brothers."[4] Guy Clark and Van Zandt continually fueled each other's creative fires. "The inspiration was not to be like Townes, but to be able to find that place within yourself to write," says Clark, who called Van Zandt "the Van Gogh of country music."[5] Van Zandt acknowledged their bond in the song "Pueblo Waltz." "If I have to go, I won't be long / Maybe we'll move to Tennessee," he sings. "Leave these Texas blues behind / See Susanna and Guy."[6]

Guy Clark played an important role in reshaping Nashville's songwriting community. With strong connections to the Austin-based progressive country scene of the 1970s and 1980s, Clark (along with fellow Texan Kris Kristofferson) helped push traditional country music themes beyond cheating and drinking and into more literate and meditative narrative storytelling.[7] Clark's major-label debut album *Old No. 1* (1975), widely considered one of the era's defining collections and a primary influence on younger songwriters such as Steve Earle, Rodney Crowell, and John Hiatt, includes two songs made popular by Jerry Jeff Walker—Clark's "instant classic" "L.A. Freeway" and the tribute to his grandmother's "wildcatter boyfriend," "Desperados Waiting for a Train."[8]

Each tune displays Clark's trademark ability to deliver the buoyant melody in workaday language. "Pack up all your dishes / Make note of all good wishes," he sings on "L.A. Freeway." "Say goodbye to the landlord for me / That son of a bitch has always bored me."[9] "Guy does this better than anybody, writing something very specific and detailed in his own life, yet it has universal meaning," says Lyle Lovett, whose career Clark helped launch in the mid-1980s. "You take more from Guy's songs every time you listen and go farther in."[10]

Some music critics consider Jerry Jeff Walker's version of "L.A. Freeway" one of the greatest all-time country music singles.[11] However, "Desperados Waiting for a Train" better exhibits Clark's keen eye for sketching strength in vulnerability, a recurrent theme especially in portraits of independent women. Early peaks such as "Rita Ballou," "Better Days," and "She Ain't Goin' Nowhere," as well as later efforts such as "Arizona Star," "Sis Draper," and "Dancin' Days" all portray flawed yet determined heroines. One shelter for battered women has employed "Better Days" as its theme song.[12]

Although Clark earned moderate success as a singer in his own right—charting "Fools for Each Other" (1979), "The Partner Nobody Chose" (1981), and "Homegrown Tomatoes" (1983), also a hit for John Denver in 1989—he has arguably had his greatest impact as a songwriter, penning hits for others. Several major singers including Johnny Cash ("Texas 1947," "The Last Gunfighter Ballad"), David Allen Coe ("Texas 1947," "Desperados Waiting for a Train"), and Bobby Bare ("New Cut Road") have had success with Clark tunes. Ricky Skaggs took Clark's "Heartbroke" to the top of *Billboard*'s country charts in 1982. Many others including Vince Gill ("Oklahoma Borderline"), the Highwaymen ("Desperados Waiting for a Train"), Jimmy Buffett ("Boats to Build," "Cinco de Mayo in Memphis"), Brad Paisley and Alan Jackson ("Out in the Parking Lot"), and Kenny Chesney ("Hemingway's Whiskey") continue the tradition.

By the time his album *Better Days* appeared in 1983, Clark's vivid vignettes had long established him as one of Nashville's most highly regarded lyricists. "Guy's is a really true, honest voice," says singer Ryan Bingham, who won an Academy Award for cowriting "The Weary Kind" with producer T-Bone Burnett for the 2010 *Crazy Heart* soundtrack. "His songs will always be around for hundreds of years."[13] Although music critics may have overused the word "craftsman" to describe Clark's precise writing, several albums, including *Texas Cookin'* (1976), *Guy Clark* (1978), and *The South Coast of Texas* (1981), seem to validate that term.[14]

Guy Clark closed out his major label years with *Boats to Build* (1992) and *Dublin Blues* (1995), two critically praised albums on Asylum Records.[15] Many songs such as "Baton Rouge," "Boats to Build," "The Cape," and "Dublin Blues" became standards in Clark's live repertoire, and Van Zandt recorded "Dublin Blues" on his stark collection *The Highway Kind* (1997). However, the emotional masterwork perhaps was not tested enough for Clark's *Keepers—A Live Recording* (1997). Instead, he largely shaped the concert album around his back catalogue with songs such as "L.A. Freeway," "Heartbroke," "Let Him Roll," "Homegrown Tomatoes," and other "greatest hits."[16]

In 1998, the American Society of Composers, Authors, and Publishers (ASCAP) honored Guy Clark with its Lifetime Achievement Award for outstanding accomplishments as a songwriter, recording artist, and mentor in the field of country music.[17]

Meanwhile, *Keepers* issued in Clark's vital second act as an independent artist. Each following album—starting with *Cold Dog Soup* (1999) and *The Dark* (2002) on Sugar Hill Records—recalls his folk beginnings more directly than the last. Townes Van Zandt has played an integral role posthumously. While Clark occasionally recorded Van Zandt tunes throughout early albums (for instance, "Don't You Take It Too Bad," "No Deal," and "To Live's To Fly"), he has purposefully included one each on *The Dark* ("Rex's Blues"), 2006's Grammy-nominated *Workbench Songs* ("No Lonesome Tune"), and *Somedays the Songs Write You*.

Townes Van Zandt might as well have written the latter album's anchor about his friendship with Guy and Susanna Clark. Consider "If I Needed You" purely as a devotional absent desire. "If you needed me, I would come to you," Van Zandt sings. "I'd swim the seas for to ease your pain."[18] "There's something so sweet and genuine and unaffected about it," Guy Clark says. "I guess because he dreamed it. He wasn't posing. I like Loop and Lil in the lyric. Those were his parakeets that he'd carry in the inside pocket of his jacket. Steve Earle does it pretty good, but I'm always changing his songs. I was always like, 'Man, if you'd just change this one word, it'd be so good.'"[19]

■ ■ ■

GUY CLARK

The first time I met Townes, he was with Jerry Jeff Walker. There was a little public radio show in Houston that a friend of mine put on in his living room. Townes and Jerry Jeff came to the taping one night. I liked Townes. We kept running into one another in Houston, and we just became friends. I liked his sense of humor mostly.[20] He was the funniest son of a bitch I ever met in my whole life, and he was incredibly bright, maybe one of the smartest people I've been around, except maybe besides Susanna. That's why they were such good friends. They're off the chart with their IQs.[21]

Townes had written about two songs when I'd met him. I think maybe they were "Waitin' Around to Die" and "I'll Be Here in the Morning." Houston was a bunch of people who liked folk songs. It's been described as the "big folk scare of the '60s." It was people of a like mind just trying to find a place to play. The Jester Lounge was a little earlier than Sand Mountain. The Jester was a bar, what they call in Texas a "pressure cooker club." They have a big, high wooden fence around the back so women could come down in the afternoon and park behind and go in these bars. They'd put their dinner in the pressure cooker for their husbands, and then go drink all afternoon. That's what it originally was, but then the guy who owned it decided he wanted to capitalize on folk music. There were seven or eight different people who played there all the time. Townes got there kind of in the middle or toward the end of it. Sand Mountain, on the other hand, was a coffee house run by Mrs. Carrick. She was pretty cool, but we were always sneaking in wine and doing things we weren't supposed to do.

I think Bob Dylan was a big influence on Townes and me both, but also equally Woody Guthrie. We were both fans of Lightnin' Hopkins, but especially Townes. Lightnin' was a pretty fair songwriter himself. We were able to go see him play quite a bit in Houston, and we played on bills together. You know, he was a real songwriter, not like kids writing songs at home. Lightnin' was the real deal.

I loved Townes's use of the English language, the words he chose. They were really good, really clean, well educated. Plus, he was writing about some pretty weird stuff, and a lot of it I still don't get. Every time Townes and I started thinking we were pretty hot shit, we'd get a tape of Dylan Thomas reading his own work and put it on. That'd put a stop to that shit. From the time I can remember, we were both fans of Dylan Thomas. It was kind of hard to get his work that was recorded in the early 1950s before he died. It's just breathtaking to hear Dylan Thomas read that stuff. It's far out. Of course, Townes's songs stand up against literature. That depends on your definition of literature, but mine is Dylan Thomas.

Townes was really at the top of his game at the Old Quarter in the '70s. He was playing great, he was singing great, he was writing great. He was fairly sane. He was just really good. That two-volume *Live at the Old Quarter* set is still the best recording of Townes. He was a really good guitar player, especially on those fast songs. He had that little click in the rhythm that he could get going. That's really hard to do. He wasn't necessarily trying to be a guitar player, but he was. He was a pretty good blues player, and he played the songs that he wrote really, really well.

I always thought Townes was done a disservice in the way his records were produced over the years. I don't think anything even comes close to a live performance like *Live at the Old Quarter.* However those studio albums were being made, that really high quality part of Townes never cut through. There was always too much other stuff going on for me. He cared, but it just got very unwieldy, the parts that I saw. That's the way it was. I would go hang out in the recording studio once in a while, but not really a lot. I kind of stayed away, but everybody seemed to have a good time.

Songwriting never was a competitive sport for Townes and I. I couldn't wait to play him my new song and get his approval nor he me. Townes was always calling me up and saying, "Man, listen to this." He'd have a new song to read over the phone to me. I would do the same. We respected one another and that was a good way to play it for whichever one of us it was, but Townes was a real snob. He didn't like anything. He could keep his mouth shut louder than anybody, but I liked everything thing he did. I talked to Townes on the phone a couple times when he called [near the end of his life], and he read me the lyrics to "Sanitarium Blues."

I thought "Don't You Take It Too Bad" is just one of the best songs I've ever heard. I think it was his favorite, too. There's something about it that's just exactly right. He had a great sense of humor and wrote really funny talking blues like "Talking Karate Blues" and "Talking Thunderbird Wine Blues." The songs I've done are usually ones that were written when we were hanging out together, and I've known them since the day they were written, like "No Lonesome Tune." I always like doing one of his songs on my records, because I think the more people who hear them, the better off we all are. I do the songs I like of his, and I like a lot of them.

Some songs I can't do, because they're too dark, too scary, pretty dark stuff that I'm not in the mood to say or to sing. It's just a matter of taste. "To Live's To Fly" is a wonderful song. There's a couple verses in "Two Girls" that I think are just far out and quote all the time: "The clouds didn't look like cotton / They didn't even look like clouds / I was underneath the weather / All my friends look like a crowd / The swimming hole was full of rum / And I tried to find out why / All I learned was this, my friend / You gotta learn to swim before you fly."[22] I thought that was pretty.

I think Townes loved [Merle Haggard and Willie Nelson's chart-topping version of] "Pancho and Lefty." He was very pleased that they would do it. We're in the business of writing songs, and it's always nice to be able to support yourself with your artistic endeavors. It means that you can keep doing it. You've gotta have money to live.

I think we tried to cowrite once when we were real drunk, but we never did really even think about it. It never seemed to be the right thing to do for either one of us. Why, I don't know. We could just write songs by ourselves, I guess. I wasn't into cowriting at that time. I started that much later. Townes was in and out of Nashville quite a bit, but he was a big part of the scene in the '70s. He wasn't living here permanently, just in spurts of a year or two, but everybody knew how good that stuff was.

On the pro side of living with Townes, he's very neat. He picked up after himself, made his bed every morning, would cook breakfast and wash any dish that was laying around. I mean, he went to military school, you know. You could walk into his motel room out on the road and everything was perfect. The bed was made, and you could bounce a quarter off it. For the rest of his life being such chaos, I thought that was pretty funny. On the con side, Townes would bring some really unsavory characters around, some guy he met at a bar or a girlfriend. You know, just unacceptable to me.[23]

He would come home from the airport with people during that period after he had been our best man. . . . So we're all in this little house in Nashville, and Townes just comes home from there and goes, "Hey, man, meet my new friends, you know, they can sleep in . . ." And Susanna's just, "What in the fuck have I got myself in now?" Or he'd come home with the news editor from the *Baltimore Sun*, who just worships the fucking boots Townes stands in, or some wino who had just gotten divorced. That was just a part of having Townes be part of your life. He saw this beautiful, good thing in each one of them.

Townes thought he was better than Chevy Chase at pratfalls. I mean he really did, and it got to the point where that was part of his show. He'd act like he lost his balance or he was too drunk to stand up and fall with his guitar on his strap and roll and come back on his feet. You know, if he had to do two sets, he'd do it twice. He seriously entertained being that quality acrobat, but his lifestyle didn't support it. He always wound up flat on his back [holding] his guitar up there. "I didn't break the guitar. I think my hip's shattered, but the guitar's okay." I mean he'd really do it, and he did hurt himself a couple of times.

One time we were in Madison, Wisconsin, and Townes played first. He was drunk, and he was sitting in a chair. He was playing, crying, singing, and telling stories, and right at the very end, you know, he just fell over backward in the chair and just hit the floor. He couldn't walk, but he had the guitar up. "I saved the guitar, man." Doctors were there, and I've got to go on right now. Townes is in the dressing room, and the doctor came in. "How many fingers can you see?" I made sure the dressing room door was open, and Townes is just kind of laying there in a daze, and I just walked up and went, "If I had no place to fall and I needed to, could I count on you?"[24] I mean, that was our sense of humor. It was, "Okay, man, you're that fucked up, you ought to laugh a bit."

Townes and I one time got into Lightnin' Hopkins's dressing room in L.A. through an innocent friend, drunk off our ass. All of Lightnin's kinfolks were there, the L.A. part of his family. He's on his absolute best behavior. The room is full of nothing but his entourage, nice middle-class kind of people. Townes and me were roaring drunk and playing some kind of gambling hand-slap game. I accidentally threw my hand back and hit Lightnin's aunt in the breast with the back of my hand. Townes is going, "Lightnin,' hey, man, are you sobering up or drunk, man? Goddamn, man. Boy, I'm so glad, man, thanks. Man, you got the

(L-R), Guy Clark, Townes Van Zandt.
Winnipeg Folk Festival, Winnipeg,
Manitoba, Canada, July 1991.
Courtesy Eric Ambel

blues? I got the blues. Come on," and on and on. And finally, somehow somebody convinced us that we needed to move on. I mean, it was very gentle, but it was like, "You guys need to move on."

Townes and I played a lot of gigs together over the years. Sometimes we just got to a point where we would just go onstage together and never have two separate sets. We'd just walk on together, have a coin toss, and call it for who goes first. "Okay, heads. You go first." That's the way we'd start the show. And then we'd sit there and trade songs if we felt like we wanted to, or if you had to go pee, the other guy would do two. We'd just do that for like two or three hours. It wasn't real musical because neither Townes nor I could play with anyone but ourselves. We would each hit a little groove once in a while, but sidemen we were not.[25]

When Townes was really playing good, he floored people. It was obvious how good he was. It didn't take long to convert an audience, because we've always tried to play to people who knew what they were coming to hear. Touring together was fun, and it was usually fairly easy. He knew how to do it, and I knew how to do it. But if he was drinking, it was really hard.[26]

One time we were coming back from this gig in North Carolina. We had a rental car, and we go to turn it in. By the time we hit the rental car parking lot, I notice Townes has got a half pint of vodka, and he's still very together and coherent, but then we get out of the car. By the time we each grab our bags and our guitar and walk across the street in this small airport to the ticket counter, Townes is falling down, blitzed. And

I know on one level he's fucking with me, on the other level he really is [drunk], you know. That was the deal with Townes. I say, "Just sit down here, Townes. Give me your ticket, and I'll go check us in."

I go get in line, and there goes Townes. "Sit down, just sit down." So, I get us checked in, and by the time we get to the electronic x-ray machine where you walk through to get on the concourse, Townes is screaming. Just like, "White man. Shit, man. Goddamn, stole my fucking land, man. Goddamn. Fucking slit your throat and drink your blood." You know, I finally get him through the checkout and the x-ray machine and go down the end of this hall to get on this small prop plane from Charlotte to Nashville. Townes proceeds to squat at the end of the concourse, right in front of the ticket booth. We were there a little early, and he squatted and just mumbled under his breath, "Goddamn white motherfuckers, stole my land, stole my father's land. Fuck you, motherfuckers."

You know, by then the airport cops are coming up. The pilot gets off the plane, says, "This motherfucker . . ." Obviously, I'm with him, but I'm dead straight. It's like, I'm impatient, and I'm pissed. "Townes, I know you're fucking with me, and I don't do this." He'd grin at you and just keep doing it. He could have stopped. The pilot came off and said, "Alright, this drunk son of a bitch . . ." And I said, "Look, man, his best friend just committed suicide, and he got really drunk." And the pilot's like, "I don't give a shit." He said, "I don't care if his fucking mother died, but I tell you what. If you promise me that you can control him, I'll let you on this plane and get you to Nashville. But if he opens his mouth one time, I'm calling the police on the radio, they're going to meet you at the gate, and that's the end of it."

So here we go to get on a twelve-seat, two-engine prop plane. Townes sits down and begins to sulk and go into his Indian mode. I just had to sit there the whole fucking trip. Every time he'd start to go like this, I'd just reach over and grab his hand. He's like, "Oh, bet you thought I was really going to do something, didn't you?" And we did this the whole way back to Nashville. Finally, they didn't call the cops. Got off the plane, the minute we crossed the threshold of the airplane walls, the door, you know, I just put my shit on my shoulder, and I started walking. I said, "Fuck you. Fuck you." I walked all the way to the baggage, got my baggage, and walked out the door. Didn't blink twice to make sure he got his shit, didn't ask him how he was getting home, absolutely not.[27]

Obviously, Townes didn't want to be better known. Townes did exactly what he wanted to do, and nobody made him do anything different. He drank too much. He was crazy. What do you think? He was psychotic. He was blitzed way too much of the time. I put up with it because he was my friend, but it wasn't fun.[28]

He said his whole life was built around one moment in time in the third grade. A teacher came in and said, "Okay, class, it's time now for science. Today we're going to study the solar system and the planets and the moon. The center of our solar system is the sun and the sun's a star, and by the way, they're all burning out." And she proceeded to keep telling him more. It froze in his mind. He said, "You telling me the sun's burning out? Are you serious? The fucking sun's burning out? Why do I have to be here on time and shine my shoes, comb my hair, and sit up straight?" He said from that moment on, he lived his whole life like that. It was like, "Excuse me, ma'am, are you hip? The sun is burning out."[29]

Ray Wylie Hubbard,
Long Center, Austin, TX,
September 19, 2010

RAY WYLIE HUBBARD

New Mexico ain't bad, Lord, the people there they treat you kind
White freightliner, won't you steal away my mind
—TVZ, "White Freightliner Blues," from *The Nashville Sessions*

Ray Wylie Hubbard, born November 13, 1946, in Soper, Oklahoma, initially gained widespread recognition as the songwriter behind the Jerry Jeff Walker hit "Up Against the Wall, Redneck Mother," from Walker's groundbreaking 1973 album *¡Viva Terlingua!*

Hubbard's trademark tune crackles with wry observations based on a real-life experience of trying to buy beer at the D-Bar-D bar in Red River, New Mexico, from an Oklahoma-born woman who disapproved of his scruffy appearance. Later featured on his *Off the Wall* (1978) and *Live at Cibolo Creek Country Club* (2000) albums, "Redneck Mother" came to be one of the best known songs of the entire 1970s progressive country era.[1] Hubbard, a longtime Wimberley, Texas, resident, continues to write with a dry wit and a sharp pen and remains one of the most prolific songwriters in the Lone Star State.[2]

As a pioneering figure in Texas' progressive country movement, Hubbard's early major-label albums *Ray Wylie Hubbard and the Cowboy Twinkies* (1975) and *Off the Wall* fortified his reputation as a freewheeling spirit who served as a rowdy precursor to Robert Earl Keen's declaration a decade later that "the road goes on forever, and the party never ends."[3] During this time, Hubbard often performed with Lone Star legend Willie Nelson and helped inspire a new generation of songwriters, including Pat Green, Randy Rogers, and Casey Donahew, to write about a lifestyle that celebrates Saturday night revelry rather than Sunday morning regret.[4]

Hubbard's excessive use of alcohol and drugs during those early years eventually crippled his creativity, and his 1984 album title *Caught in the Act* hinted at a new direction in his personal life and professional career. Hubbard got sober on his forty-first birthday. In fact, he met his second (and current) wife and manager, Judy Stone, at an Alcoholics Anonymous meeting. "I prefer spiritual awakening to religious conversion," Hubbard says of his decision to rehabilitate himself. "There are certain spiritual principles that I try to follow, and I believe there are certain spiritual laws in the universe."[5]

Accordingly, sobriety and spirituality played a key role in Hubbard's evolution as a songwriter. He also focused on improving his abilities as a performer. Legendary blues guitarist Stevie Ray Vaughan, who also struggled with alcohol and drugs, worked with Hubbard to strengthen his guitar skills. "Stevie Ray was the first guy that I had ever met who'd gotten sober who hadn't turned into a square," Hubbard says. "He still had this edge and coolness. Stevie Ray said that once he got sober, it was like he took off the boxing gloves and he could really play the guitar."[6]

Hubbard's mystical Hill Country blues enliven later albums such as *Growl* (2003), *Delirium Tremolos* (2005), and *Snake Farm* (2006), directly echoing the Texas songwriters and guitarists that Townes Van Zandt most revered, such as Lightnin' Hopkins and Mance Lipscomb. In turn, Hubbard admired Van Zandt's novelistic eye. "Townes would write these incredible songs, but he understood the craft of it," Hubbard says. "He had the rare combination of inspiration plus craft."[7]

Ray Wylie Hubbard's most recent album, 2010's metaphysical meditation, *A: Enlightenment, B: Endarkenment, Hint: There Is No C*, well suits Austin's Cactus Café, the intimate University of Texas listening room where he witnessed many Van Zandt concerts. Today Hubbard advises and collaborates with several up-and-coming Texas artists such as Cody Canada, Randy Rogers, and The Trishas. On his latest album, Hubbard cowrote "Drunken Poet's Dream" with Houston-area native Hayes Carll, who had recorded a version "about 60 percent the same" on his 2008 album *Trouble in Mind*. "I'm such a big fan of Ray as a person and as a songwriter," Carll says. "In my perfect world, Ray Wylie Hubbard would be winning Grammys."[8]

■ ■ ■

RAY WYLIE HUBBARD

One of the first times I ever really remember Townes was in the late 1960s or very early 1970s when Jerry Jeff Walker was playing in Nashville, Tennessee. It was kind of Jerry's big debut there, but I don't remember where it was. Everybody showed up, and Townes was there. Of course, we were all drinking, and Jerry was out front playing. Townes bet me $100 that he'd go onstage and stand on his head for the whole song while Jerry did "Mr. Bojangles." I bet Townes the $100. Jerry started playing "Bojangles," and Townes went out there and stood on his head the whole time. That was the last time I gambled with him.

Earlier on, back in the 1970s, he was really witty, sharp, and funny. He had a certain charisma about him. Later, you know, he was drunk a lot and wasn't as "on." But there were times when he was. *Live at the Old Quarter* was Townes in his prime. He was always gracious, cordial, and funny when I'd see him.

I played with Townes at one of his last performances in the States before he died. This was around October 1996. The show was in Granbury, Texas, of all places, at the Granbury Opera House. It was a fundraiser for the opera house in this little town because they were refurbishing it. They had Townes, Terry Allen, and me do a songwriters-in-the-round, and with the three of us, I think the term would be *irreverent*. Townes got there a little drunk and everything, but he pulled it together.

We had a great night. There were all these elderly ladies with their minks and the tiaras and the evening gowns, and they were all down front, because this is an opera house. Townes went off on some story about how he was playing at a wedding and he had to borrow some sex toy to play slide or something. The whole evening was like that. It was a lot of fun, but I knew that was one of the last times I'd see Townes because he was leaving for a tour in Europe. He was very frail at that time, and both Terry and I knew. Europe can really wear you out.

Townes and I weren't like running buddies, but I'd go see him play in Dallas, and we'd hang out. He did this benefit in Dallas for an Indian school or AIM, the American Indian Movement. Townes was the singer, the fundraiser. So, I show up just to see Townes, but he's like, "Hey, man, it's really good to see you. Do you want to get up and sing a song?" I said, "No, not really, it's your gig." "Ah, come on up, do a song," he says. He gets up there and does about three songs. Then he says, "Here's my good friend Ray Wylie Hubbard," and gives me his guitar. I start playing, and then all of a sudden I see Townes walk out the front door. He's walking down the street. I finished my song, and he's still gone. I had to do like three or four songs, and then finally he showed up again.

I saw him perform the spring before that gig with Terry Allen, and he was sober. He had been on the wagon for about three weeks or a month, and he just came out and did the deal. There were nights when it was just magical to watch him perform. He's out of the old school of folk singer, the guys who would tell the stories and then play these incredible songs. There were the nights when it was magical, and then there were the nights when you got this feeling in your stomach and would just think, "Okay, Townes, that's enough."

When it comes to his songwriting, though, the question is, "What's not to admire?" To another songwriter, you look at his songs and they're just as powerful as anything you've ever witnessed. Whether it's Hemingway or Shelley, you know. Those songs are just the best there are. His songwriting is on the level of Whitman. You could hold his songs against any of the great writers. They're just so well done— every word, every idea. They pull you in and reach something within me that's just somewhere else. They're remarkable.

In Austin, he set the bar at places like the Cactus Café, which is really good because there are now so many of these young writers in Texas who are aware of him. I think it's nice to have someone like Townes, and they can really aspire to that level of writing. I don't think anyone will ever surpass Townes, though. Onstage at the Cactus Café, there's a picture of Townes, so you walk in and say, "Okay, this is the real deal. It is about the song. It is for the sake of the song." You better have it together when you play there.

Townes's reputation is awesome. My big three, of course, are Townes, Guy Clark, and Billy Joe Shaver. But there hasn't been a young Townes or a young Guy or a young Billy to come along. There are a lot of really good writers in Texas, like Slaid Cleaves and Hayes Carll, but there hasn't been that Townes to come along yet. And I don't think there ever will be. All the planets need to line up or something for that. In certain circles, you say "Townes," and everyone goes, "Ahhh," and everyone is aware of him. He's the pinnacle.

If it were a perfect world, Townes would be as well known as Bob Dylan. There's a mystique about Townes. When people discover him, it's just enlightening. I try to turn people on to him, and that's just it. Enlightened. They're instant fans. But it's like William Blake, who I don't think was published in his own lifetime. Now it's like, "Wow." Townes deserves to be recognized, but the way the music business is, I don't know if it'll happen, if he'll achieve as much fame as Bob Dylan. But if he would, it would raise everybody's standards. Once you hear Townes and you compare everything to him, it's gotta be pretty good to work.

A lot of it with Townes is the subject matter and the way he could turn a phrase and tell a story. It was a complete songwriting package. I mean, "Bad news from Houston / All my friends are dying" [from "White Freightliner Blues"]? It's like, "Whoa, man." He just said it so nonchalantly, but it's so powerful. The word "poet" just keeps coming to mind. I mean a *real* poet. There are lots of people out there who have poetry books who aren't real poets. Townes was.

I think Townes had an effect on me as a songwriter in a subconscious way. I didn't try to write like Townes, but I want to write with quality. There's a certain quality and integrity about his writing. I try to put forth the best time and effort to make the best song I can, and that's something Townes might have affected. Somewhere in there, maybe about fifteen years ago, I wanted to be a real songwriter. I always played in these honky-tonk bands, but I realized that to be a better songwriter I'd have to be a better guitar player.

Townes was a really good guitar player. His finger picking, his Lightnin' [Hopkins] licks and things, he was really, really good. So, for me, I didn't want to be Townes Van Zandt or Guy Clark, because I knew I couldn't write that caliber of a song, but I wanted to be able to play in front of Townes's audience. I wanted to write songs so that I could play the kind of places Townes would play. So, it wasn't a conscious thing about Townes influencing me, but I did want to be a better player and really write songs that had a little depth and weight to them.

His music, his albums still are some of my favorites. I listen to him quite a bit, and even though Townes is not here, his songs are pretty timeless. They'll be around, because what he did was, he created art—not just art, but great art. It's not disposable tunes. They have incredible value , and they can still knock you down today. I think the more people find out about Townes, the more it'll make them strive to reach that quality of songwriting. Townes was just a natural.[9]

Peter Rowan, Telluride Bluegrass Festival, Telluride, CO, June 21, 2003

PETER ROWAN

In the kitchen mama sneezed, and he grinned big as you please
Said 'bless you' and a tear come to his eye
—TVZ, "No Lonesome Tune," from *The Late,*
Great Townes Van Zandt

Peter Rowan often matches Guy Clark's sharp storytelling with Townes Van Zandt's nonlinear dreamscapes (for instance, "Panama Red" and "Midnight Moonlight"). Rowan, who developed interest in bluegrass, rock, and social protest music at an early age, gained intimate access into one of Texas music's great friendships on occasional triple-bill tours with the two songwriters throughout the United States and abroad. "Townes leaned on Guy in a way that probably enabled him to stay alive longer," Rowan says, "but Guy needed Townes in his life just like Townes needed him."[1]

As a young man, Rowan, born July 4, 1942, in Boston, Massachusetts, took measures necessary to enter into elite bluegrass circles. In the early 1960s, Rowan moved to Nashville to meet bluegrass pioneer Bill Monroe, and he ended up performing with Bill Monroe & His Blue Grass Boys for nearly four years, from 1964–67. Rowan's time with the legendary outfit offered a solid foundation in the genre's traditional style, but diversity has defined his path since.[2] Rowan has continually explored new variations that span a variety of genres, including art rock (Earth Opera), jazz fusion (Seatrain), "newgrass" (Muleskinner), and country (Peter Rowan and the Free Mexican Airforce).[3]

In the late 1960s, Rowan relocated to California, where he joined Seatrain in San Francisco. The group's first two albums, Sea Train (1969) and the follow-up Seatrain (1970), garnered critical acclaim. "Seatrain was really interesting," Rowan says, "because they were classical musicians. There was no fooling around. It was back to the strict tempo approach that we'd used with Bill Monroe." One critic called Sea Train "the best country album since The Band." Seatrain's flautist Andy Kulbert categorized its sound as "sort of bluegrass, because the thing that stands out is Richard [Greene]'s violin."[4]

Rowan later formed Old and In the Way with the Grateful Dead's Jerry Garcia, renowned fiddler Vassar Clements, mandolin player David Grisman, and bassist John Kahn. The group's self-titled debut (1975) infused bluegrass sensibilities into country (Rowan's "Panama Red") and rock tunes (the Rolling Stones' "Wild Horses") and traditional songs ("Pig in a Pen"). The quintet released four albums after Garcia's 1995 death, including Breakdown (1997) and Live at the Boarding House (2008).[5]

In the 1980s, Rowan found success writing songs that were recorded by mainstream country artists such as Ricky Skaggs ("Walls of Time") and George Strait ("Dance Time in Texas") while living in Nashville.[6] By nature a philosophical man, Rowan approaches the songwriting craft altruistically. "I don't seem to play in a militant style that's trying to shake the foundations of the empire," he says. "I just write songs about what I see and hear and people I know. I don't have an agenda, really. I think music is a healing force, and it helps people."[7] Rowan recorded Townes

Van Zandt's songs "No Lonesome Tune" on the Rowan Brothers' album *Tree on a Hill* (1994) and "To Live's To Fly" with celebrated guitarist Tony Rice on *Quartet* (2007). Rowan frequently performs both in concert.

■ ■ ■

PETER ROWAN

Townes and I played a bunch of shows together at an Irish pub in Harvard Square in Cambridge, Massachusetts, back in the 1970s. He was always so unique. He dressed in this kind of beige corduroy suit and moccasins. The suit was perfect and the moccasins were really comfortable. We were on the road together, Guy Clark, Townes and me, and we played this festival in England. I guess he'd been on kind of a tear, and he bought himself a leather jerkin. He had on this beautiful white shirt and jeans and this jerkin. He kept saying, "Man, do you know what this is? This is a *jerkin*." I was like, "Well, yeah?" He said, "This is what they wore here for centuries, *jerkins*." He wouldn't take the thing off, and he wore it the whole tour, that giant leather vest. He wore it until it looked like the middle ages. He was so proud of that jerkin. Then he gave it to somebody at a festival up in Scotland.

What we had was on the level of a poetic friendship. Every time I saw him near the end of his life, he'd throw lines at me, challenging me to rhyme with him. Like saying, "Look what I came up with." I really couldn't keep up so much with the lifestyle. I just don't have it in me. I don't have the gene. I mean, there were some serious drinkers in our family, and I saw what it did to them. My philosophy is to just trust the mind as it is. That's just my way.

So, Townes and I hung out, and I would drink with him. I mean, it can't be any secret, the man would have a measure of vodka before breakfast. Mostly he was fine. That's what fueled him, kept him going. Sometimes when he'd go over the edge, it became scary; he became prophetic. He'd be very dramatic, kneel down in the middle of the floor and talk, just spouting poetic phrases that were almost terrifying in their honesty.

Being friends with Townes meant bearing witness unto Townes and with Townes. Guy Clark was probably the best man because Guy really knew how to lasso him. Townes was American to the core; he had the wild, crazy heart of an American Indian. He could have either become a successful businessman or a statesman or been the wild child, and he chose the wild child.

I remember we were playing in Berlin, and it was the beginning of Townes's last big run, probably between 1979 and 1986. By 1981 or so, Townes was gearing up for probably the last big touring effort of his life. The Germans and the Dutch loved him. Townes had the energy and the lubrication, and the warmth of the alcohol helped him deal with the pace that he set for himself. I mean, this guy never sat still. He'd book a thirty-day tour in Holland, I have no idea where he'd play, but it was just a-go. It was all a green light. He did everything to get his message out, to say what he had to say. He was always on the road. Then he took a break, and he died.

He always had to keep the party going, basically. Townes and Guy and I did this tour in England, and after the show, of course, we're all at the hotel bar. There's a big entourage of followers, and Guy would shush the entire room and hand Townes his guitar. And Townes would very humbly sing some of his great tunes. Guy was just adamant—*shush, be quiet!*—and he was gracious about it, but Townes's ability, his genius *was* to be heard.

There was a night on that same European tour when I was up in my room working on a song, "I'll Be There," on a Rowan Brothers record, and Townes was downstairs gambling, the nightly poker session. Maybe dice. He also liked to pitch pennies. I was struggling with the bridge, and Townes comes upstairs and says, "Can you loan me ten quid?" He's lost all his money. So, I say, "sure," and give it to him. He goes back downstairs, loses that money and comes back up again for another ten quid. This time I give it to him and show him what I'm having trouble with, the lines in the song.

I played the guitar part, and he sang the lyrics right there, put them in the song: "Followed my footsteps where I wander / Followed my dreams

I found you / Feel your heartbeat here beside me / All my dreams come true." I wrote them down, and he went back downstairs. Townes comes back up a while later, and he's lost his shirt, literally. He asks me for some more money. I say, "Hey, man, what about the second bridge? Check this out." He came up with the lines to another bridge: "Sure as morning follows nighttime / Sure as moonlight follows the sun / Sure as wind blows cross the prairie / I'll be there when you need someone." So I gave him the ten quid, and then he won it all back. It was a good night, a good song, and a good gamble, too.

I got very friendly with him at the end of his life. That fall of 1996, I went down to Nashville to stay with him and [his third wife] Jeanene [Van Zandt] and his little boy and girl. We were all going to have dinner and Townes went out for some cigarettes, and Jeanene said, "Well, I don't know when he'll be back." And at about 11:00 that night, he called from a bar. I think maybe he was afraid of closeness. What we were going to do was just hang out, but when he called me he was out at a bar. So, I got in my rental car, and I went out to the bar. And there he was, out on Hillsboro Road at this bar, playing pool, and he was taking comer after comer and losing and putting money on every shot. The stakes had to be high.

He was playing pool with someone that he had known when he was in the sanitarium, when he was under psychiatric evaluation. It was this person that he had picked up who knew Townes and who was talking about killing himself. And his mission that night was to hang with this guy and basically make sure that he wasn't going to kill himself. There was just no privacy with Townes; he had to be with other people all the time. At the bar, there was an audience, a whole barroom full of people. Townes was holding court. I didn't have much to do with the conversation. This guy was just goin', "You know, Townes. You know what it's like, man. You know how it is, man. . . ." Townes gives him some cryptic reply.

It was kind of like he was a guru to people who were on the edge. We were basically up all night, and I ended up getting a hotel room. We were ten miles from Townes's house and I thought, "Man, he still has to be in a hotel." We stayed up all night drinking and talking and by sunrise that guy was too tired to do anything dramatically violent. I said, "Townes, where did you find this guy?" And he told me that it was someone he'd known in the sanitarium. He said, "I didn't find him. He found me." He said they always found him. I think it was a combination of them finding each other.

Anyway, after I left that weekend, I heard Townes was in the hospital. The last show I did with him, I have pictures from it, was in Arkansas. They are the most moving pictures I've ever seen; Townes was almost transparent in them. We played together on stage that night and Townes was so fragile. I remember while we were playing together looking at him and thinking, "Brother, you're outta here." He was always mentally there and "on," but physically he was gone.[8]

Rodney Crowell, Telluride Bluegrass Festival, Telluride, CO, June 20, 2004

RODNEY CROWELL

Living on the road, my friend, was gonna keep you free and clean
Now you wear your skin like iron, and your breath's
as hard as kerosene
—TVZ, "Pancho and Lefty," from *The Late, Great Townes Van Zandt*

Rodney Crowell topped mainstream country music charts a quarter century ago, but in many ways he's always been a workaday songwriter at heart. After all, it was Crowell's writing that elevated him to iconic stature, earned a Grammy Award for the song "After All This Time" (1990), and notched ASCAP and Americana Music Association lifetime achievement awards (2003 and 2006, respectively). Along the way, Crowell managed an unprecedented string of five consecutive Number One Billboard country singles (from the album *Diamonds and Dirt*, 1988), and earned membership in the Nashville Songwriters Hall of Fame (2003).[1]

Crowell, born August 7, 1950, in Houston, Texas, met Townes Van Zandt as a young songwriter entering into Nashville's creative community in the early 1970s. Crowell took away some sustaining lessons from the experience. "[Townes Van Zandt and Guy Clark] instilled me with the right attitude, which is that the craft, the process, and the creativity of songwriting is far more important than the material rewards," Crowell says. "The late-night song-swapping sessions were always about, What are you working on? Are you getting any better? Can we take the music away and have it stand as poetry?"[2]

After two years with Emmylou Harris's Hot Band in the mid-1970s, Crowell formed his own road band, the Cherry Bombs, with a young Vince Gill and future record producers Richard Bennett, Emory Gordy Jr., and Tony Brown. Crowell parlayed wisdom he had gained into his debut album *I Ain't Living Long Like This* (1978). It produced two frequently interpreted songs—"Leaving Louisiana in the Broad Daylight" (recorded by the Oak Ridge Boys, Harris, and others) and the title track (Jerry Jeff Walker, Brooks and Dunn, and Harris). Notably, legendary "Outlaw Country" pioneer Waylon Jennings's unapologetic version of "Ain't Living Long Like This" on his album *What Goes Around Comes Around* (1979) became tantamount to a personal mission statement. In 1983, rock singer Bob Seger found success with Crowell's "Shame on the Moon," taking the song to *Billboard's* Number Two position.

Rodney Crowell peaked as a commercial artist with *Diamonds & Dirt* and its Number One singles "I Couldn't Leave You If I Tried," "After All This Time," "She's Crazy For Leaving" (a cowrite with Guy Clark), the Buck Owens cover "Above and Beyond (The Call of Love)," and "It's Such A Small World," his duet with then-wife Rosanne Cash.[3] Crowell later chronicled his divorce from Cash in the album *Life Is Messy* (1992), which produced the two Top Ten singles "Lovin' All Night" and "What Kind of Love."[4]

Crowell gravitated toward country music naturally. "I came from a household that was big into Roy Acuff and Appalachian country music," he says.[5] After *Jewel of the South* (1995), Crowell took a six-year hiatus to help raise his children. At millennium's turn, he reemerged with priorities arranged accordingly. Crowell led a group of artists, including Steve Earle, Emmylou Harris, Kelly Willis, and Nanci Griffith, who abandoned increasingly pop-oriented mainstream country music in favor of Americana, a newer genre owing to traditional country and folk influences such as Acuff, Woody Guthrie, Leadbelly, and Hank Williams. Crowell's following three albums—*The Houston Kid* (2001), *Fate's Right Hand* (2003), and *The Outsider* (2005)—offer equal measures social and spiritual commentary with an eye on the common man.[6]

Crowell's Grammy-nominated album *Sex and Gasoline* (2008) highlights his disdain for superficiality and a disenfranchised view of popular culture, particularly through songs such as "The Rise and Fall of Intelligent Design," "Truth Decay," and the title track. "There's a spirituality about Rodney that I haven't seen in anybody else," says country star Keith Urban, an occasional songwriting collaborator. "He's really, really calming to be around and effortless to write with. Plus, he's one of my favorite songwriters for sure. I'm not sure why all the great ones come from Texas, but they do."[7]

■ ■ ■

RODNEY CROWELL

Townes was fond of me, but he picked on me, man. He was smarter and faster and quicker than me, and I was always on guard. Townes would have been the fastest gun in the West. We played this game where you put your hands together and hold them in front of you, and the other guy puts his hands on his hip and he tries to slap your hands before you can move them away. I couldn't get my hands out of the way because he was so quick. He had lightning reflexes. Then, you know, he'd say, "My turn," and he'd hold his hands out and I'd put my hands on my hips and try to whack his hands, and I'd miss them. He was lightning fast, and he had a lightning-fast mind, too.

Guy Clark was the center of the group, the curator. Townes was Guy's pretty exotic friend. Townes was closer to Guy than he was to anybody else. In the beginning, Townes just thought I was a punk, you know, but I'd gladly let him smash my hands to pieces just to hang around and pay attention to what was going on, to see what I could pick up about writing songs.

On occasion over the years we'd play on the same bill together. Early on, it was breathtaking to see Townes perform. He was so good. Later on, I couldn't watch it. It made me too sad; the alcohol had really diminished his capacities. In the early- and mid-1970s, probably from 1972 to 1977, he was just so good. Townes or Bob Dylan would be the pinnacle of the singer-songwriter-performer, but I think Townes saw to it pretty well that he wouldn't be as well known as Dylan.

He fed his enigma. Townes would be in town sometimes, and we'd be downstairs drinking wine and playing guitars, and Townes would be upstairs kicking heroin. He was just this exotic guy, like, "Townes is upstairs coming off smack." It was kind of romantic.

I had a panel truck, and one night we'd been out on the lake drinking and playing music all night. I was driving this truck, like a bread delivery van with one seat in it. Had a couple lawn chairs in it. Townes and Skinny Dennis were riding in the lawn chairs. When we drove back into town, I was gonna drop Townes off at this girl's place, but he and [bassist] Skinny Dennis [Sanchez] had gotten into sort of an argument. Dennis was serious about it, but Townes was playing, lying in the weeds. They got into this real escalated argument. I'm in the front and said, "Look you guys, I'm trying to drive." We're all drunk, and I didn't want us to all get hauled to jail.

So, when we finally made it to this place, Townes flung the door open, took a beer bottle, and broke it open on the side of my panel truck. He grabbed Skinny Dennis, who was about six-foot-seven, 120 pounds, held him down with the broken bottle and said, "I'm gonna cut his throat, I'm gonna cut it right now, I'm cuttin' his throat up—I've had *enough* of him." Skinny Dennis thought it was for real, and I was trying to pull Townes off of him, trying to stop it. It was 4:00 in the morning and on the sidewalk. I'm grabbing at Townes, and he seemed out of his mind. All of a sudden, he stopped and started laughing and said, "I got you both." He wasn't anywhere as near as drunk as he was acting.

There's one thing I was always mad at Townes for. I had a girlfriend, and we were all at Jack Clement's studio in Nashville. I brought this girlfriend around, and we were doing some recording. They had this kind of exotic mirrored room upstairs, and while I was down in the studio playing, Townes took my girlfriend upstairs and fucked her. "You son of a bitch," you know? And then he didn't tell me about it until later. She didn't mention it. But he said later, "Hey, man, you didn't want her anyway if she'd do that. You don't want her." I was really mad about it, but you know what—he was right. She didn't love me, and I didn't love her either.

When you caught Townes in the afternoon, that's when you'd get to know the sweet boy. He was a really sweet, sensitive guy, very charming. Susanna Clark was the access to his sweet side. Townes would usually be a gentleman around her, and Susanna was always saying, "Ah, that other thing, that's just his act. He's really a sweet, smart boy." And he was—extremely smart, extremely charming, extremely talented. He was an absolute enigma of the highest degree.

I've said this to everybody: Steve Earle emulated Townes, and I emulated Guy. When you're younger, you emulate someone you admire, and then eventually you find your own thing. That's what I did. That's what Steve did. I'm sure Steve would say that. Townes's influence on Mickey Newbury was profound. Newbury was one of the great, sensitive poets. For him, it was the Beatles and Townes Van Zandt as the starting places.

I play "Pancho and Lefty" almost every night. They're all great—"If I Had No Place to Fall," "Greensboro Woman," "Tecumseh Valley,"

"White Freightliner"—but "Pancho and Lefty" is my favorite. "Pancho was a bandit, boys / His horse was fast as polished steel / He wore his gun outside his pants / For all the honest world to feel." Don't get no better than that. I grew up with crazy, drunk people who were poets, but he was plugged into a different light socket.[8]

(L-R) Michael Grimes, Kris Kristofferson, author. Four Seasons Hotel, Austin, TX, August 2009. Courtesy Tamara Saviano

KRIS KRISTOFFERSON

The name she gave was Caroline, the daughter of a miner
  Her ways were free, and it seemed to me the sunshine walked
    beside her
–TVZ, "Tecumseh Valley," from *For the Sake of the Song*

K ris Kristofferson, born June 22, 1936, in Brownsville, Texas, has quite an eclectic and impressive resumé that includes Golden Glove boxer, Rhodes scholar, helicopter pilot, and movie star (*Pat Garrett & Billy the Kid*, *A Star Is Born*, *Lone Star*, and dozens of others). However, songwriting remains his most potent creative anchor. As a key figure in the 1970s "Outlaw Country" movement, Kristofferson's early albums *Kristofferson* (1970) and *The Silver Tongued Devil and I* (1971) immediately established him as a top-tier songwriter whose tunes have been recorded by Johnny Cash, Janis Joplin, Ray Price, Roger Miller, and many other prominent artists.[1]

Plainspoken poetry forever unites those kindred spirits, but Kristofferson crafts more cerebral narratives. Unlike most songwriters, he addressed a broad range of social, political, cultural, and personal issues largely taboo in country music at the time that he began writing professionally. Kristofferson has always written in a succinct yet highly nuanced style that is more akin to John Steinbeck than to most Nashville tunesmiths of the early 1970s. Indeed, few writers as fluidly convey human kinetics as Kristofferson does on songs such as "For the Good Times," "Sunday Morning Coming Down," and "Loving Her Was Easier (Than Anything I'll Ever Do Again)."[2]

By nature an outsider, Kris Kristofferson often writes songs about better days for those who are down-and-out ("Shipwrecked in the Eighties") or disenfranchised ("Sandinista"). In fact, these themes of "personal liberty" and the "daily struggle of the dispossessed" are so common in his work that Kristofferson's long-time friend and guitarist Stephen Bruton once reportedly told him, "If you take freedom and sidewalks out of your show, you'd be speechless."[3]

In his song "The Pilgrim, Chapter 33," Kristofferson may have been referring directly to Johnny Cash and actor Dennis Hopper, but he just as well could have been describing Townes Van Zandt. "He's a pilgrim and a preacher and a problem when he's stoned," Kristofferson sings. "He's a walking contradiction, partly truth and partly fiction / Taking every wrong direction on his lonely way back home."[4] As Kristofferson himself said, "I heard so much about Townes from Mickey Newbury, who was really serious about songwriting. He said Townes was the best, and that included Mickey and me, so I figured he was serious."[5]

As a songwriter, Kris Kristofferson has earned commercial success mainly through others performing his songs. Perhaps most notable of

Townes Van Zandt in field (1970s), courtesy
Al Clayton

these was fellow Texan Janis Joplin's version of "Me and Bobby McGee,"
from her 1971 album *Pearl*. The song became a posthumous hit for Joplin,
a personal friend of Kristofferson, and provided the hippie generation
with a resonant mantra: "Freedom's just another word for nothing left
to lose."[6] Some music critics also consider Sammi Smith's rendition
of "Help Me Make It Through the Night" (1970) the greatest all-time
country single and place Ray Price's version of "For the Good Times"
(1970) above Willie Nelson's classic interpretation of Fred Rose's "Blue
Eyes Crying in the Rain" (1975).[7]

According to Don Was, who has worked with Kristofferson for years
and produced his recent albums *This Old Road* (2006) and *Closer to the
Bone* (2009), "there isn't a songwriter out there today who hasn't been
influenced by Kris. He's a giant."[8]

■ ■ ■

KRIS KRISTOFFERSON

The first time I met Townes was when we were filming *Songwriter*, which
was that film Alan Rudolph directed with Willie Nelson and me. We
were filming in Austin, and I got the word that Townes was out there

in the audience as an extra. Alan let me do this introduction of him, as a "songwriter's songwriter." He kept it in the movie. I remember when Townes stood up, when I introduced him, I could see, it was so sad to see, that he had no idea of the respect that so many had for him.

I don't know why that was, but I just thought that somebody should tell this guy how good he is. He was so pleased just to be recognized, and it was obvious to me that he hadn't gotten the feedback that I thought he deserved, the respect that people like Willie and Merle Haggard and I had for him.

Like a lot of us, he was in love with the beautiful loser ideal, the guy who was trying to be Hank Williams and die when he's twenty-nine. It's a very seductive role model because it's everything that you admire in somebody like Hank Williams. It was the same way with Johnny Cash when he was killing himself. A lot of people thought that was the way to go—to burn out rather than to rust.

It's a sad thing for me because it's so obvious that that's who Townes had decided to be. It's a sad way to go. People should know that Townes was the brains behind "Pancho and Lefty," and that self-destructive stuff kept him from being famous.

Townes wrote with a writer's eye. It's like the difference [between] the stuff that Willie Nelson was writing and what the Tin Pan Alley writers were writing. It's all real creative writing, as opposed to being a hack. Townes's songs are completely original poetry, but he's a real poet because he wrote from the heart. He had the tools.[9]

VERSE

CORY CHISEL

For temptation let me ply
  Be my wings, Lord, be my eyes
—TVZ, "Upon My Soul," from *The Nashville Sessions*

ory Chisel and the Wandering Sons' debut EP *Cabin Ghosts* (2008) weaves corresponding measures of Billy Joe Shaver's grit and Townes Van Zandt's grace through six portraits of infinite motion. The album's closing song "Home in the Woods" provides Chisel's mission statement of searching and solitude: "Don't mess with me, mama, I'm a mighty good man / I'll take a home in the woods by myself if I can." Cory Chisel, born in Elko, Wisconsin, followed with the full-length album *Death Won't Send a Letter* (2009).[1]

"If I do believe in spirituality, the only evidence I have is songwriting," Chisel says. "There is a haunting of sorts that can often be confused as a spiritual intervention. My father was a minister, so there are some things I can't figure out if I learned or if it's something miraculous. Have you ever seen a Baptist minister pour into the closing segment of a sermon? The cadence of a sermon can be so close to a song that a minister can almost start singing. It's like a hypnotic state, and you get to this place that's affecting you and really close behind it is melody.

"There's a state you can get into where finding a song is just cracking the surface. It's like picking a potato. It was already growing there, and you can just pull it out. I don't know if it's a different form of songwriting, but I know when I hear it.

"Townes Van Zandt would definitely be one of those people. People always call his music otherworldly, and that's why. It's not bizarre; it's very familiar to you. It's worth talking about. So many people say, 'Oh, I love how Townes has such a plain way of saying things.' Yeah, but it's eerily plain. It's very similar to a scripture being handed down. My friend [the songwriter] Richard Julian used to hang with Townes. He'd say that you'd talk and there'd be the normal Townes, and in a minute, he'd find a point and become elevated and transcendent.

"I've seen that happen to my father when he's preaching. One minute, he's my father; the next, he's a preacher; then, he's in possession of something of more importance, something of higher value. The religious aspects—the dogma, the Bible, stuff like that—none of that was interesting to me, but I definitely at times have felt in possession of a power that feels strange, and songs would come out of it.

"You almost learn to hate a guy like Townes so much. Instead of writing volumes to convey something, he could write two lines and sum up every complex entity that you were trying to put together in fifteen pages."[2]

Billy Joe Shaver, South by Southwest, Hotel San Jose, Austin, TX, March 16, 2007

BILLY JOE SHAVER

Now, the Lord resides inside a house of golden
And faith is the door and love is the key
— TVZ, "Two Hands," from *High, Low and In Between*

Billy Joe Shaver's earthy yarns link sacred and secular with a devil's grin. "Faith gets in there almost every doggone time [I write a song]," he says. "I don't want to say anything bad about it, man, but it kind of gets me looking like some kind of preacher. Waylon [Jennings] called me a Bible-thumper. I said, 'I'll thump you, buddy.'"[1] Shaver and Van Zandt wreaked havoc together as rising songwriters in the 1960s; in fact, *Crazy Heart* screenwriter Scott Cooper partly shaped the film's unruly protagonist Bad Blake (Jeff Bridges) around the duo's early days. Shaver says their interests were more saintly later on: "Townes was a Christian. We talked about that a lot."[2]

Shaver, born August 16, 1939, in Corsicana, Texas, has anchored his songs in spirituality, organized and otherwise, from the beginning. For example, while his debut album *Old Five and Dimers Like Me* (1973) featured worldly classics such as "I Been to Georgia on a Fast Train" and the title track, it also included the country hymns "Jesus Christ, What a Man" and "Jesus Was Our Savior and Cotton Was Our King." Shaver has continued to balance sin and salvation throughout his career. For every "You're as Young as the Woman You Feel," "That's What She Said Last Night," and "Hold on to Yours and I'll Hold on to Mine," he has answered with "If You Don't Love Jesus," "Jesus Christ Is Still the King," and "You Can't Beat Jesus Christ."[3]

Billy Joe Shaver entered into public consciousness through Waylon Jennings's landmark collection *Honky Tonk Heroes* (1973). Shaver wrote or cowrote eleven of its songs, including "Old Five and Dimers Like Me," "Willy the Wandering Gypsy and Me," "Ride Me Down Easy," and the title track, which one writer called the "national anthem of the Outlaw Country movement."[4] *Honky Tonk Heroes* reached *Billboard*'s Top Twenty country album chart and earned a Top Thirty single with the Jennings and Shaver cowrite "You Asked Me To."[5]

Shaver songs frequently redefine threadbare cliché as universal truth ("Try and Try Again," "Live Forever"). His most wistful (for instance, "Magnolia Mother's Love," "Corsicana Daily Sun") and weary ("I Don't Seem to Fit Anywhere," "Blood Is Thicker than Water") also blur lines between life and art. In fact, Shaver, who lost parts of four fingers in an early sawmill accident, has lived through several tragedies that could serve as blueprints for teary country songs. Most notably, he endured the "cosmic misfortune" of his mother, first wife, and only son (the guitarist Eddy Shaver), dying within a year of each other. Additionally, Shaver suffered a heart attack onstage at Gruene Hall in New Braunfels, Texas, in 2001.[6] One writer supposes that his life "might read like the Book of Job as filtered through Hank Williams."[7]

Shaver, who recorded Van Zandt's "White Freightliner Blues" on the album *Poet: A Tribute to Townes Van Zandt* (2001), claims his first songs poured forth by age eight. He considers nearly all circumstances as creative inspiration.[8] "I really believe I was born to write songs," Shaver says. "I have a lot of songs that people discover later on. If I'd heard one of these songs that I wrote now, I guess I'd just shoot myself if I didn't write it. I just love my songs."[9] Shaver's no stranger to firearms. In 2007, he shot acquaintance Billy Coker in the face with a .22-caliber pistol after an argument at Papa Joe's Texas Saloon in Waco, Texas. He was acquitted on aggravated assault charges and pleaded no contest to a misdemeanor gun charge. Shaver performed in Houston the night that he was acquitted. He says he will not write a song about the incident.[10]

■ ■ ■

BILLY JOE SHAVER

I met Townes in the early Sixties in Houston, Texas. He and I used to play this place called the Old Quarter. I had been writing all my life, but I was just getting started playing in front of people a little bit. Townes coaxed me to get in front of them, but he was just dangerously good. Then Townes and me got to running around together and raising hell, and he's crazy as a damn bat. We'd go out and get all tanked up, take LSD or anything we could get our hands on.

My wife Brenda just hated Townes. She always had to come pick us up in the middle of the morning after we'd gone off to raise hell some-where. Then there was this time Townes had somehow acquired these leather pants, and he had his face all painted up with tears like a clown. She knew we was higher than a kite. She said, "This is it," and reamed his ass, chewed him out real good. She took him wherever he had to go, then she got a hold of me. I mean, that night, she quit me. Left me with $10. I said, "Just take me out to the highway," and she did, she took me to the interstate.

Actually, I was on Highway 10, trying to get to L.A. Couldn't get a ride. Finally, I decided I'd just get on the other side of the road and go to

Nashville. First guy that came by gave me a ride all the way to Memphis. He gave me a hell of a ride, and I didn't have but that $10. So, Townes is probably the reason I went to Nashville. It was just an accident. Brenda went back to Waco, and we got divorced again.

Brenda just hated Townes so bad, but she got cancer, you know, and she died in 1999. The doctor told me this one time that she probably wouldn't last the night. In my last desperation, I told her that I had a dream that she went to heaven, and Townes was there to meet her. She says, "By God, I'm gonna live." And she did. She lived for another year. She hated him, but I laid so much stuff on him. I'd go out and get into trouble, then I'd say, "Well, Townes. . . ." And that didn't help him. "That son of a bitch," she'd say. But you always got to have someone to lay it on.

We were playin' one night, me and Townes and Guy Clark and Gary Nicholson at the Bluebird [Café] in Nashville, not long before Townes passed. We set four chairs down around a table, didn't even have a microphone. I mean, it was so packed, but everybody could hear because they were quiet as a mouse. We just had a big old time. Townes and me got to playin' spiritual songs. Guy don't really like that, I don't think, but we sang spiritual songs, and we talked that night. I said, "If you go, you're ready, aren't you?" Because I'd known him longer than anyone, I guess. He said, "Yes, I am." I'm sure Townes went to heaven. If there's a heaven, and I'm sure there is, Townes went. He was a good-hearted man with a good soul, and a real sweet person.

But he'd fight, and he had a good punch. I didn't see that very often, but if it came down to it, we could go. I could fight, too; I boxed. If we'd get thrown down on, it wouldn't take much until everybody would leave us alone. We'd get thrown down on many times, and sometimes people would try to roll us. We was always wobbling around, screwed up on something, but there wasn't no sense in them trying. Him and me together, we could probably whip six, seven men, I'd bet. It just didn't hurt because we were on stuff. That was mostly early on in Houston. Houston is really rough.

When Townes came to Nashville, he found a new group of people that he'd hang out with—Skinny Dennis and Guy Clark and all the great writers. Guy was a great writer, and still is. Guy has his head together enough. He'd get crazy, but he's smart enough to figure things out and get you out of them. Townes and Guy are both good guys, but together they were just dangerous on the stage. They're both such great writers. That night at the Bluebird in particular—man, I wish I had a tape of that.

After Townes got married to Jeanene, I didn't see him much. At that point, there were just so many friends. I'd go over there, and there'd be so many that I didn't know. Steve Earle was just a baby, and he was hanging out there. My boy Eddy was just a baby, and he was hanging out there, too. Eddy just hung out with me and played [the guitar]. He played with Guy for a while.

Townes knew I cared about him. We'd go up to Vermont and play a lot. One time we were playing cards and—I couldn't believe it—I won money off him. If I hadn't won that money, we wouldn't have had any to leave town, the way Townes spent it. I always thought he let me win it, because you just couldn't beat him. Townes or Guy, you couldn't beat either at pitching pennies. I didn't gamble with Townes much because he'd take you for all you had.

Sometimes he'd get drunk and borrow money. He'd borrow $30 off me, and then he'd come back around and say, "Hey, can you loan me $30?" I'd say, "Damnit, Townes, I'm the same guy you borrowed $30 from a while ago." He was making the rounds, just picking up anything he could get, but he did give away more than he ever got; I do know that. If you needed money, Townes would give you every damn thing he had. If he had $10, he'd give you $10.

I have a real funny story about Townes. We were out in Arizona, and it winded up being just him and me out there wandering around. Neither of us had a car, so we were just out there hitch-hiking. He had this little Indian kid who was hanging around. Townes had this eagle feather hanging from the end of his guitar, and he kept tryin' to give it away, this real nice Martin. I mean, there ain't no telling how much it was worth, it had one of those three-piece backs. I said, "Townes, I'm just not gonna let you do this. I'm taking this guitar right now." And, of course, he didn't give me no fuss about it.

I told him I was gonna send it to Guy, because Guy would take care of it. I put it on an airplane and sent it to Guy. Brenda would wire me money because I was doing good with *Honky Tonk Heroes* out, all that stuff Waylon did. I was making a little money, but I'd usually run out of it around Townes, which is why I had Brenda wire some to me.

I went to the airport, and I taped up the guitar case. But before I did, I looked inside, and there were three or four songs in there. I didn't even look at them. I just wrote on them "C-," "D," and put an "F" on one. Then I wrote things like "needs work," like the way somebody would grade it in school. I never told anybody this. Guy would laugh his ass off, because he was the one that ended up with the guitar. I don't think they ever knew where that came from. Anyway, I taped up that guitar, and I sent it on.

About a month later, Guy says, "That danged guitar, it ain't got here yet." I said, "God, I can't believe that." So, he gets to checking on it, and it turns out that thing's gone all around the world. It had stickers on it from China, Alaska, everywhere. For some reason or another, that guitar got Shanghai'd, and I dared not say what I'd done inside of it. It might have been "Pancho and Lefty" that I put the "F" on. I never did tell Guy that I messed with them songs, but that was way the hell-and-gone back there, man, way back in the 1970s.

Townes as a songwriter had his own deal. We're all from Texas, but for some reason Guy and me have more of the Texas flavor. Townes went all over the place. Townes actually came from a real wealthy family, and I remember he always had a really nice place to stay, when he stayed put. Of course, my wife, she'd say, "Get out the razor blades. Townes Van Zandt could make a lot of money selling razor blades at his shows." I'd say, "Brenda, that's art." She'd say, "Shit."

I didn't get to see Townes much after Houston. We'd just hang out every now and again. That night at the Bluebird was the last time I'd sit down that close to him. He seemed to be in pretty good spirits. I was asking him about that, probably because when I hugged him, I felt a bone. I knew he was back on that stuff again. I asked him if his heart was in the right place, and he said, "Yeah, I've got Jesus in my heart."

Behind the wall, there's something on the other side. You can't destroy nothing here. Try to burn something, and it turns into smoke, turns into something different every time. Townes appreciated it. I loved old Townes; everybody did. You just couldn't help it. You couldn't keep from it. I mean, he was a mess, so you had to have unconditional love for Townes. He wasn't gonna try to win you over—you either loved him or you didn't. Brenda claims that she didn't, but I know that she did. If she didn't, she wouldn't have come and picked us up so many times."

Chip Taylor, Waterloo Records,
Austin, TX, December 1, 2010

CHIP TAYLOR

I rode my old guitar to heaven
*   But heaven didn't feel too much like home*
*   —TVZ, "Heavenly Houseboat Blues," from The Late,*
Great Townes Van Zandt

Chip Taylor, born James Wesley Voight on March 21, 1940, in Yonkers, New York, adopted his golfing nickname as a young songwriter. His seventh solo album *Hit Man* (1996), which bridged his careers as a briefcase country songwriter and traveling folksinger after a long absence from music, captures him better. Janis

Joplin, who recorded a version of Taylor's "Try (Just a Little Bit Harder)" on her album *I Got Dem Ol' Kozmic Blues Again Mama!* (1969), is only one of many singers who have had success with Taylor's tunes. Signed to CBS's Blackwood Music in the 1960s, Taylor wrote hits for a variety of artists including Willie Nelson ("He Sits at Your Table"), The Hollies ("The Baby"), Waylon Jennings ("Sweet Dream Woman"), Ike and Tina Turner ("Country Girl, City Man"), Bobby Bare ("A Little Bit Later on Down the Line"), and Anne Murray ("Son of a Rotten Gambler").[1]

Taylor is best known as the songwriter behind two transcendent classics—"Angel of the Morning" (recorded by Juice Newton and Chrissie Hynde, among others) and "Wild Thing" (The Troggs, Jimi Hendrix, comedian Sam Kinison, and countless others). One critic called Merrilee Rush and the Turnabouts' 1968 version of "Angel of the Morning" one of the top all-time country songs, while rapper Shaggy reached Number One with the song in 2001. However, "Wild Thing" remains Taylor's most widely popular composition. Its volatile three-chord riff and suggestive lyrics—"Wild thing, you make my heart sing / You make everything groovy"—likely have launched as many garage bands as The Velvet Underground.[2] "I loved Reg Presley and the Troggs," Taylor says of the band that topped the charts with "Wild Thing" in 1966. "They reminded me of the people I grew up with, real street guys. I never met Hendrix."[3]

One particular songwriter friend spoke to Taylor with reverence about Van Zandt during that time. "I had known of Townes, but I was always on the periphery of knowing who the other writers were unless they were thrown in my face," Taylor says. "I got to be friends with Kris Kristofferson in the late 1960s or early 1970s, and I'd go to see him and always heard about Townes. Kimmie Rhodes and Townes Van Zandt's 'I'm Gonna Fly' just may be my favorite duet recording of all time. The chill I get from that just doesn't go away."[4]

Taylor's raw storytelling often personifies his own personal passions and complexities. For instance, "Son of a Rotten Gambler," which Taylor wrote for his son, Kristian, directly addresses the career path he took during the 1980s and into the following decade. For fifteen years, Taylor quit music entirely to become a successful professional thoroughbred handicapper and card player. At one point, he was a blackjack champion who was banned from casinos throughout Atlantic City, New Jersey.[5]

Taylor returned to songwriting and performing in the mid-1990s as a solo artist with the albums *Hit Man, Seven Days in May . . . a Love Story* (1999) and *Black and Blue America* (2001). However, he truly hit his stride when he met fiddler Carrie Rodriguez at the South by Southwest music conference in Austin, Texas, in 2001. Taylor and Rodriguez's duet albums *Let's Leave This Town* (2002), *The Trouble with Humans* (2003), and *Red Dog Tracks* (2005) became Americana radio staples and launched Rodriguez's career as a solo artist.[6] "When I got the gig to play with him, I was so thrilled," she says. "I'd never even tried to sing before, other than in the car with the windows rolled up. It helps me connect with the songs on a deeper level."[7] "I can't say that I don't like the work I do by myself," Taylor says. "But as a vocalist, we're way better together. I get way more chills singing with her."[8]

Chip Taylor acknowledged his own deep connection with Austin's Cactus Café by penning the song "Jesus Christ—Don't Let the Cactus Fall" upon receiving news that University of Texas officials planned to close the revered venue in February 2010. (After significant protests and social media campaigns against the movement, the university ultimately kept open the listening room under different management.) Taylor released the song as a single through Austin's Waterloo Records during South by Southwest that spring. Its pointed message directly links Van Zandt to his "home club": "Some will say, Who gives a damn for that sacrificial lamb? Well, Townes and Lu and Guy and Joe and Ray, they have answered that call."[9] "I walk in the Cactus and feel like I'm home," Taylor says. "It's very reverent. You give your total, honest self when you play places like that, and you are who you are because you play places like the Cactus."[10]

■ ■ ■
CHIP TAYLOR

The Townes song I liked a lot was "For the Sake of the Song." I don't even remember when I first heard that, but I do remember specifically hearing it another time in my gambling years. I remember where I heard it. The station was cutting out, and I was trying so hard to listen to it, getting the feeling that it was such a wonderful song. I think maybe because of Townes's spirit it didn't end up being as commercial as it might have been, but it was magical.

You have to understand that from 1980 until 1996 I hardly listened to any music whatsoever. It was mostly just the addiction to gambling that took me away from music and into the science of gambling. It wasn't until I came back to making music in 1996, and then it was a whole different thing for me. My car was strewn with Townes records and John Prine things and a couple of Guy Clark, but mostly Townes. All of a sudden I got totally involved with Townes. It was so inspiring.

I love the spirit of his songs. They sound like they're so connected to his being, to his heart. Townes's songs were so not cerebral. At the time, I'd just gotten to know Guy Clark a little bit. Just when I was coming back, I performed with Guy at [the New York City folk club] The Bottom Line, and he had said, "Whenever you're ready, come on down, and I'll get on stage with you in Nashville." So, I started to talk to Guy every once in a while, and in doing so I was talking to Susanna. Maybe once a week, I'd call up and speak to Susanna, who always had just gotten off the phone with Townes.

It was so fun for me to be going back and forth, talking to Townes through Susanna. I was such a lover of his music and I was so interested in his spirit, and Susanna used to talk to me about that. I was really looking forward to meeting Townes, and I never did. It's one of the things I feel terribly sorry about. I love singing "Pueblo Waltz," which I used to sing once in a while.

I like the obvious ones. I thought "Pancho and Lefty" was wonderful, and when it was first getting popular I absolutely loved the song. I still do. "Tecumseh Valley" is one of my favorites. One of my favorite albums is that one he did when [former disc jockey on Austin's NPR affiliate station KUT 90.5] Larry Monroe did the commentary, the interview with him, *Last Rights.* That was part of what I loved about Townes, listening to him speak. It was just his character.

My favorite singers are the ones who attach their spirit to the music. So, my favorites without question are Townes Van Zandt, John Prine, Lucinda Williams. I like to listen to Guy, too, though he's a little more cerebral than the other people I listen to. For a guy who does that type of writing, he's just the top of the list, but I love Townes's voice. I was talking to somebody the other day about how much I love Kris Kristofferson, and he said, "Yeah, but it's better when you hear someone else sing his songs." I said, "Not for me." It's the same with Townes.

Townes lived a roguish life in many ways. He was a drinker, and he wasn't settled, but listening to Townes and John Prine is more like going to church than anything I know. In fact, I wrote a song, one of my favorite new songs that I've written, called "What Would Townes Say about That." My idea is that feeling of a certain . . . well, I say right in the song, "No, it ain't how I thought it would feel / I thought I'd feel bad, but I've taken a turn for the worse / Think I'll get me to church / Singing, what would Townes say about that? / Would he just sing me off to some place in the sky where the sad angels fly? / Love's worth the hurting / Because all in good time / Everybody's waving goodbye."[11] I love that.

Listening to Townes is what lifts me to a better place in my being and in my work. I think if taken correctly, raising the bar means really, absolutely getting in touch with your spirit and letting that take you and move you in your music. That's what Townes and John Prine do at their best—in fact, almost always Townes does that. When I listen to Townes, I just get a real heart. It makes me feel like absolutely being myself, as true to myself as I can be—not a craftsman, not somebody who's trying to write songs to make people smile.

We're all songwriters. You listen to Kris talk about his early days and how important it was for him to be successful making a living at writing songs and have his poetry accepted. I guess with Picasso or Rembrandt, all these people, their goal was to have their work looked at and cared for, but they were true-hearted people. Their work was inspired by their own absolute inner being, and that's what Townes was about. At my best, I can really enjoy myself from that level. Not as somebody saying, "Didn't I write a good song," but letting my spirit move.

Townes could have written "For the Sake of the Song" a different way to make it sound more like the way people like, but what I loved about it was that he didn't. Like in "If I Needed You," he says, "Loop and Lil agree." And you go, "Okay," you know, "why not?" I don't care who Loop and Lil are. I found out later, but that's great because you know it's coming from a true place. In the best kind of music, I don't care if I don't know the specific names or the specific places. If it's told from a true heart, I'll be there and I'll know those people and I'll get that feeling.

Townes is like a Rembrandt. You're going to find that over the years, as all the crap folds and falls apart and all the celluloid and the plastic things get thrown in the junk pile, there's nothing you're going to want to dig up 1,000 years from now except for a few things. Townes will certainly be one of those things. Sure. He's growing and growing. People are finding out more and more about his genius, his heart. And how wonderful he was.

I'm not out there enough to know the real magical people, but you take even just like a talent, someone like Norah Jones, what a wonderful spirit she is. Here's a girl, she's not claiming to be a genius or anything like that. She's just starting to write, and she's not claiming that her writing is at the top of the world. But her magic is her soul and what comes through her heart as she sings words attached to her keyboard, and she's a one-of-a-kind. Even though some of the stuff she may be doing right now is lightweight, as a person and a talent she's never lightweight. She's humble and she's honest and she's special. She recorded one of Townes's songs ["Be Here to Love Me"] on her album [2004's *Feels Like Home*].

When I tour Europe, I run into Townes stories all the time. It seems like almost everybody tells me, "This was the second-to-last show Townes played," or something like that. I love that. Up in Norway, one promoter is such a fan of Townes, and he's always so supportive of me. I've played places in Norway that Townes played, but I've played lots of different places where he was, too. I just hit the same places all the time, and it's always nice to hear about him. I don't think I've ever heard of anyone who didn't love him. Most of the time, they just kind of let you know they loved him, but in those later days they had to help him get through shows. There's a lot of talk about that, but there's always still a reverence.

I forget where it was, maybe the Cactus Café—somewhere I played recently—where they told me Townes was onstage, and all of a sudden he just went to sleep. And that was it. He was drunk and he just nodded off and everyone waited a few minutes and let Townes go to sleep. But the stuff I love listening to is the concerts, listening to him talk. There wasn't much difference between him talking and him singing. He had a very true spirit when he talked about his stuff because he was very honest about it, and about how he wrote different things or what he was thinking about. Then he went onto the song, and it was the same sort of feel.

It was so sad I never got to see him perform. I would talk to Susanna so often, as she became like one of my phone mates. I'd talk to Guy and Susanna, just before Townes died, and Susanna was always telling me, "Townes said this, Townes said that." She used to tell me about their early days together, so did Guy. Showed me pictures when they were all hanging out together, a bunch of hippies living together and working on their craft. It's all very inspiring. That gets me closer to whatever you think about God.[12]

Tom Russell, Kerrville Folk Festival, Kerrville, TX, May 25, 2008. Courtesy Susan Roads

TOM RUSSELL

So, I reach for her hand, and her eyes turn to poison
*   And her hair turns to splinters and her flesh turns to brine*
    —TVZ, "Our Mother the Mountain," from *Our Mother the Mountain*

Tom Russell, born March 5, 1953, in Los Angeles, California, has an eclectic background that includes criminology student, taxi driver, folk artist, art collector, and regular correspondent with late Los Angeles poet Charles Bukowski, detailed in the book *Tough Company* (2008). In Bukowski, who wrote frankly and often comically about those destitute and down-and-out as well as his own employment at several menial labor jobs, Russell found a kindred spirit. Both writers employ protagonists who calculate time by number of daydreams between the morning alarm clock and afternoon shift bell. "Bukowski wrote about the working-class life with a fresh, outrageously honest viewpoint," Russell says. "It was a very European approach, like Celine—hardcore and hip and irreverent. The best of Bukowski resonates with truth."[1]

Russell, who has lived many places including Nigeria, Spain, and Norway, moved from Vancouver to seek his own truths in Central Texas in the 1970s. He and pianist Patricia Hardin released two albums that contained a "cosmic folk" mix of Beat poetry and Southwestern-style music.[2] During that time, Russell occasionally ran in similar circles as Townes Van Zandt, whose song "Snowin' on Raton" he later recorded with Gretchen Peters on the album *One to the Heart, One to the Head* (2009). "I met Townes on and off in the late 1970s when I lived in Austin," Russell says. "My first impression was that he was a shape-shifting, half-breed, Navajo trickster."[3]

Tom Russell's own songs have been recorded by a variety of notable country artists, including Johnny Cash ("Veteran's Day"), Suzy Bogguss ("Outbound Plane"), Nanci Griffith ("Canadian Whiskey"), Doug Sahm ("St. Olav's Gate"), and Joe Ely ("Gallo de Cielo"). He's closely linked to Southern California songwriter Dave Alvin, who recorded and regularly performs Russell's "Blue Wing," a song that displays the songwriter's sharp economy of language. "Writing with Tom is remarkably easy," says Alvin, who matched wits with Russell on the songs "Haley's Comet" and "California Snow." "We both think similarly. Of course, we'll write a song and then have an argument—a friendly argument—over a word. If you listen to Tom sing it later, he'll be using the word he wanted, and in mine I'll use the one I wanted. Everybody wins."[4]

Russell's carefully plotted story songs parallel songwriters such as Guy Clark, Ray Wylie Hubbard, and Robert Earl Keen, but his lyrical aim draws straighter lines to more politically minded artists such as Steve Earle and Kris Kristofferson.[5] For instance, "California Snow" reports "a true story about a California border agent who finds a husband and wife frozen to death while trying to cross the border."[6] "There's a Mexican dead on a power line / He's deader than yesterday's communion wine," sings the current El Paso, Texas, resident on the similarly focused ballad "Stealing Electricity." "He's trying to get something he could not afford for free / Just a poor man stealing electricity."[7] Beat poet Laurence Ferlinghetti recited "Stealing Electricity" on the Russell tribute album *Wounded Heart of America* (2007).

Tom Russell personalized his focus on immigration with the folk opera *The Man from God Knows Where* (1999), a "bizarre soundscape" based on his family's move from Ireland and Norway, and politicized it with the album *Borderland* (2001). Russell recorded *Blood and Candle Smoke* (2009), an album based on his studies in criminology and time living in Africa, with the Tucson, Arizona, band Calexico. One writer reviewing the album effectively described Russell's entire catalogue: "Maybe the CD's message is that there is no such thing as untroubled times or an untroubled mind."[8]

■ ■ ■

TOM RUSSELL

I heard Townes in Austin in person in the mid-1970s when he was playing the joints. I recall having an LP of *The Late, Great Townes Van Zandt* and thinking "Pancho and Lefty" was an odd, cubist cowboy song. Then there was "Our Mother the Mountain." I thought he had tapped into some deep level of folk myth I wasn't aware of.

I always thought Townes was some sort of beat-up bronc rider from Gallup, New Mexico. I had no idea he came from Dallas wealth, had played high school football, and all that. I can identify with his past, now, and the mental health deal. In the end, he was a minstrel—he had that vibe—like he walked right out of a Chaucer poem.

I never really hung out with Townes. I said hello and chatted. I was shy around guys like that when I was learning the trade. He challenged me to a foot race, once. While I was taking off my boots, he took off and won five bucks off me. I recall another time I went to visit him in a dressing room in New York and he looked rather lost. It was during one of his sober periods, and he kept telling me that his kids really loved my song "Navajo Rug" that I wrote with Ian Tyson. But he looked like he was in pain. Being sober was a hard road for him.

I saw him perform both drunk and sober. Saw an amazing performance once at Kerrville where he told this long story about walking down to the edge of a river with one boot on. It was typical Townes, just an offbeat anecdote that went on and on. It was really dry and odd and funny. He was a very funny cat. He walked along that tightrope as he performed, and he fell off occasionally and landed in the crowd or hit the ground. Usually there wasn't any safety net. He got beat up. You could see it in his face over the years. Gradually, it looked like something Picasso had painted.

I love "Snowin' on Raton." It speaks to what we do as singers on the road, and it hits the note. I really liked "Two Girls," because it had that odd line about the water moccasins treading ice. I tried to learn "Mr. Mudd and Mr. Gold" once, but I ain't a poker player, and I didn't get a handle on it. It sounded to me like something out of *Alice in Wonderland*, kind of scary—cards talking and all that.

The songs are odd and honest and full of myth, a myth that only Townes could tap into. I heard once that he used to read a lot of Gothic history novels, and his songs sound like it. Like knights riding through the woods and all that. Townes clearly tapped into the dark mystery, and it's a hard thing to pull off, unless you are a true poet. Most people don't have the guts, mind, or heart to dig down into that netherworld. Townes lived there.

The whole talk about Townes not reaching a wider audience during his lifetime is a lot of bullshit. They lay that on me all the time, too. He led the life he was meant to lead. There's no sense in trying to figure out why he wasn't as popular as Springsteen or Dylan or any of that. That's some trip journalists are on. It certainly did not help for people to compare him to Dylan and say he was the best in the world because his lack of financial success confused him at times. He made his own road. So did [jazz trumpeter] Chet Baker.

None of us is versed enough in deep psychology to delve into the reasons some people fall out of high windows. We should be glad he was here for a while. Townes's lasting contribution to folk music was creating an intensely personal body of honest, deeply etched work that will stand out. He didn't cop to any message or political routine. He went deeper than that, and he paid the price of the journey.[9]

Graham Leader. Courtesy
Graham Leader

GRAHAM LEADER &
HEARTWORN HIGHWAYS

I guess I'll keep a-gamblin', lots of booze and lots of ramblin'
  It's easier than waiting around to die
  —TVZ, "Waitin' Around to Die," from *For the Sake of the Song*

Many music critics consider the documentary *Heartworn Highways* (1981) to be a primary reference point for the 1970s New Country music movement.[1] The nonlinear film draws parallels between the songwriting communities in Austin and Nashville by highlighting clear emphases on art rather than commerce. Furthermore, *Heartworn Highways* illuminates Townes Van Zandt's nature as an outsider versus Guy Clark's more communal approach to the songwriting craft. While the filmmakers find Clark, Steve Young, and youthful pupils Steve Earle, Rodney Crowell, and John Hiatt staking claim to Clark's proclamation that "Nashville in the '70s was like Paris in the '20s," Van Zandt alone represents Austin.[2]

The movie's producer Graham Leader and director James Szalapski capture important insight into Van Zandt during a passage filmed inside his neighbor "Uncle" Seymour Washington's small house in Austin's Clarksville neighborhood. The scene shows Washington, a 79-year-old "walking blacksmith" who "might've made a good preacher," explaining the equal measures of deliverance and damnation in drinking whiskey. Van Zandt immediately betrays his idiosyncrasies. After Washington says, "People condemn whiskey, but they have no right to," Van Zandt exclaims, "Amen." However, Washington quickly aims his attention at Van Zandt and lectures, "But you don't have to drink a barrel of whiskey because you see a barrel sitting there." The songwriter appears ashamed.[3]

The visceral power of Van Zandt's music soon emerges. As he plays his song "Waitin' Around to Die," Washington openly weeps under the weight of its lyric, "I tried to kill the pain / I bought some booze and hopped a train."[4] Van Zandt later recalled the lighter free-for-all aspects of the day. "It was winter, and they wanted to have a Seymour-style barbecue where we lived," he said. "A couple friends and I tried to get a fire going. There were people driving past looking at us like we were nuts."[5]

Earlier in the film, Van Zandt and his young girlfriend (later his second wife) Cindy Morgan give an animated tour of their ramshackle yard. The songwriter cradles a rifle, a bottle of whiskey, and a soft-drink mixer. He's charismatic and reckless and clearly at ease in front of the camera. "He was the best thing in that movie," Guy Clark says. "Townes is the only guy who didn't try to play it like the camera wasn't there. He's just the most extraordinary character, the best as far as I'm concerned."[6]

However, guitarist Mickey White remembers this time during the mid-1970s as a creative low point for Van Zandt. "It wasn't a very productive time for him," White says. "He didn't do too many gigs. He mostly sat around drunk all the time."[7] In fact, Van Zandt overdosed on heroin in front of Cindy while they lived together in Clarksville (not his first heroin overdose). In a separate incident, he was discovered unconscious in a dumpster two months before the filmmakers arrived in Austin and was admitted into the alcohol and drug abuse treatment ward of Austin's Brackenridge Hospital.[8]

Townes Van Zandt's contributions to *Heartworn Highways* nevertheless remain invaluable. Notably, his syrupy early version of "Pancho and Lefty" with its measured delivery and unpolished lyrics proves a distinct highlight of bonus footage included in the film's 2003 re-release. "I wrote this about two Mexican bandits that I saw on the TV," Van Zandt says, "two weeks after I wrote the song." Equally loose extras, including performances by Clark ("Desperadoes Waiting for a Train"), Earle ("Darlin', Commit Me"), and Hiatt ("One for the One"), mirror Leader and Szalapski's haphazard approach. "The film was really shot from the hip," Leader says. "We went down there with an idea of what we were after and the musicians we were interested in and culture that we wanted to discover. There was no script, no blueprint, nothing."[9]

■ ■ ■

GRAHAM LEADER

Townes was going to be a central character in the film, to the extent that you can capture Townes. He's fairly elusive in many ways and is very open in many ways. We didn't have much time to make the film and very little money. We spent a total of three days in Austin, and we just took Townes as we found him. Everything Townes gives you is a gift.

I think he's clearly one of the most freethinking, original poets, and he's a performer. He's got the gift of the gab. He's a performance artist. That whole thing in the film in the garden and around the cabin, the rabbit holes and everything, that's completely off the cuff. He shows the chicken coop and the champion chicken and the piece of fur nailed to the coop, and says, "It was either that or a hungry midget." That was off the top of his head.

He's inspiring, exhilarating, extraordinary. Whenever he's on camera, it's riveting. You just have to be able to capture those moments. That's really the gift of the guy who shot and directed the film, James Szalapski. I think all the footage is interesting. You have to realize that we were down there to spend time with Townes to see what we could get. He played a club there, but he was too out of it and the performance wasn't really anything we could use. With Townes, you take what you can get.

Townes is a very sophisticated intellect. He's not just a great songwriter and singer; he's a very interesting guy, and he sees the world through his own prism. To be with Townes—as with all these guys—there's a matter of being trusted. Everybody has their defenses up a little bit. There were only six of us, and we were all about the same age, doing everything the best that we could. I think most everybody felt comfortable having us around. We didn't move in and start pulling things apart. We did things as unobtrusively and thoughtfully as possible.

Townes was always aware of the camera. He used it as a foil in a way the other characters didn't. There are so many contradictions in Townes. He's masterful, and at the same time completely guileless; he's a very smooth performer, and he's falling down drunk; he's a clown, a genius. He's just a mass of contradictions. I think he used the camera, and he made it part of his show. In a way, it was very disarming and very revealing and interesting in the way only Townes could be.

There were things we shot at Guy Clark's house or [Nashville photographer] Jim McGuire's where we'd be up all night but just be a part of it while it was happening. The camera became another character in the situation. Maybe with Guy—I wouldn't say it was more structured,

Townes Van Zandt in *Heartworn Highways*, 1975, courtesy Graham Leader

because it was pretty crazy—there was an opportunity to let the characters interact and for the music to take over and the evening and night would unfold. Jim [Szalapski] was very, very intuitive, and I think it was very beautifully shot.

We were shooting a performance of Guy at the Exit/In singing "Texas Cookin'" or "L.A. Freeway," and he was performing for the camera. Guy is a craftsman, and just a very different character than Townes. Of course, when we were shooting at his home, there'd be eight other musicians there. Why did people pretend the camera wasn't there? At that point, it was as if it wasn't. We'd become so integrated into the situation. The Christmas Eve sequence, I would say that isn't just pretense when you feel the camera isn't there. We as filmmakers, as a team, I think we earned that. When we were interviewing him, Townes was the center of attention. I think he could have tackled that many ways, and to take the camera on how he did—directly—it made perfect sense.

What got me interested in this film in the first place was that I was rather bored with what I was doing, which is the prerogative of someone so young who doesn't realize how tough things can be. I was very naïve about that, and I met the filmmaker, and we became very close friends very quickly, just hit it off. He had been nurturing this dream and had a very clear vision of what this world was all about. He started playing this music for me. I had been listening to the Rolling Stones, Bob Dylan, the Beatles, all that kind of music at that time. I just had an interest in music, and we went down to Nashville together just to see what was going on there. I didn't meet Townes on that trip. He was in Austin, and we didn't go as far as Texas.

I arrived at Nashville on a night Guy was playing at the Exit/In, and I met Susanna and some other musicians. I was coming from Paris and this was a completely different world, very authentic, then. I don't know what it's like now, but it seemed to me to be a world that was very gritty and authentic and full of colors that I had never seen before, let alone music I was just beginning to appreciate. I thought, Gosh, that's a world that could be interesting to anyone who doesn't know it. It's not exactly a secret society, but it's very hard to penetrate that tight-knit of a group of people.

Through Skinny Dennis and Jim, it felt like we had access to something very rare and special. If we could capture that on film with the music, I thought the energy and the music and the whole thing was very fresh and compelling. Literally a month later, we were shooting the film. I basically bankrolled the first part of it. The experience of making the film was brutal. We had very few resources, and I was learning as I was going along. It was quite the complicated process, producing a music film with all that's involved with the managers and recording companies and song rights and all that. It was all just happening as it was happening, very spontaneous. I think just as a filmmaking work experience, it was one of the most exciting things I've ever done.

The last time I saw Townes perform was in '93 in London. He was playing acoustic with Guy. I saw him actually a couple times in London. Townes traveled quite a lot. I'd say through the last years of his life I didn't keep in close touch with him except through his music, but if he was playing in town and I was there, I would go see him and we'd hang out and go drinking.

I saw him in London in the late '80s, maybe 1990, and he was drinking heavily and living hard, and we were up the whole night. He was really right out there. The last time I saw him he was on the wagon. Actually, he kept the show together. It was at a college auditorium, I want to say in northeast London near the British Museum. The sound equipment was completely messed up. Guy got really ticked off and went and drank a bottle of vodka. I mean, that wrecked the performance, but Townes kept it going. He was totally together and held the show together. Guy was understandably ticked off. He'd come all the way to London, and they couldn't even get the sound system working. Townes took the situation and made the best of it, really put on a great performance. It was really amazing. I'm not saying that as a put-down for Guy, just to say that Townes was very clearly sober and very together.

To mark the film's re-release on DVD with the bonus footage, there was a screening in Nashville, and it was one of the highlights of my career. There was a question-and-answer that went on for about an hour and a half, and I'd say 80 percent of the audience stayed for that, which is unheard of. Guy Clark and Steve Young and I were there to talk about it. At the end, Guy was introduced singing "Desperadoes Waiting for a Train," and he'd never seen that footage before. It's really pretty amazing. That's a beautiful song, so powerful. I think it's the most moving song in the whole film.

Then Steve Young was introduced singing "I'm So Lonesome I Could Cry," which he'd never seen before. At the end, the moderator asked if anyone would be interested in seeing any more bonus footage with John Hiatt and Townes, the royalty check scene. Everyone just stood up and clapped and they wanted to see as much as they could. It was really an amazing screening. It was packed, people filling the standing room in the back. I suppose it was a receptive audience, but it was just a magical kind of thing.

The film really wears its heart on its sleeve. It's a love story. It was made with such warmth and compassion and care. Everything that needs to be said about someone as original and talented and authentic and real as Townes has been said in the film. I was very, very moved by the film when I saw it recently. Townes, like the filmmaker, died prematurely and rather unnecessarily. Townes was a candle. He was incandescent, and we caught a little bit of that light, that brilliance and beauty, and I'm very happy with the small contribution that I could make. I'm glad we have that to remember a life that was fully lived but was too short.

I still listen to his music all the time. I hadn't seen the film in years, so when I saw it again in Nashville it was extremely gratifying. I've sat on it for many, many years thinking it would eventually see the light of day and be acknowledged. I really feel it's a strong piece of work and to see Townes in it, I'm of course sad that he and the filmmaker are no longer here, but I'm very grateful for the experience to be close to him and his music.[10]

Steve Young. Courtesy www.steveyoung.net

STEVE YOUNG

If I had no place to fall and I needed to
   Could I count on you to lay me down?
   —TVZ, "No Place to Fall," from *Flyin' Shoes*

Steve Young, born July 12, 1942, in Newnan, Georgia, appears to be skimmed over in many country music compendiums, but the singer-songwriter played a key role in the Outlaw Country movement of the 1970s. His debut album *Rock, Salt & Nails* (1969), which features prominent guests such as legendary country-rock singers Gram Parsons and The Byrds' Gene Clark, established Young as a rising songwriting talent.[1] His following album *Seven Bridges Road* (1972) includes Young's two most widely known hits—"Seven Bridges Road" and "Lonesome, On'ry and Mean."

Several major artists, including Rita Coolidge, Joan Baez, Dolly Parton, and Alan Jackson, recorded "Seven Bridges Road." However, the popular Southern California country-rock band The Eagles had the most success with their up-tempo version of the tune on the double-LP *Eagles Live* (1980).[2] Perhaps more importantly, Waylon Jennings's gritty reading of "Lonesome, On'ry and Mean" became one of the Outlaw Country movement's primary calling cards. Jennings quickly became an outspoken supporter of the songwriter. "Young is the second greatest country music singer, [next] to George Jones, of course," he said. "[Young] has no earthly idea how great he is."[3]

Young likely was heartened by Jennings's focus on his skills as a singer rather than as a songwriter. "One thing I don't like about songwriters is that a lot of them can't sing and play," Young says. "I like songwriters interpreting songs, which maybe was more fashionable in the 1960s and 1970s. It takes a musician to do that."[4] Accordingly, Young provided groundwork for the albums *Honky Tonk Man* (1975) and *Renegade Picker* (1976) with an equal measure of originals ("Alabama Highway" and "Old Memories") and interpretations (Hank Williams's "Ramblin' Man," Guy Clark's "Broken Hearted People"). Two years later, Young employed Townes Van Zandt's song "No Place to Fall" as the title track to his final album for RCA Records.

For years, Steve Young shared Van Zandt's view that excessive drug and alcohol use was necessary to become a "tortured artist." In fact, one writer claims "Lonesome, On'ry and Mean" could "easily be the title of [Young's] autobiography," considering his battles "against the music business and his own personal demons."[5] Young struggled with drug and alcohol addiction throughout the 1970s, but he achieved sobriety soon after releasing *No Place to Fall* near the end of the decade. Young credits heightened spirituality with helping him make the lifestyle transition. "There's a lot of dark and brilliant humor that comes out of places you can't go unless you're drunk or loaded," he says. "In my opinion, a lot of musicians have problems with drinking because of self-image. Buddhism helped break me free of that."[6]

Steve Young reinvented himself personally and professionally during the 1980s and released *To Satisfy You* (1981), *Look Homeward Angel* (1986), and *Long Time Rider* (1990) on a series of small record labels. He recorded the critically acclaimed albums *Solo/Live* (1991) and *Switchblades of Love* (1993) on Watermelon Records after moving to Austin, Texas, in the early 1990s. The latter was named the year's best folk album at the Nashville Music Awards in 1995.[7] The previous year, the small Australian record label Raven Records released a greatest hits collection appropriately titled *Lonesome, On'ry and Mean: Steve Young, 1968–1978*.

■ ■ ■

STEVE YOUNG

I met Townes at Guy Clark's house out in Mount Juliet, Tennessee. We used to hang out more in those days, which was probably in the 1970s. Townes and I always had a contentious relationship. We'd argue or debate things about history or what kind of person I was. We got into an argument, and Guy was sort of the referee. Townes was like that. He'd antagonize and stir up things, and he liked to do that. Nevertheless, we became friends and were friends as time went by.

Nashville never wanted real artists. It's a hyped town without any originality to offer, and it has little regard for people except after the fact. I don't know how that applies to the old guys who I grew up with, like Marty Robbins, but Nashville is one of the toughest towns for people who write real, quality, heartfelt songs, and Townes was writing real life-and-death stuff. People like that were ignored as a rule, but the group of guys in *Heartworn Highways* were the exception. Looking at it, you see how different and daring and reckless we were. It's odd that we were all congregated in Nashville. Townes liked rough people. Alkies are that way.

I say *Heartworn Highways* is hard to look at, because we were all just such drunks and drug addicts. I liked to do speed and cocaine and drink together. I used to try different things to control the drinking, so on that night they filmed us on Christmas Eve at Guy Clark's house, I didn't show up until around midnight. One of my plans was that I'd only start drinking at midnight, so I looked pretty good compared to some of them. But sometimes during the filming I was in very bad shape. I've experienced the influence of *Heartworn Highways* in places like Scotland, where my gigs are much better attended with a lot of young people idealizing and romanticizing the lifestyle.

In those times, I thought it was pointless to try to get a record deal, yet a friend of mine kept badgering me to go talk to this guy, Roy Day. Finally, I went down, and, sure enough, Roy Day says, "I want to record you if they'll let me." He was a pretty big producer at the time. The same friend showed me Townes's song "No Place to Fall." I started fooling with it, and it wound up on an album. "Snowin' on Raton" is a really great song. I really like "Waitin' Around to Die," though I used to think differently in the days when I was around Townes. I used to think, "Man, I'm depressing, but that's over the limit." As I've gotten older, I can see the wisdom and truth to it. It's a very honest song. Townes was able to find unique melodies in simplicity. I certainly think that can be done. You feel it. He probably felt it like I do. You discover it and go with it, and it's basically a simple thing.

Back in the day, Townes would play to only a few people in the audience. It was a grim thing. There used to be a place called Mississippi Whiskers on Church Street in Nashville, and there'd just be a few people there. Townes would just be droning on with his songs. It's like, "Here we are, the few outsiders, isolated."

I got sober near the end of 1979. I changed so much over those next few months. People would see me and say, "Is that you?" I looked so different, so much better. So, Townes saw me at Mississippi Whiskers, and he decided that he'd quit drinking, too. He lived out in Franklin in a shack by a river. Typical of Townes, he went home and chained himself to a tree so he wouldn't drink. He ended up staying dry for a time in the 1990s, but he was absolutely miserable the whole time, whereas I enjoy being sober.

One day after however long he'd been sober in the 1990s, he called me up and said, "I've gone back to drinking, and I want to tell you myself." I said, "Well, okay, whatever you want to do," and then probably said something in defense of being sober. He said, "My friends all think I'm an asshole sober." "Well," I said, "maybe you're just an asshole." From that point, he carried out the drinking. He felt compelled to call me because I'd been his mentor—his influence or example, momentarily—for sobriety and what might be possible.

I think any time anybody dies, the romanticizing starts. No doubt, Townes was a great songwriter. In the end, he couldn't write so much because he was just so messed up, but that's when it's really a daily survival mode. You don't really have time to let songwriting come forth that much. A lot of people will say he's the greatest songwriter of all-time, and maybe he is. I don't believe in the greatest anything because it's all just opinion, but he'll be this ongoing, legendary figure. I don't know how long that'll go on, though. Most kids don't know anything about the past, and some don't even know who The Beatles were. This whole legend stuff may fade away because of stuff like that, but there'll still be that small group who'll dig into all this.[8]

Jay Farrar, Fox Theatre, Boulder, CO, June 19, 2005

VERSE
JAY FARRAR

What can you leave behind when you're flyin'
  Lightning fast and all alone
  —TVZ, "High, Low and In Between," from *High, Low and In Between*

s a founding member of the influential bands Uncle Tupelo and Son Volt, Jay Farrar, born December 26, 1966, in Milstadt, Illinois, played an important role in the alternative country movement of the 1990s. In fact, music critics and historians frequently cite Uncle Tupelo's albums *No Depression* (1990) and *Anodyne* (1993) and Son Volt's *Trace* (1995) as the genre's defining hallmarks.[1] Farrar often closes concerts with the richly detailed travelogue "Tear Stained Eye,"

which Australian songwriter Kasey Chambers covered as a B-side to her hit single "Not Pretty Enough" (2002), from the latter collection. "I was listening a lot to Townes Van Zandt when 'Tear Stained Eye' was written," Farrar says.[2]

Farrar has also released several solo albums including *Sebastopol* (2001) and *One Fast Move or I'm Gone* (2009), a musical adaptation of Jack Kerouac's 1962 novel *Big Sur* with Death Cab for Cutie's Ben Gibbard. "To a certain degree, I've always identified with Kerouac's method of writing, just getting your first thoughts out there," Farrar says.[3] In 1995, Jay Farrar and Austin-based singer Kelly Willis recorded Townes Van Zandt's "Rex's Blues" for the *Red Hot + Bothered* compilation. Farrar occasionally performs Van Zandt's "White Freightliner Blues" in concert.

"Hearing Townes Van Zandt for the first time was like getting hit by a ton of bricks," Farrar says. "I had heard of Townes, but had not heard his music until about 1994 when a friend recommended *The Nashville Sessions* . . . Townes represented a link to some other music I was into from Ramblin' Jack Elliott to Bob Dylan, but the irreverence and pathos he brought to his songs was all Townes. I was a Townes junkie for a couple of years in the mid-1990s. People were perpetually sending me CDs and cassettes of his live shows . . . The first chance I had to see him perform was at the Maple Leaf bar in New Orleans. The next and last time I saw Townes perform was in Bethlehem, Pennsylvania, during a break in a Son Volt tour. We met briefly after the show. The one thing he said to me was exactly what I wanted to ask him: 'Are you taking care of yourself?'"[4]

Ramblin' Jack Elliott, Kerrville Folk Festival, Kerrville, TX, 2006. Courtesy Susan Roads

RAMBLIN' JACK ELLIOTT

Ride the blue wind high and free
    She'll lead you down through misery
    —TVZ, "Rex's Blues," from *Flyin' Shoes*

amblin' Jack Elliott, born Elliot Charles Adnopoz, on August 1, 1931, in Brooklyn, New York, has been a rodeo rider, street musician, student of Woody Guthrie, and mentor to Bob Dylan. At eighty, he retains a steel-trap memory. Elliott can recognize a city by area code, recite concert venues within its ZIP codes, and recount tales about guitar retailers by name.[1] However, his first encounter with Townes Van Zandt remains tellingly murky. "I can't remember when we met, but we might've both been drunk," Elliott says. "I know he was. I've never seen him sober."[2]

Elliott's close apprenticeship with Guthrie and its link to an aspiring Dylan secured his place in history well before meeting Van Zandt. As a twenty-year-old college dropout "fascinated by horses, cowboys, and the mythical West," young "Buck" Elliott bonded with Guthrie at a Brooklyn hospital in the early 1950s. Elliott sang songs for the ailing activist and folksinger until he became Guthrie's "perfect mimic." Guthrie was flattered by the attention and invited Elliott to bunk with his family for more than a year. "I think [my father] was grateful to have a protégé right there," Woody's daughter Nora Guthrie says. "I think my dad was happy to hand over everything he knew and everything about himself that he could pass on."[3] Elliott remained close to the family as Guthrie suffered from the Huntington's disease that claimed his life in 1967.[4]

Legendary folksinger Pete Seeger called Elliott "one of the finest pickers and singers and all-around entertainers I've ever seen on a stage." Seeger observed that Elliott adapted his entire way of living, including wearing cowboy hats and boots and expertly playing the guitar, to become the embodiment of the guitar-slinging cowboy he'd dreamed of being as a young man.[5] Several of Elliott's earliest recordings, including *Woody Guthrie's Blues* (1955), *Ramblin' Jack Sings the Songs of Woody Guthrie* (1960), and *Songs to Grow On by Woody Guthrie, Sung by Jack Elliott* (1961), directly saluted his mentor and established Elliott as one of Guthrie's foremost interpreters.

Elliott became a beacon of the thriving 1950s and 1960s folk music scene. During that time, he "liberated" a young Bob Dylan to change his name from Robert Zimmerman, and frequently introduced Dylan as his son onstage at gigs in New York City's Greenwich Village. In turn, Dylan, who achieved unparalleled fame during the 1960s, invited Elliott to be a part of his acclaimed Rolling Thunder Revue tour (1975), a union of highly regarded folksingers including Joan Baez, Roger McGuinn, and Joni Mitchell. Elliott's campfire singing style, an approach that has remained the same throughout his sixty-year career, well suited the outing. In fact, there was no "debate about including Ramblin' Jack, whose cowboy-errant lifestyle . . . paralleled the Revue's vagabond ideology." Some believe including him in the Rolling Thunder Revue was Dylan's way of paying back the significant debt he owed Elliott for helping launch his career.[6]

After spending the majority of the 1970s and 1980s away from the recording studio, Ramblin' Jack Elliott enjoyed a creative comeback with such albums as the Grammy-winning *South Coast* (1995), *Friends of Mine* (1998), and *The Long Ride* (1999). Elliott dedicated *Friends of Mine* to the recently deceased Townes Van Zandt, who in 1981 had opened Elliott's fiftieth birthday show at McCabe's Guitar Shop in Santa Monica, California.[7] Elliott included a wistful version of "Rex's Blues" with Van Zandt devotees Nanci Griffith and Emmylou Harris on the album. "Recording 'Rex's Blues' was Emmylou Harris's idea," Elliot says. "She liked that song."[8]

Elliott brought history full circle by closing his recent collection *I Stand Alone* (2006) with "Woody's Last Ride," a spoken-word story that details a nearly penniless cross-country road trip with Guthrie. The journey detailed ultimately mirrors Elliott's philosophy as a singer. "I think to be a good song interpreter," he says, "you have to have lived enough to understand where the person who wrote the song is coming from."[9]

■ ■ ■

RAMBLIN' JACK ELLIOTT

I liked Townes's musicianship and his style and mood and his way of expressing himself. He was a true poet. He also was a gambler, which I admired but appreciated from a distance, because I've never been a successful gambler. I don't know anything about card playing, and he was obviously a master at it. He tried to get me in a game like liar's poker every time I'd see him. I didn't know what he was talking about, but he was going to get all my money, that was for sure.

I figured gambling might spoil our friendship, but perhaps my approach kept us apart a little bit. The few times we were together, it was purely about Townes and me and the music. There wasn't any card playing going on, although he always did have a deck of cards nearby. I think I met Townes between seven and ten times, and I did a brief tour with him. He was traveling in a Chevy pickup with a camper on the back, and I was traveling in some other kind of car. He had another guitar player, Mickey White, with him. Townes certainly was a compelling performer.

A photographer friend of mine named Chris Felver, who recently shot a film about the poet Laurence Ferlinghetti, shot a two-hour film of Townes teaching me how to play the fiddle in New Orleans. It's probably the most boring film I've ever watched. I watched the whole two hours hoping I might learn something about fiddle playing, but it wasn't very entertaining. There was a bottle of cheap Smirnoff vodka there at the hotel. Townes's manager was there, and whenever it appeared that Townes was getting a little bit too deep into the sauce, the bottle would somehow miraculously, mysteriously disappear. It would stay gone for half an hour or so. After half an hour of no drinking, Townes would pretty much sober up, whereupon the bottle would miraculously reappear.

We consumed a good deal of the big bottle during the two hours, at which point we had a sandwich. Then we decided to go for a swim. Townes didn't have a bathing suit, so I went up to my room, where I had a spare pair of hiking shorts. I loaned them to Townes, and we decided to go for a swim. Now, there were a lot of very stylish ladies hanging around the pool, and Townes was feeling shy about his physique. He didn't look like a muscle man, and he didn't want to walk out there in his swimming trunks in front of all these bathing beauties.

I had an idea. I said, "Hey Townes, make believe you're Ray Charles and I'm your manager. You're blind, so I'll just guide you over to the pool. We'll just go for a nice swim. Okay, Ray?" He went along with that game and had his eyes closed and was groping around in the air with his arm and I had his other arm around me. I was guiding him to the pool. There was one more step. I said, "This one's a step up about six more inches, Ray."

Then he pulled a funny on me. As we were about to think about diving in the pool, he reached around and gave me a shove. I flew about twenty-five feet through the air, and there was a big splash in the middle of the pool. That distracted all the nice ladies, so they didn't see Townes as he slipped into the pool behind the echo of my splash. Once we were in the pool, we had a swimming race. We swam about four laps, and he beat me by about fifty feet. I was amazed. He was a really good swimmer.

Townes did one of the best jokes I've seen in a long time in that movie *Heartworn Highways*. There's Townes with his young girlfriend and his dog. He introduces the dog first, and then he introduces his girlfriend. I thought that was cute. Then after some folderol, he disappears into a hole in the ground. He was obviously drunk, but he had perfect control over everything, because Townes was used to performing drunk. He'd perform drunk at the Cactus Café, my favorite club in the whole world. I love playing there. Townes is much more loved in Texas than anywhere else, but I know that he has fans just as passionate everywhere else. I have a record of him playing in London, and I can really hear the applause and feel the appreciation they gave him there.

Anyway, I was invited to come down to New Orleans by the historian Doug Brinkley. This is when we had that two-hour fiddle lesson. I had never met Mr. Brinkley, but we were talking on the phone, and he said, "Jack, I want to ask you a favor." "Sure, what's that?" "When you arrive, someone will pick you up and take you to the hotel and you can drop your bags off. There won't be a lot of time to waste, because Townes Van Zandt is playing in a blues club, and with your permission, I'd like to bring you to the club as soon as you get rid of your bags. I want to go over and surprise Townes. I think it'll be a fun thing."

I said, "Well, do you know Townes?" He said, "Well, I never met him, but I'm a fan and I know his work." "Townes is a very sensitive person, and I don't know if he would appreciate me just barging in on him in the middle of a gig like that. It might disturb him, and I don't know how I feel about this." He says, "Oh, I think it'll be all right, just trust me, Jack." Here's a total stranger asking me to trust him, but I liked him and picked up something from his voice that sounded like he's a good guy.

So, his girlfriend picked me up at the New Orleans airport, drove me into town, and we dropped the bags at the hotel. We stopped briefly to get a bite to eat. We paid the bill and hurried out and zipped on over to the blues club and tip-toed up the back stairs to the upstairs dressing room and came through a fire escape. We walked in, and Townes saw me and his face lit up with a big smile and he said, "Jack." Everything was fine. He says, "Hey, will you play?" "Well, I guess." So, he played a few songs, and then he invited me to get up. He sat in the front row dictating all the songs I should play, and I think he made me play six or seven tunes. Of course, I realized that we were even better friends than I had formerly supposed.

I called Guy Clark on New Year's Eve day [1996] to wish him a happy new year, and we talked a little bit. Guy said, "Hey, Townes is here, do you want to say hi to him?" I said, "Oh, please, put him on." Townes got on, and he told me that they were listening to a record of a song of mine that he liked. Now, I've written five songs in forty years; I'm not a songwriter, but it's one of the gooder ones called "912 Greens." I don't perform it anymore because it's too long. Townes says, "We've been listening to '912 Greens,' and I sure do like that song." I said, "Thank you, Townes, and y'all have a good new year." He said, "I will," and he hung up the phone. He died about eight hours later.[10]

David Olney, Heart of Texas Motel, Austin, TX, October 28, 2010

DAVID OLNEY

Lie in circles on the sunlight, shine like diamonds
    on a dark night
Ain't no mercy in my smiling, only fangs and sweet beguiling
—TVZ, "Snake Song," from *Flyin' Shoes*

David Olney, born March 23, 1948, in Providence, Rhode Island, remains largely a mystery outside Nashville, but he's quite highly regarded within its scope. "Nobody else in the whole world knows when Mac's gonna open the Radio Café, but we do—and we tell each other," Todd Snider says in "From a Rooftop," a spoken-word tribute to his East Nashville neighborhood. "We stand around down there and smoke during Dave Olney's break."[1] The song suggests that fellow songwriters gather around Olney to offer attention and study closely his craft, which has shaped songs performed or recorded by Linda Ronstadt ("Women Across the River"), Johnny Cash ("Jerusalem Tomorrow"), Del McCoury ("Queen Anne's Lace"), and Emmylou Harris ("Deeper Well").[2]

Steve Earle often performed Olney's "Saturday Night and Sunday Morning" during the 1980s. "This is one of the most perfect songs I've ever heard," Earle has said by way of introduction. "I'd been singing this song for four, five years before I realized that I'd run across a song that was so perfectly constructed that it doesn't have a rhyme in it anywhere."[3] After several years with the Nashville band the X-Rays (The Contender, 1981), Olney began a solo career with the albums Nashville Jug Band (1982) and Customized (1984). Two years later, Eye of the Storm, featuring "Saturday Night and Sunday Morning," paved the way to a turning point. "[1989's Deeper Well] was just a convergence of the right songs and being lucky and Emmylou Harris getting into it," Olney says. "Even without [Harris's interest], I think it was a very solid work that caught what I was doing."[4]

Olney formed a lasting mutual admiration with Townes Van Zandt during his first decade as a solo artist. "He'd come to stop by the house to visit, and it was like George Washington had shown up," Olney says. "It wasn't as deep a friendship as I have with Steve Earle or Guy Clark, but he liked my songs."[5] Olney might well underestimate his impact on Van Zandt. "Anytime anyone asks me who my favorite music writers are, I say Mozart, Lightnin' Hopkins, Bob Dylan, and Dave Olney," Van Zandt said at least once.[6] Olney repaid the compliment by anchoring his album One Tough Town (2007) around Van Zandt's evocative "Snake Song": "The future, he don't try to find me / Skin I been through dies behind me / Solid hollow wrapped in hatred / Not a drop of venom wasted."[7] "Who would think to write that?" Olney says. "It's a song about snakes, a straightforward way to talk about frightening things. It's not music for a feel-good generation."[8]

Olney's enthusiastic Dutch fan base taught him that "what I was writing was translatable into other cultures." He has acknowledged the support by releasing no fewer than four concert albums recorded in Holland—*Live in Holland* (1994), *Women Across the River: Live in Holland* (2002), *Illegal Cargo: Live in Holland* (2004), and *Lenora: Live in Holland* (2006). Olney's recent album *Dutchman's Curve* (2010) imagines a 1918 Nashville train wreck as "life as a series of more manageable collisions."[9] "'Dutchman's Curve' is close to where I live and record," Olney says. "This was also a way to give a tip of the hat to Holland."[10]

■ ■ ■

DAVID OLNEY

The first time I heard Townes was at a gig in Athens, Georgia, in January of 1973. I was opening for him at a club called The Last Resort. I was living in Atlanta at the time but was about to head for Nashville to try my luck there. One of the reasons I was leaving Atlanta was because I was splitting up with a girl I had been living with. The breakup was her idea, and I was heartbroken. She came to the gig in Athens as a kind of goodwill and goodbye gesture. So, I had a lot on my mind.

I had written maybe ten songs at that point. They weren't bad, but they were very derivative of old folk songs. This is to say that I had not yet found my own voice. I played my set, hoping to perform so movingly that my soon-to-be ex-girlfriend would change her mind, then found a seat to hear Townes play. It's very rare that we get to experience something or someone without any preconceived notions. We read reviews and blurbs of movies and books and recordings before we actually confront the work and artist for real. Hearing Townes play that night was one of those times when there was no hype in front. I was totally unprepared.

He came onstage wearing a cowboy hat, jeans, and white cowboy boots. He was very low-key in his interaction with the audience. I believe he had just flown in from Europe and was exhausted, jet-lagged, hung over, whatever. Then there were the songs. They were exquisite without being pretentious; sad without being maudlin; funny without being cheap; personal without being narcissistic. The poetry was so natural and so unguarded and unashamed. "Pancho and Lefty," "Columbine," "St. John the Gambler," one after another they poured out.

Suddenly, the breakup with my girlfriend became, not unimportant, but even more poignant, as if Townes's songs were intensifying every experience, good and bad. I was stunned. Doors were opening in my mind, leading to new ways to think about songwriting. A song could be a folk song and still be alive with emotion, not stuck in a previous time. I guess "Pancho and Lefty" is the one that hit me hardest. I would leave for Nashville a few weeks later and get to know Townes better, but there is only one chance to hear someone for the first time. That night in Athens was my chance, and I cherish it."

Richard Dobson and I went down to Houston in 1974, and we got there a week early. Townes was playing at the Old Quarter. We got to hear him night after night, and they were great shows, but hanging around he was just so crazy that I knew I couldn't keep up. I noticed that everyone was sort of like a satellite going around him. I felt like that would be disastrous for me to do, not just physically but artistically.

I did one tour in Townes's car with Cindy. We got to the gig at a place called the Iron Horse. These people drove up from Texas and were like, "We drove up to hear you, Townes." I thought this was going to be great. We go in the club, and they're the only people there. They proceeded to get completely wasted. Townes got up to play, and these fans from Texas got in a fight and were thrown out of the bar. There was nobody in the club. It was a very strange gig.

He went into a Goodwill store while we were in Little Rock and came back with this sport coat and said, "Hey, try this on." It probably cost five bucks back then, but it was such a completely unexpected act of generosity. That kind of was Townes's thing. I wore it for years, but I left it someplace.

A guy in Ireland had a tape of Townes doing a song I'd written called "Illegal Cargo." The idea that Townes would do a song of mine in public was thrilling. I'd run into people, and they'd say, "Oh yeah, Townes said I should listen to you." It wasn't just that he'd compliment you while you were there. He actually seemed to like the stuff. Just the fact that Townes liked my songs was a huge boost to me. I could put up with any amount of abuse, as long as I knew that. He wasn't the only person in the world, but he was such an important figure to us.

Think about "Dollar Bill Blues." It has that line, "Mother was a golden girl / I slit her throat just to get her pearls." Who is going to write a thing like that? I mean, he went into his unconscious and pulled this thing out and didn't go, "Ahh." He said, "Okay, that's it." It's a very powerful moment in the song. That struck me. If you're really going to go deep inside yourself, then maybe some things that come out will be pretty weird, but you have to try the best you can to get those things in the songs, too. He was very brave like that.

Townes's songs will be studied in schools. There are so many songs that it takes a long time to separate what's good and bad and exceptional. Townes's songs will be there forever. It's kind of like Hank Williams. Hank has a core of deep, rural Southern listeners, but also college professors can go, "That's pretty good. That's getting to it." There'll always be hardcore, rebellious outsiders who will be drawn to Townes. The lyric writing is so strong. It's just a matter of time before they'll be teaching it.

When I was playing solo, I'd have to do these gargantuan drives. Sometimes late at night I'd go through every word of "Pancho and Lefty." How did he do that? Every word is perfect. He didn't labor over every word and the flow would've come to him naturally, but look at "Lefty split for Ohio." It comes in the middle of the song, and at that moment the song isn't just a mythical tale of the southwest. It's one word: "split." Suddenly, it carries the song to a new time and place—from a splendid desert in a mythic past to a cheap Cleveland hotel in a tawdry present. That's the fifty-yard line. This is past, and that's the future. There's the movement of the gray *federales*, every verse they're getting older. I'd keep myself awake for hours with that. There's a lesson in that one.

Look at the first verse and the lyric, "You sank into your dreams."

That's in the second person. It's not Pancho or Lefty. It's Townes. Well, I don't know who it is, but it's a different person. Suddenly, you go into the story. It's like a prologue. You've got to sink into your dreams to pull that story and those images out, I guess. That floored me.

There are songs like "For the Sake of the Song." "Why does she sing her sad songs for me? / I'm not the one." There are two people, the girl singing and the "I" of the song. To me, that's two different parts of Townes's brain. It's like, Why do I sing these songs? He was able to feminize himself. Why do I do this? Why would anyone sing these kinds of songs? There's the lyric, "Does she actually think I'm the one?" To me, that's Townes saying, "Do I really think this song is going to change anyone's behavior? Will I make people happier or sadder or better with this song?" Then he brings the hammer down: I do it because the song demands that I do this. That's so cool.

I always think when I'm playing, my first obligation is to the song. A distant second is the people listening. You have to give a good gig, but there have been too many with no one showing up or showing up drunk or being assholes. It's great when people show up and get into it, but you can't count on them. You can count on the song. You owe it to the song to sing it like it's supposed to be sung, which is what pissed me off so much about the last year of Townes's life. He was dragging the songs through the mud.

Townes was poison to the big labels in Nashville. They wouldn't even acknowledge him. Yeah, "Pancho and Lefty" was cut, but if that became where the bar was set in Nashville a lot of people would've been out of work pretty quick. At the same time, I remember seeing him again around 1976, and he looked a lot worse for wear. Health-wise he was really starting to go downhill. So, right at the moment where he was starting to get a little bit of recognition and the underground songwriters were getting to know him, he was physically starting to show it and was going the opposite way.

When I first heard him, his finger picking and flat picking were really so good and different. Around the time he did *The Late, Great Townes*

Van Zandt, his playing skills began to deteriorate. He was very crazy, and there was no way he was going to be able to walk into a Nashville label and get a deal. He was just too outside, but he didn't care. He thought songwriters were gypsies who wandered. Maybe on some level it pissed him off that he wasn't recognized more. Some part of him wanted to be recognized, but maybe it was more as a poet. He had emotional demons to deal with that I can't even imagine.

It's hard to figure out why he was so extreme with the drinking. I've always thought if he was going to go that route, I kind of wish he died a couple years earlier. It was just so painful to see him play in the last couple of years, knowing what it used to sound like. He played at a place called the Boardwalk in Nashville one time. It was just a bunch of drunk people trying to buy him a drink. He got up onstage, and he couldn't get through a song. He was babbling on and burst into tears and all this crap that he did in the last year. I would never do this, but it was so horrifying to see this, I went up there and said, "Townes, you've gotta get off stage. You've got to leave now." He just went, "Oh," and left. It was so awful to see.

It seemed like he was writing a whole lot more when he started drinking again [in the early 1990s]. Maybe they were connected. It's like Billie Holiday. Jesus, it was terrible the way she abused her body with drugs and drink and all that stuff. People imagine what she could've done if she didn't do that stuff. Well, she might not have done anything. She might've become a seamstress. For some people, the drink bone is connected to the create bone. I think Townes was Townes like Django Reinhardt was Django Reinhardt. That's just the way he was. I don't think people realize the commitment. It's like, are you right-handed? Are you committed to being right-handed? It's just what you do. That's what Townes was born to do.[12]

Todd Snider, Rocky Mountain Folks Fest, Lyons, CO, August 21, 2005

TODD SNIDER

I've always been a gamblin' man
Roll them bones with either hand
–TVZ, "Dollar Bill Blues," from *Flyin' Shoes*

Todd Snider's increasingly political songwriting crested during the George W. Bush Administration ("Conservative Christian, Right-Wing Republican, Straight, White, American Males" and "You Got Away with It: A Tale of Two Fraternity Brothers") and peaked with the pointed anti-war EP *Peace Queer* (2008).[1] However, Snider, a satirical writer who often addresses serious cultural and political topics with skewed humor and plays himself the fool, keeps a lighthearted viewpoint. "With political songs, I risk sending out the message that I have knowledge that I clearly do not have," he says. "Anyone who knows me could tell you that."[2]

Todd Snider, born October 11, 1966, in Portland, Oregon, admits to being "the natural bullshitter in the neighborhood."[3] That locality changed frequently as he moved through an itinerant early adulthood from Oregon to Texas to Tennessee. Before settling for a time in Memphis and eventually for good in Nashville, Snider cut his teeth at Central Texas roadhouses such as San Marcos's Cheatham Street Warehouse and the nearby Devil's Backbone Tavern, both of which he has written autobiographical songs about ("The Ballad of the Devil's Backbone Tavern" and "Cheatham Street Warehouse").[4] "Cheatham was the first place to hire me, and [its owner] Kent Finlay was the person to tell me I was good enough at songwriting to go for a living at it," Snider says.[5]

Todd Snider draws inspiration from several Texas singer-songwriters including Kris Kristofferson, Guy Clark, Robert Earl Keen, Willis Alan Ramsay, Nanci Griffith, Al Barlow, and Aaron Allan.[6] He employed their sensibilities and developed a niche following with such early albums as his debut *Songs from the Daily Planet* (1994), *Step Right Up* (1996), and *New Connection* (2002). In the mid-1990s, the minor hit "Talkin' Seattle Grunge Rock Blues," from *Songs from the Daily Planet*, briefly made Snider a popular MTV staple.

However, Todd Snider's buoyant stage presence has always been his main attraction. Snider typically appears barefoot with plastic beer cup in hand and introduces himself with a short monologue early in each set. "My name's Todd Snider," he says, "and I've been driving around [for] fifteen years, making this shit up and singing it for anybody that'll listen to it. Some of it's sad, some of it's funny, some of it's short, some of it's longer than others, and sometimes I'll go on for as many as eighteen minutes in between the songs."[7] "I sort of go into a trance," Snider says. "It feels like once I say that part, I can relax."[8]

Several major artists have recorded Snider's songs, including Jerry Jeff Walker ("Alright Guy"), Cross Canadian Ragweed ("I Believe"), and Gary Allan, who made "Alright Guy" the title track to his 2001 album.[9] Country music superstar Garth Brooks recorded the same song for his 1999 album *The Life of Chris Gaines*, but later cut the track, reportedly fearing that his mother would disapprove of its reference to marijuana. "[Brooks] was really gracious about it, and he gave me a bunch of money just for my time," Snider says. "That was a cool experience. I got to play guitar and the harmonica. Boy, it was on the record until the last minute. I mean, like the day before."[10]

Snider, who performs most frequently as a solo acoustic troubadour like Townes Van Zandt, met the songwriter at a John Prine gig in Nashville in the early 1990s. "I thought it was cool that people used to say that Townes would always have five new songs every time you'd see him: long, sad songs," Snider says. "Of course, he'd never remember them if you saw him again. That's what Jerry Jeff told me one time."[11]

■ ■ ■

TODD SNIDER

I know how to play "To Live's to Fly," "Lungs," "I'll Be Here in the Morning." I could probably do more if I thought about it and had a couple more beers, like "White Freightliner Blues." The one I play out most is "To Live's to Fly." He played "To Live's to Fly" the night I met him, and then he played "Pancho and Lefty." The only ones in Townes's league are Guy Clark and John Prine, Randy Newman, Bob Dylan, and Neil Young. Like Prine or Randy Newman, I'd put Townes in the same category as Dylan because he found this thing that he made his own.

The first record I got was that one where he's sitting in the kitchen [1970's *Townes Van Zandt*]. I can't remember when that was. He's always been on the abstract side, and I've always liked that, although I've never incorporated that sort of thing in my own songs. I like his words, I guess, just like everybody else, but I never usually knew what he was talking about. I always thought that was cool because a lot of folk singers don't pull that off.

I can't remember what year it was, but Keith Sykes, a songwriter whose house I was living in, was trying to get me going. I didn't have a record contract yet, and John Prine was having this Whole Damn Family party. That's what's listed in the paper, and nobody knows who it is, so you don't know that it's John Prine in a bar with a band. The band was like Keith Sykes, Guy Clark, and Townes. Keith didn't tell me that Townes was going to be there.

This is kind of a sad story, really. I go to the club, and Keith says, "Come on, you can go into the dressing room." I kind of knew John a little bit. So, I get in there, and it's John and Guy Clark, Townes Van Zandt, Nanci Griffith, and Keith and me. They were gambling, and they were *fucked up*. They were playing the dice, and everybody was drunk. Guy Clark was yelling, and I just sat there by myself. Right when I saw Townes, I knew who he was. I was really excited to meet him, really overwhelmed.

He seemed really sad, like a really sad person, and Keith had said that he's always really sad. So I'm sitting there watching them gamble, and out of the blue Townes comes over and sits right next to me. He grabs my arm really hard, and he'd just met me. He didn't even know I sang, and he grabbed my arm and said, "All of this is so *wrong*," and I got scared. Like, "What's going on?" He said again, "All of this is *so wrong*." And I said, "What's wrong?" And Guy Clark yelled, "*Goddamnit*," over the gambling. Townes looked at me and rolled his eyes and pointed at Guy, who was gambling and really drunk, and Townes was like, "That. All of it. This is fucked up." He wouldn't let go of my arm. "I gotta get outta here, I gotta get outta here," he said.

He ended up playing that night. He just sat there for a while, and it was his turn and he played a couple times. Then everybody else had a big party afterwards, but he didn't go to it. The band played that night, but when his songs were done, he was done. He was drinking vodka from the glass, but he was pretty upset about it. Maybe he'd taken the cure by then. This is probably about '92, maybe '93. Jack Ingram saw him onstage in the last year [of his life], and Townes started crying. Jack said he played about four songs, started crying, and Guy Clark came out and took him offstage.[12]

Shawn Camp, (L-R) Tamara Saviano, Lloyd Maines, Verlon Thompson, Terri Hendrix, Shawn Camp, Jen Gunderman, Glen Fukunaga. Cedar Creek Recording, Austin, TX, January 4, 2011

SHAWN CAMP

Ah, the sculptor stands stricken, and the artist he throws away his
  brushes
When her image comes dancing, the sun she turns sullen
  with shame
—TVZ, "Quicksilver Daydreams of Maria," from *Townes Van Zandt*

Shawn Camp, born August 29, 1966, near Perryville, Arkansas, has achieved significant commercial success as a songwriter for mainstream country artists. Most notably, the longtime Nashville resident has cowritten Number One hits for superstars such as Garth Brooks ("Two Piña Coladas"), Brooks and Dunn ("How Long Gone"), George Strait ("River of Love"), and Josh Turner ("Would You Go with Me"), as well as several other songs recorded by artists including Tracy Byrd ("Can't Have One Without the Other"), Blake Shelton ("Nobody But Me"), and Randy Travis ("A Little Bitty Crack in Her Heart").[1] Camp himself charted the singles "Fallin' Never Felt So Good" and "Confessin' My Love" from his self-titled debut (1993), which he followed with an Emory Gordy Jr.–produced album that Warner Bros. swiftly shelved. "The label said it didn't sound like the latest hit," Camp says. "They wanted me to change everything. Told me to take all the fiddles and Dobros off and put electric guitars on. I got crossways and never did it."[2]

Around that time, Shawn Camp began writing with Townes Van Zandt's closest friend, Guy Clark. The pair's creative partnership has produced arguably some of Clark's most memorable work since the turn of the millennium (such as "Sis Draper," "Magnolia Wind," and "Maybe I Can Paint over That"). "Shawn sings, plays, and writes up there in the fine, rarified air where very few can breathe," Clark says. "It's a joy to behold."[3] "I have always thought Shawn should be a star," says "Cowboy" Jack Clement, the legendary producer (Johnny Cash, Roy Orbison, and Townes Van Zandt, among others), songwriter (Cash's "Ballad of a Teenage Queen," "Guess Things Happen That Way"), and longtime mentor to Shawn Camp. "He's got the talent, the voice, and the looks to do it."[4]

Meanwhile, Camp released the critically acclaimed solo albums *Lucky Silver Dollar* (2001), *Live at the Station Inn* (2004), and *Fireball* (2006), as well as *The Bluegrass Elvises, Vol. 1* with singer and songwriter Billy Burnette (2007).[5] A multi-instrumentalist who has played fiddle, guitar, and mandolin as a sideman for Alan Jackson, Trisha Yearwood, Suzy Bogguss, and Clark, Camp also performs with The World Famous Headliners, a band that includes fellow songwriters Al Anderson and Pat McLaughlin.

"There's this sly, underlying sexiness to Shawn's songwriting that I dig," says current Warner Music Nashville President John Esposito.[6]

Esposito's appreciation recently rewarded Camp's artistic vision. Sixteen years under dust, the label released Camp's previously untitled album as 1994 (2010).[7] The collection includes high-profile collaborations with bluegrass pioneer Bill Monroe ("Worn Through Stone"), celebrated Dobro player Jerry Douglas ("Little Bitty Crack in Her Heart"), and singer Patty Loveless ("In Harm's Way"), as well as the earliest Camp and Clark collaboration, "Stop, Look and Listen (Cow Catcher Blues)," which includes vivid imagery as engines "groan" and steel rails "pop like a broken heart."[8] "Writing with Guy Clark is a lesson in honesty," says Camp, who served as recording session bandleader on the album *This One's for Him: A Tribute to Guy Clark* (2011). "Every line cuts to the bone, and he's not afraid of truth. It's a good lesson."[9]

Camp ran in the same circles as Townes Van Zandt in the 1990s, but the two never formally met. Still, Van Zandt's music has had a significant impact on Camp. "Townes's stuff is above and beyond the ability of most Nashville songwriters," he says. "He's got a huge pile of incredible songs that speak for themselves."[10]

■ ■ ■

SHAWN CAMP

I was at the same Whole Damn Family Christmas show as Todd Snider. It was at Joe's Village Inn in Nashville, such a blur of drinking and all kinds of wild stuff. I remember that night Guy and Townes and quite a crowd were back behind the stage shooting craps. When I was onstage, which is like five or six inches off the floor, Guy and Townes were shitfaced, standing directly in front of me. Guy was smoking a cigarette. I played a solo, and in the middle of it Guy reached out and flicked his cigarette ashes right on my fiddle top. Evidently, I laughed about it, which is totally unlike me, and he later said, "I liked you from then on."

So, Guy and I started writing together. At that point, though, I was young enough and too intimidated by that crowd to get into the mix. They were kind of heroes to me. I always knew about Townes and that he was around. For some reason, I never went and sought him out or went to hear him. I should have. He died before I ever met him. The day he died, I went out to the record store and bought every record he ever made. I got really depressed that I missed my opportunity. I've been hanging out at "Cowboy" Jack Clement's since 1988, and I had so many mutual friends who all loved him. Townes would be there, sometimes even in the building, but I'd be doing my own thing and wouldn't see him.

Everybody who came through that studio back when Townes started may not have been as clear-headed as they'd be today. Everyone was partying and having a good time. Cowboy came from Sun Records, where there wasn't a whole lot of experimentation, and you got what you got right then. Cowboy's an innovator, always looking for something exciting and new. One of his phrases is, "You can't leave it off until you put it on." His idea of producing a record is to cut the band, and then overdub the world. Cowboy's a mad scientist, and he's doing it all with love. He may have overproduced a few things with Townes, or at least it's been called overproduction. That's the nature of his sound. If it makes him want to dance, he'll put it on. The Townes album that Cowboy produced that I really love is *At My Window* (1987).

I have a natural tone that's similar to Townes, as far as a Hank Williams influence in my vocals. Everything I listened to, soaking him up, it was like, I can't believe I missed this dude. You know, Guy has that portrait of Townes looking down at us right over his writing desk. Somewhere along the line, we were talking about Townes. It came up that Townes died on the same day that Hank Williams did. Guy said, "Yeah, he always wanted to be Hank Williams. Lucky son of a bitch."

The poetry of "Quicksilver Daydreams of Maria" and the clean beauty of its every line is just perfection. I know what's special to me, but I don't really think about his influence. Maybe I write songs similar to him sometimes, but I also write a bunch of songs that aren't. I think every songwriter changes the way you look at songwriting, and Roger Miller, Townes, and Guy Clark did it for me. I don't know that Townes totally changed the way I go about it, but I've really enjoyed his music.

Terrell Tye worked at Cowboy's since she was like seventeen, and Townes was in and out of there. They were good friends. Terrell also ran Forerunner Music, where I was a writer for about five years. Terrell's favorite song was "Snowin' on Raton." She passed away on Christmas Day of 2010, and they had the memorial on New Year's Eve. Her sons requested that I sing that song. The funeral home was full of all of the folks Townes knew, kind of a big family of misfits. I told them, "Townes will be gone fourteen years tomorrow." That was kind of wild.

I don't necessarily play a lot of Townes songs, but I can. They're so ingrained in my mind, and I enjoy doing them. I've listened to "Snowin' on Raton" a lot. I love "Ain't Leavin' Your Love," and "Lungs"—"Won't you lend your lungs to me / Mine are collapsing / Plant my feet and bitterly breathe / Up all the time that's passing." I've been writing a lot with Loretta Lynn the past couple years, and I'm thinking about doing an album of songs I've written with her and a couple of hers and several songs with "Loretta" in the title. I think I'm going to do Townes's "Loretta" in that batch. I told Loretta about that, and she thought it was cool.

About six months ago, I dreamed that I was talking to Guy about Townes. I've had dreams with Townes in them many times. In the dream, I was talking to Guy at this house that felt like it was in Austin. We were on the back porch, and I said, "Guy, I never met Townes." Guy's smoking a cigarette, and he says, "Is that right? Well, it's about time. Come on." We walk next door, and Townes is lying on the front porch, asleep, wearing cowboy boots. Guy kicks him on the sole of his boot. Townes sits up, reaches up and grabs my hand. He's young and in good health. Guy, still smoking the cigarette, says, "Shawn, Townes; Townes, Shawn." Then I woke up. I told Guy about that and said, "Man, it was like it really happened." Guy said, "Well, didn't it?"[11]

Chorus
BEN NICHOLS

And now the dark air is like fire on my skin
And even the moonlight is blinding
—TVZ, "Rake," from *Delta Momma Blues*

Ben Nichols, born August 2, 1974, in Little Rock, Arkansas, has fortified his band Lucero's seven studio albums—including *Lucero* (2001), *Nobody's Darlings* (2005), and *Rebels, Rogues & Sworn Brothers* (2006)—with young, working-class narrators striving for better days. His hardscrabble barroom vignettes frequently highlight

Townes Van Zandt at Liberty Hall,
Houston, Texas, June 4, 1977. Photos ©
1977 by Ken Hoge, www.kenhoge.com

Townes Van Zandt at Liberty Hall. Photo © 1977 by Ken Hoge, www.kenhoge.com

relentless resolve recovering broken hopes.[1] Lucero's recent album 1372 *Overton Park* (2009) tempers garage rock ("Sixes and Sevens") and Memphis soul ("Darken My Door") with gentler ballads, such as the Townes Van Zandt–inspired "Hey Darlin' Do You Gamble." "I believe you should run with me / Until this Texas sun falls into the sea," Nichols sings on the latter. "If I shed this skin of iron and this breath of kerosene / Darlin' would you take a chance on me?"[2]

"I'm very much drawn to Townes's music," Nichols says. "I have a soft spot for the softer, darker, sad stuff, and no one really does that any better than Townes. As much as I try to emulate that, I can't get anywhere close. He was coming from a very particular place in a lot of those songs. I'm probably coming from a similar place, but I try to get there and just can't. I still listen to him all the time, even when I'm in a good mood.

"Some of his lines are just poetry, but it's the kind of poetry that you'd hear from an old guy down at the end of the bar. It makes sense that his lyrics are pretty straightforward—they're something that everybody can relate to and are put in such a beautiful but simple way. That's something I've strived to do.

"I found the song 'Hey Darlin' Do You Gamble?' in that excellent Townes documentary *Be Here To Love Me*. His third wife tells the story about sitting at a bar when [Van Zandt] walks up and says, 'Hey, darlin,' do you gamble?' She's like, 'Dear Lord, don't let this be the one', but it was. As soon as I heard that line—'Hey darlin,' do you gamble?'—I was like, 'Man, I'm stealing that.'"[3]

James McMurtry.
Courtesy Ann Woodall

JAMES McMURTRY

Where I lead me I will travel; where I need me I will call me
I'm no fool, I'll be ready; God knows I will be
—TVZ, "Where I Lead Me," from *Delta Momma Blues*

"A conservative," Franklin D. Roosevelt once proclaimed, "is a man with two perfectly good legs who, however, has never learned to walk forward."[1] James McMurtry turned those words into weapons on his album *Just Us Kids* (2008). "You keep talkin' that shit like I never heard," McMurtry sings on the collection's blunt centerpiece "God Bless America." "Hush, little president, don't say a word."[2] McMurtry's politically provocative songs ("The Governor" and "Cheney's Toy," for instance) may diverge from the Guy Clark and Billy Joe Shaver songwriting mold, but his keen storytelling (such as "Ruby and Carlos," "Freeway View," and "Fireline Road") fits flush.

McMurtry, born March 18, 1962, in Fort Worth, Texas, met Townes Van Zandt at the Leon Springs Café in Leon Springs, Texas, in 1985. "He was sober that night, so I wondered what all the fuss was about, why every-body seemed to be so scared of him," McMurtry remembers. "He was very friendly. He'd talk to you directly and look you right in the eye."[3] McMurtry nodded to Van Zandt by closing both the albums *Walk Between the Raindrops* (1998) and *Live in Aught-Three* (2004) with a swampy, electric version of his song "Rex's Blues." The current Austin resident anchors local gigs around his Wednesday night residency at the Continental Club, a longstanding and popular nightclub frequented by Van Zandt in the 1970s and early 1980s.[4]

McMurtry's early albums *Too Long in the Wasteland* (1989), *Candyland* (1992), *Where'd You Hide the Body* (1995), and *It Had to Happen* (1997) established him as a link between Flannery O'Connor's dark narrative fiction and Bob Dylan's literate folk music.[5] As the son of novelist Larry McMurtry, best known as the author of 1975's *Terms of Endearment* and 1985's Pulitzer Prize-winning novel *Lonesome Dove*, storytelling runs deep in James McMurtry's blood. However, he has required time to discipline his craft. "The songs get written when they absolutely have to be written," McMurtry said early in his career. "When I cannot avoid sitting down and working on the songs—that's when they get finished."[6]

McMurtry has never achieved commercial success in his own right. Even with major label backing on early albums, his gruff voice and syrupy delivery cut against the mainstream radio grain. However, longtime ad-mirer Robert Earl Keen has extended McMurtry's reach by recording his heartland vignettes "Levelland" (on Keen's 1997 album *Picnic*) and "Out Here in the Middle" (*Farm Fresh Onions*, 2003). The former particularly showcases McMurtry's descriptive lyrical imagery. "So, they sunk some roots down in the dirt to keep from blowing off the earth," he sings. "They built a town around here / And when the dust had all been cleared, they called it Levelland."[7]

The latter song scolds those who find "justification for wealth and greed" and foreshadows McMurtry's heightened political focus on *Childish Things* (2005). The album most tightly clenches its fists on the song "We Can't Make It Here," whose aggressive message against social inequality garnered McMurtry national attention and won two awards at the following year's Americana Music Association awards in Nashville.

■ ■ ■

JAMES McMURTRY

I only did a couple of shows with Townes, but I talked to him backstage a bit and he was quite entertaining. The last time I saw him he was talking about the last time that Harold Eggers let him drive. He was on the interstate going through Arkansas in the middle of the night, and Harold, his road manager, was sleeping under the shell of the pickup behind him. And this voice in his head said to him, "Make that exit," so he did. "Hang a right by those mailboxes," so, of course, he did. "Hang a left here," so he did. Then the voice said, "Step on it." So, Townes says, "I'm going down this dirt road at seventy miles an hour and H wakes up in the back and he says, 'How'd we get on the back road?' Finally, he gets through to me, and I come to a tearing stop about ten feet in front of one of them orange and white barriers, and the creek bridge was out."

That was the last time Townes got to drive, because he listened to the voices. It made enough sense to me that he listened to the voices. Probably where he got the songs. He didn't question the voices, but it's dangerous when you drive like that.

When I saw him perform, the result just depended on the night. When he was on a good night, he was unbeatable. If he was drunk, it was embarrassing. It ran the whole gamut. Sometimes it would come the whole way around the back side—he would be so drunk and so embarrassing that you wouldn't want to miss it. There was a show at La Zona Rosa in Austin where Townes was too drunk to make it, so Guy Clark came out and just played Townes's show for him, basically. Townes stumbled off the stage, but he went off stage left where there wasn't any door. So, he was there walking back and forth around the wall for around ten minutes trying to find the door through it, when there wasn't any. Robert [Earl]

Keen said he was at that show, and people were going out the front door in droves. The doorman's saying, "You don't know who this man is," and the customers are saying, "I don't give a fuck who he is; I want my money back."

The good nights were incredible. He was channeling something. That's the thing: he did not question the muse. If it made him write a goofy thing, so be it. He had to explain that line about Loop and Lil being parakeets, but he put it in the song anyway, because that's what the dream told him to do. He dreamed that song ["If I Needed You"], and wrote it exactly as he heard it. His songs are raw, very close to the heart.

My soundman used to own a club in San Antonio, and he has some stuff he taped off the board of Townes and Guy Clark that is killer. Had to be the last couple of years of Townes's life. I wouldn't say anything in his playing and performing had decayed judging from that, or from what I heard at the Birchmere the last time I heard him play in D.C. in '95. I've seen Kristofferson stop a room the way Townes could, but part of that has to do with the people in the room, how well they know you, and how well they love you when you walk in. You get that from working for years and years and years until you can develop a crowd like that. I never saw Townes play to a completely unfamiliar crowd, so I don't know what he could do with that. He could certainly stop his crowd. He did that by working his whole life at it, so he'd have people that'd heard him for fifteen years and they know every line in every one of your songs. They're gonna stop for you.[8]

Lucinda Williams, Harro East Theatre and Ballroom, Rochester, NY, March 13, 2009. *Courtesy Heather Ainsworth*

LUCINDA WILLIAMS

Being born is going blind and bowing down a thousand times
To echoes strung on pure temptation
—TVZ, "Nothin'," from *Delta Momma Blues*

"I took from Townes what I took from any good songwriter," Lucinda Williams says. "It's the way he puts words together." The creative osmosis paid off. Williams, whose father, the poet Miller Williams, read at Bill Clinton's presidential inauguration in 1997, has created a rich collection of literate story-songs over the past quarter century. Regular exposure to writers of literature and poetry throughout her childhood served as a primary influence. "I always love when people bring their kids to my shows," Williams said at a 2005 concert at Denver's Botanic Gardens. "It reminds me of my parents, who introduced me to people like Charles Bukowski when I was young."[1]

Lucinda Williams, born January 26, 1953, in Lake Charles, Louisiana, played a key role in the 1970s Texas folk music scene, particularly within the Austin and Houston music communities. Williams's debut album *Ramblin'* (1979) adopted influences shared with mentors such as Nanci Griffith, Eric Taylor, and Townes Van Zandt and displayed her warbling vocals on country-folk standards (for instance, "Jambalaya" and "Great Speckled Bird") and popular blues ("Ramblin' On My Mind" and "Malted Milk Blues"). Williams's first collection of original songs, *Happy Woman Blues* (1980), provided a sturdy stepping stone to her self-titled album (1988), which yielded hits (most notably, Mary Chapin-Carpenter's 1994 Grammy Award–winning version of "Passionate Kisses"), as well as longtime live staples (such as "Changed the Locks").[2]

Williams's Grammy-winning album *Car Wheels on a Gravel Road* (1998), which was produced by Van Zandt disciple Steve Earle and earned widespread recognition and commercial success, is widely considered her landmark release.[3] The diverse album blends equal measures of country ("Still I Long for Your Kiss" and "I Lost It"), blues ("Lake Charles" and Randy Weeks's "Can't Let Go"), folk ("Greenville" and "Jackson"), and rock ("Right in Time" and "Joy"). In concert, Williams often dedicates the album's centerpiece "Drunken Angel" to Townes Van Zandt and their common friend, the late Austin singer-songwriter Blaze Foley, whose songs include "Clay Pigeons," "If I Could Only Fly," and "No Goodwill Stores in Waikiki." "Blood spilled out from the hole in your heart, over the strings of your guitar," she sings. "The worn out places in the wood that once made you feel so good."[4]

"I treasure Lucinda as a songwriter and a performer," says popular rock singer Melissa Etheridge. "Her song 'Essence' just makes me want to lie down in a pool and melt. '2 Kool 2 Be 4-Gotten,' 'Can't Let Go'—these are great rock-blues songs. She has a handle on the pulse of where rock and roll comes from. Lucinda's such a purist and hasn't once sold out for anything. She's on the edge and wild and wicked."[5]

That artistic integrity helped Williams earn recognition from *Time* as "America's best songwriter" in 2001.[6] At that point, songs poured forth more rapidly. After releasing only five albums in the previous two decades, the admitted perfectionist answered *Car Wheels on a Gravel Road*'s success with as many in the first decade of the new millennium (including 2005's concert album *Live at the Fillmore*). Each studio album—*Essence* (2001), *World Without Tears* (2003), and *West* (2007)—bested the last on *Billboard*'s pop chart, and Williams reached her highest rank at Number Nine with *Little Honey* (2008).

In March 2011, she marked the release of her most recent album, *Blessed* (2011), with a gig at Lost Highway Records's tenth anniversary showcase at South by Southwest in Austin. "Everything since *Car Wheels* has been compared to [that album]," Williams says. "Frankly, [*Blessed*] is the best produced, best sounding album to me. I think my voice is definitely better now."[7]

Many younger songwriters today view Williams as a creative beacon and touchstone for self-fulfilling promise. "When we toured together, I became a huge fan," says Heartless Bastards' lead singer Erika Wennerstrom. "I think it's inspiring to open for a really great songwriter like that."[8]

■ ■ ■

LUCINDA WILLIAMS

I love "If I Needed You." That's one of his songs that really stands out. The melody and the simplicity and what the song says make it work. It sounds traditional, like an old folk song. Sometimes those are the ones that people identify with, because it sounds familiar even when you listen to it for the first time. There's one song I wrote, "Jackson," off *Car Wheels on a Gravel Road*, that's probably one of the most closely influenced by Townes. In fact, when I recorded it, Steve Earle played guitar, and he said the way it was played was like a Townes kind of sound. You can certainly hear Townes in Steve's music. Townes had his own way of playing and phrasing.

I like his darker songs, too, like the one I covered on the *Poet* tribute album, "Nothin'." I really buried myself in his songs when I was trying to pick one to play for that album. It gave me perspective on his writing because I just pored through tons of his CDs. The darkness and the mysteriousness of "Nothin'" drew me to it; I like songs that are dark and brave at the same time. "Tecumseh Valley" is a great one, of course, and "Pancho and Lefty." Those are ones that people recognize. "Pancho and Lefty" is a brilliant song, and it tells a story full of wonderful imagery.

I met Townes in 1973 in Nashville. It was when I was first heading out on my own with my guitar and starting that whole thing. I met Townes briefly through some other people. Then I ended up later in Austin, and I would see him from time to time when I was there and living in Houston.

When I first met him, I thought he was a really good-looking guy. He was very striking and very mysterious. I was quite intimidated by him. I'd known about him as a songwriter, and I think I discovered his music around 1971. The first album I heard was *Delta Momma Blues* (1971). I was pretty into him, pretty well versed in folk music and the whole singer-songwriter thing from the 1960s. I was definitely a fan of Townes's music from the start, but I admired him more from afar. He was a tall, dark, mysterious figure, a great songwriter, and I was just a kid in his eyes, just a little girl with a guitar. I wasn't on his level, so I don't think he took me very seriously until sometime later.

I never could really talk to him. He liked to talk in riddles. It's kind of hard to explain what I mean by that; you had to be around him and know his personality. He was a very perceptive individual, very smart and witty and fun, but I always felt that he kept his guard up to some degree. He was always joking around. I think underneath that there was this tenderness and perception, but I never got to know that side of him. It was always cloaked behind his joking around. I wish I could have gotten to know him better.

I knew Blaze Foley a little better because I was around him more often, but he was somewhat guarded, too. I think most people who drink a lot tend to be like that to some degree. So, Townes was always this elusive figure to me. He'd drift in and out of town. He'd show up and I'd see him out and see him play, but there was a distance, too. I was quite a bit younger and just getting started, and he was already a legend. We didn't relate in the same way he and Guy Clark related, certainly—or even he and Steve Earle. There were other people he was much closer to. It was something of a boys' club.

Townes was a brilliant artist, and also somewhat self-destructive. When you put those things together, you're not going to have the most consistent performances, but a lot of that was happening at a time when everybody was doing that anyway. A lot of people would get onstage and be stoned and drunk and whatever, and it sort of just went along with what was going on at the time. I don't think anybody made a big deal about it at the time because we were all drinking and smoking pot and getting crazy. Townes just took it a step further.

He was playing pretty regularly in Houston just before I got there around 1975 or 1976 at a place called Sand Mountain. By the time I got there, I think he was living in Nashville. When I was playing around Houston, Lyle Lovett and Nanci Griffith were just getting started. I was a peer of theirs, and we were playing in the same clubs at the same time. Townes was someone we all looked up to.

Certainly more people know who Hank Williams is and Bob Dylan is than who Townes Van Zandt is. It shouldn't be that way, but that's unfortunately the way it is. It might take some time, but maybe over the years Townes's legacy will build. If you go up to someone on the street and ask them if they know Dylan, they'll say, "Yeah." They won't know Townes, unless they've paid attention over the years. After people die, their legacy grows, and that's probably what'll happen with Townes. I've seen that happen with Blaze Foley.

The last time I saw Townes was in 1993 in Jack Clement's studio. I was with this guy who's a bass player that I was seeing at the time. Townes kind of picked up on something, and he was giving me a warning in his funny, self-effacing way, saying, "Watch out for this guy." He said to the guy, "You better treat her right." In his own way, he was protective and very sweet. He came to appreciate me as an artist.

His love songs were very romantic, very beautiful. I loved [their] earthiness. He had an obvious sense of place. Oftentimes, he'd have references to different parts of the country, like his song "Snowin' on Raton." I've done that a lot in my writing. He wrote a lot about cities and towns and rivers, and he used a lot of that imagery. When you heard Townes, you knew it was him. He had a way of writing very simply and sparingly, and yet being very evocative and effective. That's one of the things I've strived to do over the years in my writing.[9]

Lyle Lovett, Telluride Bluegrass Festival, Telluride, CO, June 17, 2004

LYLE LOVETT

Spring only sighed, summer had to be satisfied
   Fall is a feeling I just can't lose
   —TVZ, "Flyin' Shoes," from *Flyin' Shoes*

Lyle Lovett's *Step Inside This House* (1998) directly salutes his favorite Texas songwriters. Lovett's covers collection honors mentors close in sentiment (Guy Clark's "Step Inside This House"), spirit (Willis Alan Ramsey's "Sleepwalking"), and style (Vince Bell's "I've Had Enough"). He nods most frequently (four times each) to the late songwriter Walter Hyatt (including "Babes in the Woods" and "Lonely in Love") and Townes Van Zandt ("Lungs," "Highway Kind," "Flyin' Shoes," and "If I Needed You"). "I learned 'Flyin' Shoes' when I was eighteen," Lovett says. "I loved the chord changes, the lyrical idea of leaving everything you know and love behind and embarking on an unknown course. That notion's a very real thing when you're eighteen."[1]

Lovett, born November 1, 1957, in Klein, Texas, cut his teeth as a performer at legendary Lone Star venues such as Anderson Fair in Houston and Gruene Hall in New Braunfels. He recalls gigs at one of Texas' oldest working dancehalls as idyllic snapshots in time. "On Sunday afternoons, people were relaxed and just happy to be [at Gruene Hall]. The doors would be open and the breeze would be blowing through the screen doors and people would be wearing shorts. Behind the bar, Hal Ketchum would lean through the window and play harmonica."[2]

Lovett's self-titled debut (1986) matched wits with other emerging young country singers Steve Earle (Guitar Town), Dwight Yoakam (Guitars, Cadillacs, Etc., Etc.), and Randy Travis (Storms of Life). Lovett's singles from the album, including "Cowboy Man" and "Farther Down the Line," highlighted his storytelling ability while "God Will" showed more pensive qualities.[3] Lovett migrated toward big band and swing tunes on the album Pontiac (1988). "It was a really experimental time in Nashville," he says.[4] The following year's Lyle Lovett and His Large Band made official that transition, which has continued through It's Not Big, It's Large (2007).

A quarter century on, Lyle Lovett remains as unapologetically independent as his former Texas A&M University roommate, Robert Earl Keen, although with significantly more mainstream popularity. As one writer claimed, "[Frank Sinatra] might well have hung out with Lyle Lovett, in which case the Texas singer-songwriter with the Eiffel Tower hair could have told Ol' Blue Eyes a thing or two about 'doing it his way.'"[5]

Lovett's personal life became highly trafficked tabloid fodder for a time. In late June 1993, Keen reportedly found a message from Lovett on his answering machine that said, "I've met this great gal, and I'm getting married to her tomorrow, and I hope you can make it." The "gal" was movie star Julia Roberts, whom Lovett had met while filming the Robert Altman movie The Player. The marriage was frequently portrayed in the press as a beauty-and-the-beast pairing due to Lovett's unconventional looks. It lasted less than two years.[6]

Lovett's ongoing "guitar pull" concerts with Guy Clark, Joe Ely, and John Hiatt have endured considerably longer. The loose acoustic song swaps caught steam after the quartet performed together for the Country Music Association in 1990, and they continue sporadically today. "We come here with no agenda, no set list . . . no clue," Clark will often say to introduce the evening. "To sit onstage and watch Guy play is incredible," says Lovett, who alludes to the guitar pulls in his song "All Downhill" with the lyric, "Good luck, you can't buy it / Joe Ely and I sit next to that John Hiatt / We park next to Guy Clark / We sing when it gets dark."[7] On November 8, 2010, Lovett performed "All Downhill," along with the Van Zandt songs "Loretta" and "White Freightliner Blues," during the final episode of *Austin City Limits* taped at the television program's original Studio 6A set on the University of Texas campus in Austin.[8]

■ ■ ■

LYLE LOVETT

We'd just finished playing an early evening set at the Kerrville Folk Festival in 1985, and as I walked offstage, there was Townes. He shook my hand and introduced himself. He was a real gentleman. I'll always remember what he said to me: "I've never heard your music, but people whose opinion I respect say you're all right." That really made an impression on me. What a nice thing to say.

Guy Clark always talks about how lighthearted and smart Townes was, how he had a wonderful, playful sense of humor and a razor-sharp wit. That's the Townes I remember, too. I first saw him after the years he lived in Houston, after he'd made his *Live at the Old Quarter* record. I'd hear him years later and sometimes get to open for him when he'd come back through Houston to play Anderson Fair. He was always kind to me.

Townes Van Zandt was compelling, not just as a writer, but also as a person. When you're in a room with Willie Nelson, there's something about how personally quiet he is. You see people are drawn to him. He's

Townes Van Zandt at 1995
Kerrville Folk Festival,
Kerrville, TX. Courtesy Susan
Roads

the calm in the center of the storm that's happening all around him. Townes had that same quality of being a very focused, quiet, powerful energy in the middle of a room. Townes could be so still, and there's something mesmerizing about that.

In performing one of his songs, I try to live up to what Townes has written, what he has said. But really, I just enjoy living inside his song for four minutes, or however long it lasts. To be able to inhabit one of Townes's songs, to be inside it and say the words and feel their meaning is a very real thing whether you're onstage or whether you're just playing in your living room. That's the fun of it. You get to live through great pieces of music. With words as beautiful as his and melodies so strong and haunting, it's an emotional and very powerful experience.

Townes was brilliantly gifted at taking a complex emotion or complicated idea and expressing it in an accessible way. That's what's so powerful about his writing—there's a novel, a whole life behind a very simple line. I loved to listen to Townes talk about his writing, because he'd talk about it in mysterious terms. In the liner notes to one of his albums, he talks about "sky songs." They'd just seem to come out of the sky and go into his arm and onto a piece of paper, he said.

I heard him tell more than once about dreaming "If I Needed You." He said he just woke up and wrote it down. Townes was staying at Guy Clark's house. Guy says Townes got up one morning, walked into the kitchen and played it all the way through. In fact, it doesn't matter how he wrote it. "If I Needed You" is an important and beautiful song no matter how it came about, but the romance of a story like that is hard to resist. The thing is, music is emotional, not intellectual. If you have to analyze and appreciate it, it's not the same as feeling it.

Townes reminds me of the old cowboys and farmers I grew up with here in the Houston area—my relatives, my uncles and cousins. They would say something to you that would have three or four different meanings, just to see how much of it you'd get, to see how much you were paying attention. Townes had that quality—that twinkle in his eye that tests your perception. He would see what you're made of. You have to wonder if he was doing that a little bit in the stories he told about his songs. It always makes me smile to think about whether Townes was being straight up and literal when he spoke to you, or if he was really just checking you out.[9]

John Gorka, Kerrville Folk Festival, Kerrville, TX, 2007.
Courtesy Susan Roads

JOHN GORKA

Her hair did curl, and her thoughts unfurled
   Like birds upon the wings of spring
   —TVZ, "Snow Don't Fall," from *The Late, Great Townes Van Zandt*

John Gorka, born July 27, 1958, in Edison, New Jersey, discovered Townes Van Zandt while studying at Moravian College in Bethlehem, Pennsylvania, in the late 1970s. "His seem like perfect songs with such beautiful lyrics," Gorka says. "It didn't seem like anyone could write a song like that, like it'd always been there."[1]

Early on, Gorka performed with guitarist Doug Anderson in the Razzy Dazzy Spasm Band, but he earnestly developed his trademark easygoing onstage style as a solo acoustic act at Bethlehem's Godfrey Daniels coffeehouse. In 1984, Gorka entered into Texas music history as a winner in the Kerrville Folk Festival's New Folk songwriting contest. (Townes Van Zandt, who frequently performed at the Kerrville festival and served as a songwriting contest judge in 1977, was inducted into the festival's Hall of Fame shortly before his death.)[2]

John Gorka's narratives well suit a songwriting institution such as the Kerrville Folk Festival. Many follow strong-willed individualists (such as "Flying Red Horse," "I'm From New Jersey"), hopeful romantics ("Italian Girls," "Gypsy Life"), and wistful realists ("Writing in the Margins," "Always") typically emboldened by their own seeking and self-awareness. Occasionally, Gorka traces the Whitman-inspired naturalist themes ("Branching Out") so prevalent in Townes Van Zandt's tunes, such as "Catfish Song," "Snowin' on Raton," and "Our Mother the Mountain."

Seven years after Gorka made his mark at Kerrville, *Rolling Stone* magazine named him the "preeminent male singer-songwriter of what has been dubbed the 'New Folk Movement.'" While his approach matches the movement's focus on accessible story songs, Gorka disagrees with the strict categorization. "I think ['New Folk' is] probably a marketing term," he says. "I see myself as a part of the continuum—at least the kind of music I aspire to make—of music that could be called 'folk.'"[3]

A jittery and jovial stage presence, Gorka ties together his live shows, even today most frequently performed solo or with sparse acoustic accompaniment, with long, humorous monologues. "This song came from a time in my life that was terrible—when I got a job," he often says to introduce his song "Land of the Bottom Line." "Getting a job is a great thing for people who want one."[4] Gorka has steadily built a strong career split equally between Windham Hill/High Street Records (including 1990's *Land of the Bottom Line* and 1992's *Temporary Road*) and the Minnesota-based Red House Records (2001's *The Company You Keep* and 2006's *Writing in the Margins*).

Gorka recorded Townes Van Zandt's "Snow Don't Fall" as a duet with Nanci Griffith on *Writing in the Margins*, an elegant rendition that highlights lyrics likely inspired by Romantic poets such as Lord Byron and John Keats: "Snow don't fall on summer's time / Wind don't blow below the sea / My love lies 'neath frozen skies / And waits in sweet repose for me."[5] Van Zandt reportedly was proud of the song but rarely performed it. Guitarist Mickey White believes its heart cut too close to the bone: "He wrote 'Snow Don't Fall' for Leslie [Jo Richards]," Van Zandt's nineteen-year-old girlfriend who was stabbed to death. Richards was murdered while hitchhiking on an errand for Van Zandt during the Los Angeles recording session for his album *High, Low and In Between* (1972). The incident left the songwriter "a big pile of guilt."[6]

■ ■ ■

JOHN GORKA

I've been doing "Snow Don't Fall" off and on for a long time. I did a show in Michigan with Nanci Griffith, and I started asking her about Townes. She asked me to sing his songs. She was really good friends with him and had taken me to see him my first time in Texas in 1984. He was something special to Nanci, and I'd met him a few times. Didn't really know him, but I loved the songs.

My friend Doug Anderson introduced me to Emmylou Harris's version of "Pancho and Lefty" in college in the 1970s. Doug had a great record collection, and we all loved Emmylou Harris. I would always bug Doug to play that song, so finally he said, "Why don't you just learn it?" I found out that it was Townes who wrote that in her liner notes. "Pancho and Lefty" changed—it *unchained*—my idea of what a song could be. I never knew that a song could be that big and deep. It seemed like literature come to life—in what it said and didn't say, the questions that it brought up. It just exploded my idea of what a song could be. All of those things led me to record "Snow Don't Fall" on *Writing in the Margins*.

The process for that album was different. I'd originally gone in to record a Christmas album that Canadian Pacific Railway was putting out. I was going to be doing this holiday train trip to raise money for food shelters, and I went in and just felt like putting down some songs that I like. I ended up going in about once a week, or when I could. Some were my own, and others were songs that I always liked. "Snow Don't Fall" was one of them. The version that's on the record is live, very little editing if any. Nanci's vocals were live.

I can't remember exactly where Nanci took me to see Townes, but it was in Austin, between weekends at the Kerrville Folk Festival when the festival was two weekends. I'd done the Kerrville New Folk thing. Townes might've played there. I'm not sure, but then Nanci took me to see him. So much is a blur. I think the show was close to the disastrous end of the spectrum, but I saw him other times when I really enjoyed it.

I picked up a cassette of the *Live at the Old Quarter* album, and I love that collection of songs. I have others like *Flyin' Shoes* and *The Late, Great Townes Van Zandt*, and I learned "Snow Don't Fall" off *The Late Great*, which is why I originally did it on piano. I think he plays piano on the record. Those songs were like the best of the people I learned about in college and then got to see at Godfrey Daniels Coffeehouse in Bethlehem. It was so much better than anything I'd heard on radio or seen on television. Like I said, it was like literature come to life.

I don't remember hearing Townes play in the Pennsylvania and New York circles a lot when I was starting out. I think he was more like a Texas legend, though he probably didn't live in Texas anymore at that point. He did influence my own songwriting, though, quite a bit. Like I said, the idea of what a song could be was so much bigger after hearing "Pancho and Lefty," and I know there are some songs—sort of story songs, but like an overheard conversation—where you pick up enough of a story to have it be interesting but it doesn't give you all the answers. It raises more questions than it gives you answers.

A song like "If I Needed You" has the whole thing—beautiful melody, straightforward lyrics. Before the lyrics, it's the sound first that will keep you there. Then the words come out and the melody carries the lyrics—that's what really gets people, more a visceral thing. The lyrics appeal to another part of your brain. I was talking to David Rawlings and Gillian Welch recently, and they said that they never do a set without playing a Townes song. That's a neat thing.

There are lots of ways to make a song great. Songs that I like and mean something to me have specific, concrete details that are easier for people to latch onto and take in rather than a series of ideas. Townes was a master of that. "Snow Don't Fall" is, what, two verses and a bridge and then repeating the first verse? It's such a perfect song in so few lines.[7]

Bianca DeLeon. Courtesy www.biancamusic.com

BRIDGE

BIANCA DeLEON

Sleep, babe, until the moon slips away
    I'm hopin' all your dreamin' comes true
    —TVZ, "Lover's Lullaby," from *No Deeper Blue*

ianca DeLeon, born near Corpus Christi, Texas, met Townes Van Zandt while he was playing the Houston folk club circuit "somewhere around 1966." She says they formed a "deep, lasting connection that remains central to her life" today.[1] DeLeon included a version of Van Zandt's "Waitin' Around to Die" on her album

Outlaws & Lovers (2001), which she followed with *Live: From Hell to Helsinki* (2003) and *The Long Slow Decline of Carmelita* (2004). DeLeon lives in Van Zandt's former Clarksville neighborhood in Austin, Texas, one of the more gentrified areas of the rapidly growing capital city.

"There's a spiritual side to [songwriting]," DeLeon says, "but I'm not even sure that that matters. Townes would say the songs come from the sky, and I understand that, because I write most of my songs in my sleep. I dream songs. I wrote this one song, because I dreamed that I was in this club in Detroit that I used to hang out in years ago. I was sitting at a table and someone came up to me and tapped me on the shoulder and nodded their head to the stage. I saw this big band getting up on the stage and I said, 'Oh, my break's over.'

"So I got on stage to sing this one song, and at the end of the song I realized, 'Oh, I don't have a guitar, I'm only singing into the mike.' I realized right then that I was in a dream and that I should wake up and write that in a song. That happens all the time. I thought everybody did it until I started asking other people, and I guess that's what would happen to Townes sometimes—they'd come in a dream.

"Townes wrote one song for me, wrote it in front of me—'If I Needed You.' He wrote the first verse or two and then flew me to Nashville. I still have the ticket he sent me to go to Nashville. It's [dated] February 19, 1972. We were in the living room at Guy and Susanna's at Chapel and Mission, and he said, 'Now that you're here, I can finish the song.' That was it. It was amazing. He finished it the next day in a couple minutes."[2]

Michael Timmins. Courtesy
Stephane Boule

MICHAEL TIMMINS

Snake eyes cry, boxcars sigh
 Seven's stuck in the middle just wonderin' why
 —TVZ, "Cowboy Junkies Lament," from *No Deeper Blue*

The Cowboy Junkies enjoyed a symbiotic relationship with Townes Van Zandt throughout the 1980s and 1990s. "Townes's words, voice, and music were the soundtrack to our early rambling journeys across the continent," says the band's guitarist Michael

Timmins.[1] The Canadian quartet repaid creative fires fueled by offering
the songwriter widespread exposure. At the height of their popularity, the
Cowboy Junkies invited Van Zandt as tour support on a twenty-five-city
route in 1990, exposing his music to a new and likely receptive audience.
By the band's account, Van Zandt remained mostly sober and performed
superbly throughout the run.[2]

Van Zandt answered by writing "Cowboy Junkies Lament," a deliberately crafted song recorded on his final studio album, No Deeper Blue
(1994). "He said, 'The first verse is about you, the second verse is about
[singer] Margo [Timmins], and the third verse is about [drummer] Pete
[Timmins]," Michael Timmins says.[3] One of Van Zandt's more memorable later-year lyrics carries the tune. "Mama, don't you worry, night's
approaching / There's a hole in heaven where some sin slips through,"
he sings. "Close your eyes and dream real steady / Maybe just a little will
spill on you."[4] Michael Timmins later penned the song "Townes' Blues"
about their travels together.

Michael Timmins, born April 21, 1959, in Montreal, Quebec, shaped the
Cowboy Junkies' debut Whites Off Earth Now!! (1986) with syrupy takes on
Van Zandt influences such as Lightnin' Hopkins ("Shining Moon"), Big
Joe Williams ("Baby Please Don't Go"), and John Lee Hooker ("Forgive
Me"). Many consider the album a precursor to the band's definitive state-
ment. Trinity Sessions (1988) trademarked the Cowboy Junkies' "country on
Valium" sound and established the band as Canada's alternative country
pioneers.[5] Twenty years later, artists including Ryan Adams ("200 More
Miles"), Vic Chesnutt ("Postcard Blues"), and Natalie Merchant ("To Love
Is To Bury"), gathered at Toronto's Church of the Holy Trinity, where the
Cowboy Junkies recorded the original album, in order to acknowledge
their debt by recording the tribute Trinity Revisited (2008).

The Cowboy Junkies' major label follow-ups The Caution Horses (1990),
Black Eyed Man (1992), Pale Sun Crescent Moon (1993), Lay It Down (1996), and
Miles From Our Home (1998) hewed closely to that languid blueprint. The
band deepened its Townes Van Zandt connection by closing Black Eyed
Man with the trilogy "Cowboy Junkies Lament," "Townes' Blues," and
"To Live's To Fly," and included the Timmins and Van Zandt "cowrite"

"Blue Guitar" on *Miles from Home.* "I think Townes knew what he was doing was pretty special," Timmins says. "He had an understanding of his place, which is unusual."[6]

The Cowboy Junkies foreshadowed trends by entering into the new millennium on their own Latent Recordings record label to release *Waltz Across America* (2000). The band continues to capitalize on the artistic latitude self-releasing allows today. "We have never lacked a work ethic in this band," Timmins says, "but this freedom has allowed us to think as big or as small as we want."[7] The Cowboy Junkies infused the concept album *Renmin Park* (2010) with atypically political themes of social disenfranchisement and personal solitude inspired by Michael Timmins's trip to China the previous year. "That's not Mike's style, but you can't avoid it, especially when you're dealing with history so recent and well known to everybody," says Cowboy Junkies' bassist Alan Anton. "There are a couple songs that are pretty overtly political."[8]

■ ■ ■

MICHAEL TIMMINS

It was the mid-1980s, a terrible time for music. A friend of mine, Steve Cross, was passing through Toronto en route from England to Australia. He brought me a gift—a mix tape of some singer-songwriter named Townes Van Zandt. He said, "I think you'll like this guy." Meanwhile, Cowboy Junkies was being born. The tape was put into the cassette deck of our touring van, and it remained there for the next couple of years.

During one of those tours, we pulled into Atlanta and discovered that Townes was performing in town that night. We had never seen him play live. Coincidentally, it was my birthday. We dug into the gas fund and bought four tickets. He was playing two shows that night in a small folk club in the Five Corners district of the city. After the first show we were stunned; we couldn't move. It was one of those performances that reaffirms one's belief in the power of music to uplift, redeem, and heal. We managed to act inconspicuous and were able to take in the second show for free. That night he performed the Rolling Stones' "Dead Flowers." Shortly after that, we added it to our repertoire as a sort of oblique tribute to·him and to that night.

I saw Townes all over North America, and it was always a roll of the dice. There were the shows when he opened up so much that you almost didn't want to be there. It was like looking at a car wreck in a way. He'd be rambling on and not connecting, and all of a sudden he'd fall into a song and it'd be so direct and pointed and intense and he'd really open up his soul to you. You'd be like, "I don't know if I should be watching this." It was almost too intense. There were tons of shows where he was just great, a fantastic guitar player and his words and singing and guitar playing all came together and all of the beauty and strength of his songs were on display at once.

After the release of our third album, The Caution Horses, we were sitting around and planning our upcoming US tour. The subject of an opening act came up and someone jokingly said, "Wouldn't it be great to get Townes Van Zandt to come along with us?" We all laughed, and someone else said, "Why not?" Phone calls were made and soon after that we were once again rambling down those same highways, but this time we were riding a tour bus instead of a van and instead of having just Townes's music to keep us company, we had Townes in the flesh. We passed a lot of time on that bus playing dice, a game that Townes was quite anxious to teach us. Townes would also occasionally, almost reluctantly, tell us stories about some of his early days on the road, and on more than a few occasions after a show, Townes would pick up his guitar and open up his heart to us. We would sit there in our post-gig haze and be transfixed and transformed by the words, voice, and music of Townes Van Zandt.

He'd give these little preambles when he'd play songs on the bus, not necessarily about what they were about, but what they were "around." He'd circle a theme. "Flyin' Shoes" is one of my favorites and a good example. He said the song was written when he lived in Tennessee. He'd go to this field and sit on a rock to do some writing. It was the site of a very minor Civil War battle, and one day he was sitting there and imagined a young soldier lying there, bleeding and waiting for death to come. Now, if you listen to the song, there's no mention of soldiers or Civil War or battlefields. There's no mention of people bleeding to death, but there's definitely something impending coming. It's about the emotions.

I took from Townes that you get your idea for a song and take it beyond the initial place and make it much larger and open for other people to bring their own experience to it. A soldier dying was just the takeoff point for inspiration with "Flyin' Shoes." Then it transforms into this song about escape and longing, and there's so much ennui and a sense of not being in the right place. Of course, once you know that story behind the song, you think, My god, that's a beautiful way to describe someone lying there and dying. You get a sense of the scene.

One time our driver stayed with us overnight. He was a real hardcore redneck guy, very gruff. He wasn't in the same mindset that we were in, but Townes sort of took him under his wing. Townes pointedly began playing songs specifically to him. Before he played "Nothin'," he looked at him and said, "Ken, have you ever visited a mental institution?" Ken said, "Yeah." Townes said, "You know when you walk into the halls and you look at the rooms where you see the people who are worse off and you see them sitting in a corner?" Ken said, "Yeah." Townes said, "Well, that is what this song is about." Again, the song isn't necessarily about a mental patient sitting in a corner of a room, but when you hear it, you can think, Okay, this song fits that situation.

Certainly at the time when we took him on tour, people didn't know who the hell he was. He was on excellent behavior traveling on our bus as far as the drinking goes. His state of mind was solid. He was writing a ton on that tour, too, a good half of his last record, No Deeper Blue. He even made a point of saying that he hadn't been writing a lot [before the tour] but was on a real creative streak while he was out with us. After the tour, he gave us "Cowboy Junkies Lament," and I sat with it and toyed with it a bit, trying to figure out what it was about. I called him up and said, "You've got to give me a clue here." He said each verse is a reflection on us. When I knew that, I looked at it and said, "Okay, this makes sense, now I get it."

"Cowboy Junkies Lament" was an interesting analysis of our characters and personalities and how he saw us. I think we forget, but at the time we were blown over by it. You look back and think, My god, Townes Van Zandt wrote a song for us and titled it off us, and then he recorded it himself. Talk about a highlight of one's life and career. That was pretty spectacular. There's that great line, "There's a hole in heaven where some sin slips through." That one is in my verse. That's excellent. A lot of people who've come to the band later sort of think that we got our name from that song, that that song came before the band.

I wrote "Townes' Blues" after our tour. In some ways, it was a response to "Cowboy Junkies Lament." That song is based around a true story, an ongoing, nonstop dice game during a twenty-four-hour ride that we took on the bus from Boulder down to Houston. The bus driver decided to take this phenomenally long route around the mountains that added another eight or nine hours to the drive. Townes would do that drive all the time down from Colorado to Texas. The whole time, Townes kept saying, "You know, if we go through the Raton Pass [at the Colorado and New Mexico border], we'll cut eight hours off." That's where the line "Ain't this fool ever heard of Raton?" comes from.

I like to say "Blue Guitar" was written with Townes after he died. I sat down to write an elegy for him, and I wrote basically the music and the verses. That's as far as I got. I felt it wasn't a completed song. So, I put it away for a few weeks, and then Jeanene Van Zandt invited Margo and me to do a Townes tribute at the Bottom Line in New York City. When we were there, she gave all the performers this book of lyrics that hadn't been finished or published. He had one in there that I think was called "[Screams from] the Kitchen." When I saw that, I suddenly saw how I could transform "Blue Guitar" into a completed song with some of those lyrics.

I think what people are hearing now in Townes is the poetry. Maybe that's an obvious thing, but most people don't write like that. There's lots of wordplay that's based on Romantic poetry. The exciting thing is how much his work has continued to grow as people explore it. People are recognizing the name. There was a time when you'd say, "Townes Van Zandt," and people would stare at you blankly. Now, if someone has any sense of music, they know the name right away.

A few days after Townes died, I was spending my first night in the country in this isolated 200-year-old house that I had rented in order to do some writing. That night I had this dream. I was in a small rowboat with Townes. I was in the back, Townes was in the front, and we were both facing each other, although not really looking at each other. There was someone in between us doing the rowing, but that person was of no consequence. We were heading to an island where we were going to leave Townes to die. We both knew this.

We got to the island, and I followed Townes off of the boat and on to shore where he sat down on a rock. Still, there were no words spoken or any kind of communication. I turned to leave, hesitated, turned back and said, "Townes." He kept staring off into the middle distance. I said, "Thanks." He looked up at me, and his expression got hard and dark. He didn't say anything. I turned and walked back to the boat.[9]

Kelly Joe Phelps, St. Andrew's Presbyterian Church, Austin, TX, November 12, 2010

KELLY JOE PHELPS

When his earthly race is over and the curtains around him fall
  We'll carry him home to glory on the Wabash Cannonball
  —Trad. arr. by TVZ, from *Townes Van Zandt: Live at McCabe's*

"You call yourself a folksinger, and you don't know the 'Wabash Cannonball'?" Townes Van Zandt cross-examined a young Steve Earle with that challenge at the original Old Quarter in Houston in 1972.[1] Kelly Joe Phelps later walked the walk with Van Zandt. In early 1995, Van Zandt invited his opening act at McCabe's Guitar Shop in Santa Monica, California, back onstage to perform "Wabash Cannonball" and a second traditional tune, "Banks of the Ohio." Phelps's lively teardrop Dobro clearly boosted Van Zandt's already high spirits. "A little showing off there," he joked after Phelps executed a particularly animated solo during "Wabash Cannonball."

Van Zandt's loose demeanor, which is captured on the album *Townes Van Zandt: Live at McCabe's* (2003), displays his affection for the intimate venue. "When we checked into the hotel across the street from McCabe's and ate at the Mexican restaurant up the block," Van Zandt's longtime road manager Harold F. Eggers Jr. says, "Townes said, 'I want to retire here and live at this motel, so I can stumble on foot up the block to eat and drink and perform regularly at McCabe's.'"[2] Phelps frequently does today.

At thirty-five, Kelly Joe Phelps, born October 5, 1959, in Sumner, Washington, was a relative newcomer that night supporting Van Zandt with only the album *Lead Me On* (1994) under his belt. By the time of *Roll Away the Stone* (1997), he had established himself as one of the modern era's most accomplished slide guitarists and blues singers, as well as a highly combustible and exciting performer who reels like a dervish in concert.[3] As a bandleader, Phelps jolts and gyrates in his seat while shouting changes to rhythm players and nodding to extend instrumentals. As a solo performer, he loses himself as deeply in his instrument as Van Zandt would sink into his lyrics.[4]

At first, Phelps employed his innovative style primarily to enliven traditional blues (such as "Motherless Children" and "Goodnight Irene") and spirituals (such as "I've Been Converted" and "Doxology"). His uniquely emotive approach won over early admirers such as actor Colin Firth and songwriter Steve Earle, as well as a significant European following.[5] "Forget about songs in a twelve-bar, three-chord progression with a two-line repeat and answer-rhyme structure," Earle wrote about Phelps's following album, *Shine Eyed Mister Zen* (1999). "I'm talking about a feeling, a smoky, lonesome and painful—yet somehow comforting— groove that lets you know that you're not alone."[6] *Shine Eyed Mister Zen* marked Phelps's emergence as a lyricist and songwriter. The complex interpretations such as "The House Carpenter" and "Dock Boggs Country Blues" remained, but Phelps for the first time penned the majority of the album's songs (including "River Rat Jimmy" and "Wandering Away").[7]

Phelps purposefully scripted the evolution. "When I started looking over the songs I was writing before, I started feeling like the lyric side was the weakest part of the package," he says. "So, my musical energies turned to trying to figure out a way to write words that fit me, rather than trying to emulate great songwriters."[8] His more recent albums—including *Sky Like a Broken Clock* (2001), *Slingshot Professionals* (2003), *Tunesmith Retrofit* (2006), and *Western Bell* (2009)—frame outcasts from the Pacific Northwest not far removed from Tom Russell's catalog (such as those in "Tommy," "Waiting for Marty," and "Not So Far to Go").

■ ■ ■

KELLY JOE PHELPS

I was hired as an opener for Townes at McCabe's Guitar Shop in Santa Monica, California. When I showed up at McCabe's, Townes was sound checking. I'd not met him before, other than through his music. The promoter showed a friend and me to my dressing room. The door was cracked, so I could hear Townes warming up as I warmed myself up. Then it got quiet. I could hear footsteps creeping up the stairs, those infamous McCabe's stairs to the backroom. The door of my dressing room was pushed open and there standing, I knew from pictures, was Townes Van Zandt. With neither a handshake nor a hello he looked at me, and said, "Do you know 'The Banks of the Ohio'"? I said, "Yes." I knew it, sure. He said, "Well, you play it, and I'll sing it."

He crouched against the wall nearest the door, and I started an intro to the song. I looked over, and he began singing. My friend and I swapped quick glances, both feeling the crazy magic that was happening. Two other people showed up at the door to listen. Two more. Word spread through the downstairs room what was happening upstairs. Soon

Kelly Joe Phelps, McCabe's Guitar Shop, Santa Monica, California, February 10, 1995. (Standing, L-R) [unknown], Kelly Joe Phelps, Townes Van Zandt. (front row) [unknown]. Courtesy Harold F. Eggers Jr.

enough, the upstairs hallway was full of staff and customers watching and listening to Townes and me making music for the first time together. We continued our way through the tune, then reached a point where we both smiled and laughed. I stopped playing, he reached out a hand, and said, "I'm Townes." I reached out to shake his hand. He looked me in the eye and said, "You want to play with me tonight?" "Of course," I said.

We had two shows that night. The first started on schedule and finished relatively within the bounds. The second show started about 11:00 at night. I remember looking at the clock somewhere around 2:00 in the morning, and he was still going strong, still talking, telling jokes and stories, singing those great songs of his. That night he gave me one of the most important lessons of my life, not just about being a musician but more so about being human. I realized at that very moment what it was to become so much a part of yourself that nothing but honesty remained. I've thought about that moment a hundred thousand times, but we never talked about it. I never had a chance to thank him, either. Which, in the end, I think is perfect.[9]

Steve Turner, London Astoria, London, England, May 30, 2004

STEVE TURNER

If three and four were seven only, where would that leave
   one and two?
If love can be and still be lonely, where does that leave me and you?
—TVZ, "Buckskin Stallion Blues," from *At My Window*

Some say Mudhoney begat grunge rock.[1] At least, the Seattle quartet played an important role in developing the early 1990s movement. While bands such as Nirvana, Pearl Jam, Soundgarden, and Alice in Chains earned national recognition for pioneering the form, which mixes elements of punk, rock and roll, and heavy metal, many music critics and insiders consider Mudhoney to be as significant an influence. "I think Mudhoney records will always sound like Mudhoney records, which sound like Stooges records," Pearl Jam lead singer Eddie Vedder says, "which will last until the end of time." Although its origin remains debatable, some credit Mudhoney singer Mark Arm with coining the term "grunge."[2]

In 1988, Arm and guitarist Steve Turner left the regionally influential group Green River to form Mudhoney. The band's raucous shows, which included stage diving, slam dancing, and other "shenanigans and craziness," established its name throughout the Northwest.[3] Mudhoney's signature combination of heavy blues and punk rock backed by Turner's heavily distorted guitar fortified its early Sub Pop Records releases *Superfuzz Bigmuff* (1988), *Mudhoney* (1989), and *Every Good Boy Deserves Fudge* (1991). They were reluctant to sign with major labels during this time. "The majors went around saying, 'What's the next best Mudhoney?'" says bassist John Leighton of The Thrown Ups, a side project with Turner. "It was Nirvana."[4]

Nirvana's major-label breakthrough *Nevermind* (1991) instantly framed singer Kurt Cobain as the international representative of grunge rock. Meanwhile, Mudhoney signed to Reprise Records and released four albums, including *Piece of Cake* (1992) and *Tomorrow Hit Today* (1998), to decidedly less mainstream fanfare. The band returned to Sub Pop with the record *Since We've Become Translucent* (2002).[5]

Longtime Townes Van Zandt enthusiast Steve Turner, born March 28, 1965, in Houston, Texas, and Mudhoney recorded Van Zandt's "Buckskin Stallion Blues" with legendary Texas singer-songwriter Jimmie Dale Gilmore as a one-off project with Sub Pop during the band's major-label tenure. The split-single EP *Mudhoney/Jimmie Dale Gilmore* (1994) features "Buckskin Stallion Blues" as its centerpiece, surrounded by the musicians performing both country and rock versions of Mudhoney's "Blinging Sun" and Gilmore's "Tonight I Think I'm Gonna Go Downtown." Townes Van Zandt reportedly was proud to be recognized by popular younger artists. "I'm the mold," he said, "that grunge was grown in."[6] In turn, Van Zandt's impact on Turner was significant. "The first time I saw Townes was with Mickey Newbury and Guy Clark, which in retrospect was more than anyone could hope for," Turner says. "At the time, I just wanted those other two guys to shut up and let Townes sing."[7]

Another leading grunge band, Sonic Youth, played a role in Van Zandt's final days, as the band's drummer, Steve Shelley, oversaw Van Zandt's last recording session at Memphis's Easley Studios in December 1996. The unreleased sessions for Geffen Records reportedly were disastrous, with a wheelchair-bound Van Zandt suffering from a broken hip and deep in the throes of alcoholism, but he managed to cut a few tracks, including "Harm's Swift Way," perhaps his last composition. Former Led Zeppelin lead singer Robert Plant, who recorded Van Zandt's song "Nothin'" on his Grammy-winning country-roots collaboration with singer Alison Krauss, *Raising Sand* (2007), included a version of "Harm's Swift Way" on his Grammy-nominated album *Band of Joy* (2010).[8] "Another reason why I shouldn't write another song," Plant says of "Harm's Swift Way." "There's such a wearisome thing about it. Every one of [Van Zandt's] songs is a landscape for a book. What goes with that is a short time span, by the looks of it. You get too close to the sun. Maybe that's the courageous way. Songwriters sometimes get old and spend too much time in the supermarket buying health-food stuff."[9]

■ ■ ■

STEVE TURNER

I stumbled upon Townes in a thrift store. I was getting into a lot of '60s folk and saw one of his records. He had the proper look of a folkie and was standing in a New York City doorway with some dirty hippies making out next to him. Perfect. I picked it up. I had me a new, sweet lady, and by the end of "Nothin'," Townes was our new favorite, next to Rudimentary Peni, of course. I spent the next few years searching out the rest of Townes's records. It could be said I was a bit obsessed. I won't embarrass myself too much here, but let's just say I'm also from Houston, and Lightnin' [Hopkins] was my first favorite as a young man. I felt, as they say, a connection.

Townes made it to Seattle pretty often, and I saw a couple more shows. I brought the other Mudhoney dudes in, and Mark [Arm] and I somehow managed to record "Buckskin Stallion Blues" with Jimmie Dale Gilmore, which is definitely more than we could have hoped for. The next time Townes came through, he was aware of this odd fact, and we met him. In fact, there was some sort of mix-up and the promoter asked us if we had any vodka at home we could get for Townes, it being Sunday and the state liquor stores were closed.

Townes's shows in Seattle had been getting increasingly boozy, and Mudhoney had a bit of a reputation for imbibing as well. Dan Peters, our big-hearted redheaded drummer, had one of his moments of genius. His house was only a few blocks from the club, and he had a well-stocked cabinet. He suggested Townes just come on over after the show and hang out. So, he and Townes came over. We drank, talked, smoked pot, and listened to Townes sing some songs in Dan's living room. Townes kept rubbing his eyes with some smooth stones from a leather pouch and mumbling something about Indians, I think. Townes was really fucked up by the end, as was I. I wish I had a clear memory of it all, but I don't. I only know it was something very special, and kind of apocalyptic. We were trying a little too hard to have a little too good of a time.

Townes made it to Seattle one more time, I think. He wasn't at his best, and I couldn't make out a single word when I said hi after the set. I remember my mom asking about him shortly after, and I told her I really didn't think I'd see him again.[10]

David Broza, One World Theatre,
Austin, TX, December 19, 2010

DAVID BROZA

There is a home out of harm's swift way I set myself to find
I swore to my love I would bring her there, then I left my
*   love behind*
—TVZ, "Harm's Swift Way," recorded by David Broza on *Night Dawn: The*
Unpublished Poetry of Townes Van Zandt and by Robert Plant on *Band of Joy*

For the past thirty-five years, David Broza, born September 4, 1955, in Haifa, Israel, but raised in Great Britain and Spain, has played an important role in popularizing the poetry of several major international writers, including Elizabeth Bishop, Federico García Lorca, Percy Bysshe Shelly, and Walt Whitman, by adapting their words to his original music. Broza initially earned regional recognition through a celebrated collaboration with Israeli poet Yehonatan Geffen (1977's "Yihye Tov"), but his true commercial breakthrough came six years later with *The Woman by My Side* (1983), a multi-platinum album that made Broza a star in his native country. While touring internationally during the past three decades, he has shared stages with a broad range of prominent musicians such as Bob Dylan, Jose Fernandez, Spyro Gyra, Van Morrison, Paul Simon, and Sting.

Broza seems driven by a quest for depth and diversity. In addition to his musical endeavors, the current Tel Aviv resident has served as a soldier, peace activist, UNICEF goodwill ambassador, and artist-in-residence at Vermont's Bennington College. He has recorded several albums in English (including 1995's *Stone Doors*), Hebrew (2002's *All or Nothing*), and Spanish (2004's *Parking Completo*), matching his linguistic dexterity with a stylistic elasticity that frequently moves between country, pop, and rock music, occasionally within the same album. The public television special *David Broza at Masada: The Sunrise Concert* features the enthusiastic musician, who nearly lost his ability to play guitar following a 1998 car accident, performing alongside notable singer-songwriters Jackson Browne and Shawn Colvin.[1]

David Broza performed only twice with Townes Van Zandt, but the shows had a lasting impact on both songwriters. "David is dynamic onstage, and Townes was blown away by his guitar playing," says songwriter Linda Lowe, who hosted the disparate duo as a part of her Writers in the Round concert series in Houston in 1994 and took them to play at the Kerrville Folk Festival a year later. "I could physically see Townes getting involved in the songs. There was an obvious point where David just had him, and that was it."[2] In turn, Van Zandt's individuality clearly captivated Broza. "I only knew a couple of his songs—'Pancho and Lefty,' 'Flyin' Shoes'—when I met Townes, but it was his personality that really got me," Broza says. "That [four-person song swap with Lowe and orchestral composer David Amram in Houston] ended up being about Townes and me. Each of us was trying to impress the other, and I was obviously very inspired. The show lasted for four hours."[3]

Sixteen years later, Broza released *Night Dawn: The Unpublished Poetry of Townes Van Zandt* (2010), an eclectic album that sheds light on poems that Van Zandt posthumously bequeathed to the songwriter.[4] *Night Dawn* highlights common lyrical themes present throughout Van Zandt's catalog such as death ("Old Satan," "Harm's Swift Way"), isolation ("Holes in My Soul," "Southern Cross"), and yearning ("Night Dawn (Silver Dollar)"), but the Flamenco guitarist's signature percussive style often brightens dark material ("Jeanene"). "I had Townes in my mind as I composed the music on *Night Dawn*," Broza says. "[Our show together in Houston] was many years back, but I could feel it. His was not a long forgotten presence."[5]

■ ■ ■

DAVID BROZA

I wasn't born in the States and didn't grow up there. I came to America when I was twenty-seven, twenty-eight years old and already had a family and two kids and a career. I came because I was really fascinated by American culture and folk and folk-rock and jazz and poetry. When I sat in front of Townes that night in Houston, I felt that he really was the essence of American singer-songwriter or troubadour. What I had been searching for and really wanted to meet and see in person was what Townes had.

He's a very honest performer with stories that he tells from the heart. Our show in Houston was not calculated. His were very instantaneous and spontaneous, and I very much have the same approach to life onstage. He would play every night if he could, and I am also like that. I actually have played almost every night for the past thirty-five years. I felt that I'd found, not a twin soul, but certainly someone I could look up to who answered my quest for meeting that American artist. Townes had it all in him.

Townes had the thought that night that maybe we should meet and collaborate on his poetry since I was telling him and the audience most of my work was writing music to poetry in English or Hebrew or Spanish. He said, "You know, I have some poetry, too." That was the end of that because for two years we tried to get together but never managed to. I suppose we didn't try hard enough because he died before we could put it together.

I got a phone call from Linda Lowe in 1996 saying she had spoken to him. He had called a couple weeks before and dictated a poem to her and said, "Please make sure this gets to David Broza." This poem is called "Harm's Swift Way." She called and was very excited to read it to me over the phone. A couple weeks later, she called and said with a kind of sadness and alarm that he had just passed away. She said that he'd expressed that he really wanted me to work on his poetry.[6]

When I looked at the lyrics to "Southern Cross," it was so American, so Texas. For years, I'd go to Texas and tour six times a year. I love Texas and that Southern feel that reminds me of the Middle East. The hills remind me of Galilee. When you're far away from home and traveling a lot, you try to cling onto things that remind you of your roots. Suddenly, that language brought it all back to me, whether I was in Manhattan or Berlin or Madrid or Tel Aviv. The lyrics painted that kind of a familiar feeling that connected with me.

In other places, it was just a beautiful love song like "Jeanene": "If I have to go / I'll be gone forever / No Pueblo sunrise will / Shine on me." I like the word "Pueblo" because it's Spanish. It shows that Texas border culture. I like that, of course, because I grew up in Spain. That immediately catches my attention. Besides, it has a great storytelling feel. It's haunting and captivating. Some of the songs didn't take me more than an hour or two to compose, but others took me many days to figure out. It's full of riddles, but I like that.

Townes's version of "Harm's Swift Way" was very somber. I was very clear that I wanted to reflect that. I gave it a little bit more of a structured, melodic, repetitive feel. It's not a happy song. Robert Plant does a version of it that sounds like another happy, merry day out in the meadow or country fair. It's not [upbeat], "Oh me, oh my, who's gonna mark my time?"[7] There's a lot of pain. Even if a man wants to die, dying is not something you walk to happily. Dying is something you resign to. It is the end of the story. Nobody wants any story to end.

Townes Van Zandt (R) with David Broza, Main Street Theater, Houston, TX, March 16, 1994. Courtesy Linda Lowe.

Townes did not want the story to end, but he couldn't stop himself from ending it, obviously. He'd been on the path to the end for a long time with alcohol, terrible bouts of chemical imbalance. His life was one long story of a troubled soul and a beautiful human being who was a great storyteller with a great sense of humor. He wanted to experience life in the edges, but the end is the end.

I'm very close to the end. I have gone through wars. I deal with people who have gone through shell shock, and I've gone through shell shock. What we see here in the Middle East for good and bad—mostly bad—is people who end up in all kinds of establishments that are closed-door treatment for post-trauma drug and alcohol rehabs. Hell, you live with that, and you feel it. And when somebody tells it like Townes, I want to give it a little bit of an expression that will let you march along with it. It's not the end. What a poet leaves behind is something that's engraved in stone. I hope I did Townes's poetry a service. That's what I went out to do, with total respect, like I did with Walt Whitman, Elizabeth Bishop, Federico García Lorca. I totally identify with every word and every note of that song, "Harm's Swift Way."

[My instrumental dedicated to Van Zandt] "Too Old to Die Young" is like a guy on a horse riding into the horizon. I play it with a Spanish guitar, so I'm taking a thematic cowboy melody and playing it on that guitar, which changes the tone. And the minute the tone changes, the whole color changes. That's because it's Townes and me. When I was playing it, I was thinking, I'd like to play that for him. This is what I want to tell you, Townes. I want to talk to you just with the music.

I wasn't sure what to call "Too Old to Die Young," but then one day I was talking to [Night Dawn co-producer] G. E. Smith about the tragedy of Townes's life and the way it ended when he was fifty-two. I said, "I would be very, very sad, but he was fifty-two. He was already old enough to have a family, to live the good part of his life. He was too old to die young." It wasn't like Kurt Cobain or Jimi Hendrix or Janis Joplin dying at twenty-seven or [French poet Arthur] Rimbaud at [thirty-seven]. I'm thinking, I'm fifty-five now. If I go, I've already lived. You can't say he died too young. I thought of naming the album that, but they thought it was too morbid.

I think songwriting is humbling, but not always spiritual. I think Townes always talked about songs falling from the sky with a grain of salt. He never wanted to preach. He wanted to share with people his feelings. He was very, very, very honest. That hurt him a lot. A lot of times, we feel things and would rather not say them because it's scary. He didn't. He loved to scare you. He'd tell you exactly what he felt, even if it was terrible. His spirit was born on the outside not on the inside. I'm not like that. I can't live like that, but I so respect it and I feel it. He's doing it all the way.

Of course, I feel lucky to be gifted to write music like I do. I take responsibility. I write music, I sing songs, I produce albums, I tour. People pay to see me and I'm an entertainer first and foremost. I want people to walk out and say, "Hell, where was I before I came here? I feel so good now." I want them to forget. Townes wanted to do that, too. He was a real entertainer, but he always wanted to test everything to the end. To be spiritual and talk about it is to preach. To be spiritual and to accept it and understand it and be humbled by it, you have to reflect upon it. There must be a spirit, but it's not for me to say. I'm really living it. I'm not professing it.

[I identify with Townes because] I'm an outsider. I'm not part of the Austin or Nashville scene or the scene here in Israel or Madrid. I think Townes was a total outsider, a different cast. He was everybody's friend, and yet he didn't play the game that everybody played. He didn't want to be like anybody else. He wanted to be Townes, and really that's very special. You have someone like Kris Kristofferson who was one of the best singer-songwriters ever in the music scene in America, but he's an insider. He's there. He sits around with Johnny Cash and Bob Dylan.

Townes could have been with Bob Dylan and Johnny Cash and everybody every day because they so respected him, but he was never around to be caught with them. He was down the street chopping wood. Playing in a small bar because he wanted to play the small places. It's very interesting, and now look at how many people talk about him and analyze him and think about him today after his death. The man had a vision. He had a say. His poetry certainly shined on and on.[8]

MICHAEL WESTON KING

A fella across town said he's looking for a man to move some
    old cars around
  Maybe me and Marie could find a burned out van and do a little
    settlin' down
—TVZ, "Marie," from *No Deeper Blue*

Michael Weston King, born November 11, 1961, in Derby-shire, England, supported Townes Van Zandt throughout the United Kingdom during an extensive overseas tour in spring 1994. The songwriters met at Heathrow airport the afternoon before their journey's opening concert at Union Chapel, which was later released as the landmark double-disc set *Townes Van Zandt Live at Union Chapel, London, England* (2005).[1] "Townes was this tall, road-weary character with a raincoat and Davy Crockett hat," Weston King says. "He had these great moccasins on. He said he'd swapped his cowboy boots for them in Norway, and I coveted them the whole tour."[2]

Weston King soon modeled his band The Good Sons, whose albums include *Singing the Glory Down* (1995), *The King's Highway* (1996), *Wines, Lines, and Valentines* (1997), and *Happiness* (2001), on Van Zandt's craftsmanship, only with a more buoyant backdrop.[3] "My idea for The Good Sons was to write songs in that classic songwriting style like Townes or Guy Clark, but then combine it with what was happening in the beginning of the alt-country scene like the Jayhawks or Uncle Tupelo," the Birmingham resident says. "I wanted to write songs as good as [Townes's], but with that alt-country attitude." Weston King immediately furthered his goals by enlisting Van Zandt as a duet partner on *Singing the Glory Down*'s "Riding the Range."[4]

Michael Weston King's solo albums such as *A Decent Man* (2003), *A New Kind of Loneliness* (2007), and *I Didn't Raise My Boy to Be a Soldier* (2010) frequently feature mournful ballads close to Townes Van Zandt's heart.[5] Accordingly, he has made both early Van Zandt songs (such as "Rake" and "Waitin' Around to Die") and later-year tunes ("A Song For," "Lover's Lullaby") a staple of his live set for years. "It's rare that I get through a whole show without playing a Townes song," Weston King says.[6] (His version of Van Zandt's "Marie" appears on the live album *Crawling Through the USA* (2008)).

In turn, Van Zandt tipped his hat by recording Weston King's "Riding the Range" with bluegrass musicians Jim and Royann Calvin shortly before his death. Exile Records released the song as a limited pressing seven-inch vinyl single with a B-side cover of Ewan MacColl's "Dirty Old Town" (1996). "Townes looked at Mike as himself coming up the ranks," says Harold F. Eggers Jr., Van Zandt's former business partner and manager. "Townes recorded 'Riding the Range' because he liked the words, and that single went like hotcakes. It got a five-star review in the German *Rolling Stone*."[7]

By that time, Van Zandt and Weston King had toured again twice in Europe, but their first concert together remains the most fortuitous evening overall. "Eight months after [our] concert, The Union Chapel Day Centre was set up in response to the amount of homeless people sleeping rough, literally on the doorstep," Weston King wrote in the liner notes to *Townes Van Zandt Live at Union Chapel, London, England.* "Since then it has opened every Sunday including Christmas and Easter and helped thousands of London's homeless, all of whom would surely be able to relate to Townes's poignant story in 'Marie' . . . If there is a better song about the hopelessness and degradation of being homeless and poverty stricken, then I have yet to hear it."[8]

■ ■ ■

MICHAEL WESTON KING

Union Chapel wasn't the usual club or bar Townes was used to playing, so it was quite a surprise for him. It's a huge, beautiful old church in Islington. Over the next couple years, I saw many different Townes shows in varying quality, but the Union Chapel gig was unique. It was certainly the biggest show Townes had played in the UK. There must've been getting on 1,000 people, which is quite extraordinary. Townes had been over numerous times before, but I don't think he'd ever played for more than a couple hundred. He was a bit bemused.

That day everything seemed to fall right. Townes was in pretty good shape, he was playing pretty well, and the audience was on his side. As a singer and songwriter, I was struck by the quality of the songs—hearing "Marie" for the first time blew me away—but his way with the audience was what really struck me. His humor made the show so wonderful. If your in-between talk [is] as dark as those harrowing songs, it would make for a very hard evening.

That London show was the first one, and then we went off around the country. The English band The Tindersticks had covered [the Van Zandt song] "Kathleen," and it had been a hit. A lot of people who didn't really

Michael Weston King (L) and Townes Van Zandt, London, 1994. Courtesy Harold F. Eggers Jr.

know who Townes was came out to find out what this guy was all about. There was more press because a younger band had recorded his song. He did interviews with more mainstream radio stations like the BBC National and stations that ordinarily wouldn't have interviewed people like Townes.

It was a bit of a rollercoaster ride, for sure. I'd been in many bands up to that point, but that was the first time I saw firsthand somebody like Harold who had to ride shotgun for a whole tour just to make sure that Townes made it on stage. I really respected Harold for the twenty-four-hour care he had to give Townes to make it happen. I think deep down, Townes did, too. By the second or third tour—I probably played about twenty to twenty-five shows with Townes—I just sort of took it for granted.

Townes would tease Harold and wind him up considerably, but in a loving way. He would play mind games with him all the time. I think Harold knew that and went along with it. Townes played up to the fact that he had somebody who was going to look after him. It wasn't that Townes was totally incapable; it was that he had the opportunity to be incapable if he wanted. Harold was a very willing ally who doted on Townes. Certainly those tours wouldn't have happened without Harold being there. It was a lovely relationship. You weren't sure who the boss was sometimes. They were like partners.

Townes influenced me a lot in the way that he dealt with people on the road. Despite his troubles, he was always very gentle and didn't carry around a big ego. I've toured and traveled with so many people—bigger names than Townes and some smaller—and that just struck me. A lot of people can be quite assholes on the road, especially dealing with people they think are inferior to them. I never got that with Townes. You can be tired and miserable on the road, but he was always charming and lovely to everybody he came into contact with. Behavior like that stands you in good stead.

I've written a lot more songs in A-minor since, and I wrote a song called "Lay Me Down" about Townes. I took his song "Waitin' Around to Die" and stretched out the time scale and the chords. Apart from that instance, I haven't sat down and tried to write songs in Townes's style. Sometimes you might be playing somebody's song regularly in your set and then without even knowing it, you kind of make those changes similar to a song that's in your head. I wrote a song called "Cosmic Fireworks" that was heavily influenced by his song "Lover's Lullaby," which I covered.

Because I was touring with him at the time, *No Deeper Blue* still sticks with me more than anything. The songs I've tended to perform have been from that record. I still maintain that it's a fabulous record. Given that it was toward the end of his life, it's more remarkable for it. Two or three of those songs were as good as anything he'd ever written, songs like "A Song For" and "Marie."

"A Song For" is one of the most perfect songs to personify Townes. He probably felt that for all the things he'd done and tried to do, it was like, "Well, what was that all about? What was that all for?" That song perfectly encapsulates the weary troubadour who has sung and played his heart out, as the song says. You think, "What have I achieved?" You can feel like you haven't been financially rewarded. "Another relationship has fallen apart because of my desire to pursue this career." That song is almost an ending. Townes told me that was originally called "A Song for Shane MacGowan," but it seems very autobiographical to me.

"Marie" is remarkable, an incredibly agonizing and sad song. I've played "Marie" so many times, and I don't think anybody can fail to be moved by it. The subject of homelessness had been dealt with before in songs, but that is like a short movie. It talks about the hopelessness about being homeless, but it doesn't preach. It just tells the story of these two people. It's like a mini-Steinbeck book in five or six chapters. It draws you in, and then there's the payoff line at the end: "She just rolled over and went to heaven, her little boy safe inside."[9] It's a killer of a line to close a song with.

"Riding the Range" is a slightly tongue-in-cheek song about this strange phenomenon we have in Britain with working-class people dressing up as cowboys and living out that Wild West fantasy. These events usually take place in caravan parks and holiday camps. I thought it would be very bizarre to get Townes to sing on it. That was wonderful, and I didn't think anything more of it. Then on the day of the Borderline show [in London on December 3, 1996], what turned out to be his last show, he called me to his room and said, "Have a listen to this," [the version that Van Zandt recorded]. As a musician and certainly a songwriter, it's a huge, huge thrill to have him, arguably one of the greatest songwriters ever, record your song. I was blown away.[10]

Jewel, Woodland Park Zoo,
Seattle, WA, July 30, 2009.
Courtesy Kirk Stauffer.

VERSE
JEWEL

Well, Allison laid an egg on me, and every time I turn around
It's swimming through the air above my bed
—TVZ, "You Are Not Needed Now," *High, Low and In Between*

Jewel's confessional lyrics typically favor rustic idylls rather than dark recesses. However, the singer-songwriter, born Jewel Kilcher on May 23, 1974, in Payson, Utah, but raised in Homer, Alaska, clearly appreciates Townes Van Zandt's multilayered poetry. After all, she named her first born son Kase Townes in July 2011.

Jewel's debut album *Pieces of You* (1995) and its hit singles "Who Will Save Your Soul" and "You Were Meant for Me" launched a highly successful commercial career that has spanned a variety of genres, including the recent collection of children's songs *Lullaby* (2009). "Parents always have told me, 'I don't know what it is about your voice, but my kids are so calmed down when they hear you sing,'" she says.[1]

"I think some of the strongest singer-songwriters like Merle Haggard and Loretta Lynn and Townes Van Zandt come from the country genre," Jewel continues. "I've always loved storytellers and lyricists that wrote from their really strong, personal point of view. That's what I've set out to do. I've always had really strong country influences in my music and on all my albums, but I've never been able to get my label to work anything to country radio. Even 'You Were Meant for Me' I wanted to work for country radio, and they never did it.

"Townes seemed like a pure soul. He's a musician and an artist and a rolling stone that had his own little path and wrote some really lovely and really unique songs without really being constricted by hit-song structure. I think that allowed him to be really creative and tell stories. I don't think a standard songwriter would come up with 'Pancho and Lefty,' because it's too long or it doesn't go to the chorus the exact same way. That type of music is really valuable."[2]

DAVE ALVIN

You know, she cools me with her breathin'
  Chases away those howlin' bottles of wine
  —TVZ, "Brand New Companion," from *Delta Momma Blues*

Dave Alvin's stark vignettes slice life from both sides of the gas station counter. Many of his blue-collar narratives, equally informed by Dust Bowl balladeer Woody Guthrie and acoustic blues progenitor Lightnin' Hopkins, suggest that Alvin carves their essence from experience in each position (for instance, "Abilene" and "Fourth of July"). Alvin's key asset might be the ability to sketch Southwest landscapes with corresponding measures of heartbreak and hope. "She's been dancing on tables to pay rent and be able," he sings in "Abilene," "to just get by and maybe stay clean."[1]

Dave Alvin, born November 11, 1955, in Downey, California, has played an important role in Southern California's roots-rock movement for the past three decades. As a member of the influential band The Blasters, Dave Alvin and his brother Phil Alvin cut four albums, including *American Music* (1980), *The Blasters* (1981), and *Hard Line* (1985), which combine country, rockabilly, and punk rock sensibilities. The dynamic live performers toured continually with a diverse range of bands, including the Western swing group Asleep at the Wheel and the hard rock band Queen, earning an increasingly fanatical following. The Blasters invited such rising acts as Los Lobos and Dwight Yoakam as tour support before sibling tensions led to the band's dissolution in 1986.[2]

Dave Alvin immediately embarked on a successful and critically acclaimed solo career tailored more toward his goals as a singer-songwriter. Alvin boosted its start with Blasters highpoints such as "Fourth of July," "Border Radio," and "Long White Cadillac," later recorded by Yoakam in 1989, on his debut album *Romeo's Escape* (1987). Alvin followed with the collections *Blue Blvd.* (1991) and *Museum of Heart* (1993), but *King of*

Townes Van Zandt with Brownie McGhee. (L-R) Brownie McGhee, Harold Eggers, Townes Van Zandt. Courtesy Harold F. Eggers Jr.

California (1994) might be the album that best defines his solo catalogue. Recorded at the height of MTV's *Unplugged* series, Alvin clarified the acoustic album's purpose. "Current trends and fads aside, I've wanted to do a collection of stripped-down versions of old, new, borrowed, and blue songs for quite some time," he said.[3] Alvin's hushed versions again shed new light on "Border Radio" and "Fourth of July," which Robert Earl Keen recorded three years later on his album *Picnic*.[4]

Alvin acknowledged his blues influences on *King of California*'s "borrowed" tunes, such as Memphis Slim's "Mother Earth," Tom Russell's "Blue Wing," and Whistlin' Alex Moore's "East Texas Blues." In fact, folk and blues figured prominently in his following two studio albums, *Blackjack David* (1998), and the Grammy-winning *Public Domain* (2000). "[Songs such as 'New Highway' are] me playing guitar in the style of one of my heroes, Lonnie Johnson," Alvin says.[5] Dave Alvin brought blues back home with *Ashgrove* (2004), a tribute to the Los Angeles club where he witnessed concerts by bluesmen such as Rev. Gary Davis, Brownie McGhee and Sonny Terry, and Big Joe Turner as a young man. "I'd sit and stare and dream of doing what they could do," he sings.[6]

Today Alvin frequently mines Internet vaults for video footage of the country and blues influences that he shares with Townes Van Zandt and posts clips on social media outlets. "Townes's music had a stylistic imprint on me," he says.[7]

■ ■ ■

DAVE ALVIN

I'd probably be more in the Guy Clark camp, because my songwriting style is more journalistic. "Metaphysical" applies to Townes Van Zandt. I do dig Townes, but he wrote a different kind of poetry than I write. His is Romantic. One of my heroes when I was a kid—well, he still is—was Lightnin' Hopkins. I saw a Townes and Lightnin' co-bill one time, and Townes did a pretty good job for a guy who didn't record a lot of what you'd call straight blues. Townes had a lot of blues in him. In a weird way, his whole aura was that of a blues man. That show was early on, when I was about fifteen. When I was young, I was really interested in how you can adapt blues and not try to ape them.

The Texas songwriters who have influenced the most were probably Guy Clark and Terry Allen. The thing about those kinds of stories is that unless you're writing a quasi-folk story about a larger than life character like Pecos Bill or Paul Bunyan, you're trying to find a different way to comment on bigger issues without having to pull out the big club and announcing to the world, "I'm making a big comment here."

Stories are the way to do it. The drama in stories, in life, is where dreams and reality collide. We go through the day-to-day life—get out of bed, pay bills, have kids, cars break down, we get them fixed—and that's where the collision between how we think it should be and the humdrum of survival is. I mean, I'm a professional musician, so I certainly have issues when it comes to paying the rent. My sympathies lie with people who are trying to survive.

I was driving the other day and heard the Willie Nelson and Merle Haggard version of "Pancho and Lefty," the hit they had with the kind of disco beat. It struck me that Townes wrote a couple of great story songs—"Pancho and Lefty," "Tecumseh Valley." I tend to follow the Marty Robbins model—"El Paso" had the biggest influence on me—but Townes is telling a similar sort of deal. On the other hand, what he leaves out is so amazing. "Pancho and Lefty" is a great song because of what he doesn't say. The beautiful poetry is in the fine line between what he chooses to say and what he doesn't. Unfortunately, I think my biggest drawback is filling all the holes.[8]

JOSH RITTER

You cannot count the miles until you feel them
  You cannot hold a lover that is gone
  —TVZ, "Snowin' on Raton," from *At My Window*

Josh Ritter's first three albums—*Josh Ritter* (1999), *Golden Age of Radio* (2001), and *Hello Starling* (2003)—showed a talented young balladeer growing exponentially as an artist. During that time, Ritter was turning descriptive phrases that split the difference between the Guy Clark and Townes Van Zandt catalogues, such as "you look pretty good in that jonquil dress, but your smile is a wooden nickel's pride" from "Golden Age of Radio."[1] In fact, Ritter directly references Van Zandt in "Me and Jiggs," a song from *Golden Age of Radio* that unexpectedly topped Irish charts and launched a mutual admiration that remains today. "Sitting on the porch, singing Townes Van Zandt / Play guitar to burn off the hours," he sings. "Till we climb the fences at the edge of town / And paint our names on the water towers."[2]

Josh Ritter, born October 21, 1976, in Moscow, Idaho, viewed the world through an increasingly layered historical context on *The Animal Years* (2006). His major-label debut gained attention with cerebral narratives such as "Girl in the War" and the ten-minute epic "Thin Blue Flame," both pointed protests against the George W. Bush administration and the war in Iraq. "Mysterious, melancholy, melodic," novelist Stephen King said of *The Animal Years*. "['Thin Blue Flame'] is the most exuberant outburst of imagery since Bob Dylan's 'A Hard Rain's Gonna Fall' in 1963."[3]

"I wanted to write about how weird the world is without beating anyone over the head with politics," Ritter says. "I think everyone understands how weird things are. The important thing for me was to write about the ambiguity and the uncertainty in the world."[4] At this point, critics erased lines drawn toward Nick Drake, whose hushed delivery and clean finger-picking Ritter mirrored on early albums, and pointed comparisons toward Bruce Springsteen instead. Coincidentally, Ritter frequently performs Springsteen's song "The River" at solo acoustic appearances.[5]

Ritter's thought-provoking lyrics have earned a devoted fan base among college students seeking intellectual challenge. However, his cheery on-stage delivery might be his greatest appeal. In fact, few singer-songwriters match Ritter's intensity and passion in concert.[6] "Some of his songs are just superb," folk singer and former touring partner Joan Baez says, "but what I'm most impressed by is watching him perform. He's the only other performer other than myself that I've ever seen step out from the microphone and do a whole song. He's very charismatic."[7] Like Van Zandt, Ritter frequently lightens moments between his darkest songs with jokes. For instance, at a 2007 concert in Austin, Texas, he recalled an observation from a previous local appearance: "The marquee at Stubb's read, 'Gospel lunch, then Josh Ritter, then The Darkness.' That's hardcore."[8]

That same year, one music critic called Ritter "the standard bearer for a new generation of Americana artists."[9] At first, his recent albums *Historical Conquests of Josh Ritter* (2007) and *So Runs the World Away* (2010) sound far removed from the genre with their crashing cymbals, tinny electric guitars, and quavering keyboards. At heart, however, Ritter's rustic storytelling and intricate wordplay remain the same as his defining early material. At the same time, one song from *Historical Conquests* indirectly echoes Townes Van Zandt and shows Ritter's evolution. "'Next to the Last Romantic' definitely has some Townes there," he says, "but really I get much more inspiration now from the last book I read or the last train I rode."[10]

■ ■ ■

JOSH RITTER

Before I went to college, the people I was listening to were Johnny Cash and Bob Dylan. I started listening to them pretty late, but that's who I was into when I went off to college. Then at Oberlin [College], there was a girl at the end of my hall who used to give me music, and one night she gave me Townes Van Zandt. The album she handed to me was one of his live records, *Rear View Mirror*. That was a total revelation. Townes was doing things that no one else was doing. "Snowin' on Raton" is one of my favorite songs ever. I just love it. But it's really weird when you write it down and read the lyrics and see how it's structured. It's just not typical.

A song doesn't have to have a purpose. It just has to have that fuel that pushes it forward and washes over. "Thin Blue Flame" was really fun for me to write, because when you get on a roll the words just jump out and you don't even know where they come from. Sometimes they come out and they're awful, and you leave them and come back and laugh at them. I wrote so much for that song, and then pared it down.

In that song, I was thinking that the conservative Christianity and anti-Christianity movements swirling around are in a lot of ways moot points. What is there except the people around you that you can help? I feel like everything is missing the boat if we don't remember that. Why is it that community is so undervalued? God isn't going to make things better. I don't understand why spending all this time trying to be good in a certain way and hoping to get to heaven is doing any good for any of us if we're not just doing good for other people. That's part of the song. It's impossible to imagine that there's a god who's going to help you out if you're not going to help other people out.

The power of a song like ["Snowin' on Raton" or "Thin Blue Flame"] is that it shouldn't have a clear message. So many of those clear-messaged songs are just preaching to the choir these days. Is a song going to make you go out and vote for Kerry when you were going to vote for Bush beforehand? You just lose the beauty of words and emotion. Trying to fit them all into a moral sometimes does the poetry and the music a disservice. I'm a songwriter—I'm a writer—that's what I do.

So, I got into Townes Van Zandt, and then from him I found Guy Clark and songs like "The Randall Knife." People talk about them like they're poets, and they kind of are. They're like Raymond Carver, you know? There's a real sensibility to the way Guy Clark writes. It's incredible. But someone like Townes Van Zandt really blows your mind as a songwriter, and really as just a writer. The songs are just so . . . *nice.* When you listen to his songs, no one cares how many records Townes Van Zandt sells or how many people were at his shows. You just look at him as a writer and look at that incredible writing. He's making something that I feel lives beyond itself.

I think I saw Townes once during my freshman year in college. I was starting to think about getting into music, so I went down to the Kerrville Folk Festival. They have these campfires, and everybody plays around the fire. This was about the year before Townes died, and I didn't know all that much stuff about him. But I was sitting at this campfire and I believe Townes was there. I don't remember what song he was singing, but I believe that had to have been him. At least that's the way it is in my mind, anyway. I feel really close to him. He's kind of like one of the founding fathers.[11]

Scott Avett, Austin City Limits
Music Festival, Austin, TX,
October 2, 2009

SCOTT AVETT

Greensboro woman, don't you smile on me
    I do not feel like being comforted
    —TVZ, "Greensboro Woman," from *High, Low and In Between*

Scott Avett's theoretical last will winnows earthly import to a chill. "Don't bother with all my belongings," Avett sings in "Murder in the City," the unifying nucleus of the Avett Brothers' 2008 EP, *The Second Gleam*. "Make sure my sister knows I loved her / Make sure my mother knows the same / Always remember there was nothing worth sharing / Like the love that let us share our name."[1] Scott Avett's raw intimacy, as unflinching as windows allowed into his soul by Townes Van Zandt, has become a defining nexus of his songwriting approach. "When Scott discovered Townes Van Zandt, it greatly affected how he saw music," says younger sibling and songwriter Seth Avett.[2]

Scott Avett, born June 19, 1976, in Cheyenne, Wyoming, but raised in Concord, North Carolina, often fastens lyrics on themes of self-doubt and self-improvement. His confessional storytelling has rapidly risen in popularity in recent years. "We've seen a lot of temporary, disposable, plastic music in the mainstream," Avett says. "When the public becomes oversaturated with that, it's very pleasing to hear something more simple and human and with less libido, like someone's just talking to you." Accordingly, the Avetts deliver their unique blend of rock and mountain music, which at times wraps Charlie Poole's banjo blues ("Pretty Girl from Chile") and calypso great Lord Kitchener ("Pretty Girl from San Diego") around a single lyrical theme, in conversational narratives.[3]

The Avett Brothers frequently have covered Townes Van Zandt's "Greensboro Woman" in concert. "'Greensboro Woman' was easy just for its [geographic] point of reference, but I also cover 'Highway Kind' for my daughter," Scott Avett says. "She'll get real quiet when I play the piano when she's crying. It's so serious and dark, and I just love it."[4] That connection emerged clearly on the band's 2009 major-label debut *I and Love and You*, produced by Rick Rubin (Slayer, Johnny Cash), an important figure in the Avett brothers' musical development. "When we were thirteen to eighteen years old," Scott Avett says, "a lot of the records [he produced], from the Beastie Boys to the Chili Peppers, were high on the rotation."[5]

The Avett Brothers' early albums, including *The Avett Brothers* (2000), *Country Was* (2002), and *A Carolina Jubilee* (2003), owe deeply to such home-state influences as Doc Watson, Blind Boy Fuller, and Squirrel Nut Zippers. However, the high-energy concert albums *Live at the Double Door Inn* (2002), *Live, Vol. 2* (2005), and *Live, Volume 3* (2010) perhaps better capture the band's spirit. "I first met the Avett Brothers in New York [around 2003], and I was excited to be invited to North Carolina to support them at the [Chapel Hill's] Cat's Cradle not long after," says folk-pop singer-songwriter Langhorne Slim. "There were people young and old freaking out all night. I thought to myself, These guys are like some kind of bluegrass Beatles."[6]

I and Love and You caused some backlash among fans passionate for the band's leaner early sound, but the album earned significant critical acclaim.[7] One writer claimed that the Avett Brothers display the "heavy sadness of Townes Van Zandt, the light pop concision of Buddy Holly, the tuneful jangle of The Beatles, the raw energy of the Ramones."[8] Seth Avett grounds their influences in a less likely source. "[Blind Melon's] Shannon Hoon had the most joyous voice while talking about the most heart-wrenching challenges and confusion," he says. "He made it sound so sweet. What an apt description of people in general. We're all complicated, and we all have a way of being two ways at once."[9]

■ ■ ■

SCOTT AVETT

I pulled some vocal moves that Townes had used on a couple of his songs on *I and Love and You*. It was just like a Townes Van Zandt song because it was just verse after verse after verse. I love that because the song moves and never gets hung up on a chorus. That's a true folk or country-folk song. Rick Rubin was like, "Man, those two verses are just killing me, and I want to hear it again." The song was eight verses, so we cut out two of them, took the sixth and took one and turned it into a chorus, took another and turned it into a concept and theme. So now you have a chorus, a theme-slash-bridge that ends up as an outtro, and a whole new, refined song that keeps all the great elements of the verses. It doesn't work for every song, and it didn't work for a couple, but you have to be able to flex as a songwriter.

Townes's depth and despair came out in abstract wording that I relate to quite a bit. My brother is quite a formal writer who can write a very well outlined essay, whereas I just never showed the interest in school and kind of floated. As I developed, I related to Townes because I'm guessing that he developed an orderly fashion about writing songs by default because he just wrote as he felt. Sometimes I hear a line and I think, I don't even know what that meant, but, God, it makes so much sense. I'm in a very direct point of relation with that because I'm living that life and writing songs. I understand the despair that the occupation carries.

Now, his despair came in other ways—the alcoholism and things working against him—that ultimately killed him, but I try to keep that out of the equation. I have a strong family and friend network that really allows that to stay out. I was reluctant to get into Townes Van Zandt, and for a stupid reason—his name. You know, you hear that name Van Zandt all the time. How many Van Zandts are there, and how easy is it to mix them up? Who needs another folk guy? I tell you, when I engaged him, there's not another writer that I relate to more.

Townes would say stuff like, "This is a pretty song," which could come off as pretty egotistical. You think, "Well, he owns that song, so he shouldn't say that it's so brilliant or so pretty," but those of us who are serious about songwriting know that you're not the writer. [The song] found you, and not the other way. I don't think Townes ever said his songs were pretty because he made them pretty. He's thinking, "This song came to me, and I'm fortunate that it did. It's not mine, but it's a pretty little song, and I'm gonna share it with you."

We make ourselves available to catch the songs when they come. I don't think they're brilliant new things, they've all been regurgitated over and over, but if I wake up in the middle of the night and I can't go to sleep and my family's in my face and I hear a song and I choose not to put it down, that's me neglecting to accept that song. I think there's a very spiritual and godly type thing that happens, and it happens to way more people than we know. It's just that very few of us choose to engage it.[10]

Jim James, Santa Barbara Bowl, Santa Barbara, CA, July 9, 2004

JIM JAMES

When true love knocked upon my door, she'd just barely turned fifteen
And I was a little bit nervous, if you know just what I mean
—TVZ, "No Deal," from *High, Low and In Between*

My Morning Jacket's Jim James, born James Olliges Jr., on April 27, 1978, in Louisville, Kentucky, focuses on angles less frequently examined. While critics and songwriters exhaust superlatives on Townes Van Zandt's lyrics, James finds his natural aura more compelling. "It's the whole tone of his voice, his delivery; the way it sounds is like a time capsule," James says. "His voice is so sweet, but horrifically depressing at the same time." While many critics believe "Cowboy" Jack Clement too ornately produced early Van Zandt albums (such as 1968's *For the Sake of the Song* and 1969's *Our Mother the Mountain*), James believes the pairing timeless.[1] (Notably, Clement himself has admitted that his heavy-handed use of flutes, strings, and other accompanying instruments on those albums was "over-production, but I liked *For the Sake of the Song*.")[2]

My Morning Jacket's lush albums *The Tennessee Fire* (1999) and *At Dawn* (2001) carved a unique niche by employing ethereal production and reverb-heavy guitars, at core owing to influences such as the Rolling Stones, Big Star, and The Band. My Morning Jacket's major label debut *It Still Moves* (2003) extended its scope with Memphis horns ("Easy Morning Rebel"), arena rock ("One Big Holiday"), and introspective ballads ("One in the Same"). The album earned widespread critical acclaim, and one music critic called the collection "by turns beautiful and possessed, by others raucous and fiery."[3]

It Still Moves did not break through commercially, despite heightened praise. However, My Morning Jacket grew its fringe following with the albums *Z* (2005) and *Evil Urges* (2008). Its energetic performances at such festivals as Bonnaroo, Lollapalooza, and the Austin City Limits Music Festival increased the band's popularity among the jam-band circles.[4] In fact, My Morning Jacket's interpretations of Sly and the Family Stone's "Hot Fun in the Summertime," James Brown's "Cold Sweat," and Erykah Badu's "Tyrone" during a more than three-hour set at 2008's Bonnaroo, exhibited the group's diversity. Metallica guitarist Kirk Hammett joined the band onstage to perform "One Big Holiday."

At the same time, Jim James began diversifying his own interests. "I don't want to do the same old shit over and over again," he said that year, "but there are people who would be most happy with us if we kept remaking *The Tennessee Fire*."[5] James's aim eventually took shape as the Monsters of Folk, a side project loosely formed four years earlier with fellow songwriters M. Ward and Conor Oberst and Mike Mogis of the Omaha, Nebraska, band Bright Eyes.

The Monsters of Folk's debut album *Monsters of Folk* (2009), which James recorded under the stage name Yim Yames, proved at heart a more direct link to Townes Van Zandt. Although the quartet employs modern devices, such as electronic drums, the band's "sun-dappled, well-worn folk tunes" frequently exhibit such traditional themes as coming-of-age weariness ("Say Please") and searching ("Dear God (Sincerely M.O.F)") backed by lilting harmonies ("Slow Down Jo").[6] In concert, the band members, who frequently swap instruments and takes turns on lead vocals, have been compared to Portishead and The Traveling Wilburys. "It was and still is a fresh and new feeling, like starting your first band in high school," James says. "Lots of adventure, fun, and laughs."[7]

■ ■ ■

JIM JAMES

We played Austin a lot, and some of my buddies there were always trying to get me into Townes. They kept saying, "You gotta hear this guy. You'll love him." I remember hearing about Townes and seeing articles, but back then I didn't really know anything about him. A friend of mine gave me a twenty-song mix in 1999 with a bunch of Townes songs. The first time I listened to it, I didn't like it at all. A few months after that I found the CD again and said, "I'm gonna try this once more," and I've never stopped listening to it since.

I don't know exactly why it took me so long to get deep into his music, but I find that most of my favorite artists or albums are like that. I'll listen to something and think, "Well, that's okay," and put it back for a few weeks. Then I'll find it again, and it'll hit me when the universe somehow knows I'm ready. Lots of times, I think you have to mature somehow before you're ready for something like that, sort of how kids don't like brussels sprouts until they are much older. It's deep in the melody, the production of his songs—I'm big on soundscape—where the magic comes alive for me. Like the flute on "Come Tomorrow."

I grew up on everything from the Muppets to Janet Jackson to The

Beatles, but in high school, like many other souls out there, I gravitated to heavier, sadder sounding music and bands like The Red House Painters and the slower side of REM, who could sometimes sound influenced by traditional country music in very subtle ways. There was a song called "Country Feedback" in particular by REM, as well as seeing Johnny Cash on *Austin City Limits* by chance on TV one night that got me curious about the dark gateway of real country music: Hank Williams Sr., Johnny Cash, John Prine, Waylon and Willie and the boys. After loving those guys so much it was a real gift, the cherry on my country sundae, to find someone like Townes. I thought I had heard all I needed to hear as far as country music went, but the spirits proved to me that that is never true. There is always something new waiting to surprise you. You get a funny Townes song like "No Deal," or you get a really dark song like "Kathleen." There are so many variables, and that's what I like the most. I think that he is great at conveying sadness, but then he'll have something goofy like "Turnstyled, Junkpiled" that's fun and frolicking.

Most of the time when I first hear new music my brain doesn't really pick up on the lyrics. I just get sucked into a song because of the way it feels, the dance that a particular song does and what it does with you, the way Townes's sad music uplifts. You feel it even if you can't quite pick up on literal aspects of what he is saying, or perhaps if what he is saying specifically doesn't even relate to your life situation. There's a comfort in being there and staying in that place. You're there with him, and you get through it. I strive to do that in our recordings, too, to keep it sounding Technicolor but still futuristic. I hope there is some thread within where a person feels it even if the specific song might not be addressing an actual issue in their life. The feeling is there, and we are connected.

I've covered "Be Here to Love Me" sometimes, and I like that one a lot. I've really been into "Come Tomorrow" lately just because it's such a sweet song. We tried to cover "No Deal" on our first Monsters of Folk tour, and we sat around in the basement drinking beers working on it, trying to get to that place, but we couldn't master the delivery. That song is hilarious.

I think the thing that strikes me so much about Townes is that out of all the legends that we all hold up so dear, to me he's one of the most human [and] ordinary people. I think that makes it more special. I just feel like he's touchable somehow. He's such a giant, but he's also a normal guy. Being a musician, you're always living in the shadows of "the greats." Maybe because Townes is a little more current and died so recently, he's more tangible and still feels like "one of us." His voice, his delivery is so real. He doesn't sugarcoat it at all.

You hear about Townes from people you love and trust, [which is] the best way to be turned on to new music and the best way to start a lasting relationship with any artist. Sometimes the world has a way of bastardizing a person's legend, focusing on their social standing or the circumstances around their death or the fact that they're an alcoholic or a drug addict more than the music they made. It's so sad to see someone's legacy get lost in all that. Hopefully by having remained so down to earth, future generations will just focus on Townes's music, which he knew was the most important part.[8]

Adam Duritz, Wilmont Theatre, Montclair, NJ, August 17, 2010. Courtesy Michael J. Trojan.

ADAM DURITZ

But maybe she just has to sing for the sake of the song
    And who do I think that I am to decide that she's wrong?
    —TVZ, "For the Sake of the Song," from *For the Sake of the Song*

Adam Duritz, born August 1, 1964, in Baltimore, Maryland, and Counting Crows earn day wages as a popular modern rock band deeply influenced by folk and country songwriters. In concert, Counting Crows has performed songs written by such Americana artists as Steve Earle ("Fearless Heart," "CCKMP"), John Hiatt ("Crossing Muddy Waters"), and Townes Van Zandt ("Pancho and Lefty"). Lead singer Duritz, who lived an itinerant youth traveling between Boston, Los Angeles, and Houston, before settling in Northern California in the early 1980s, most appreciates Van Zandt's craftsmanship. "Townes is a perfect songwriter," Duritz says. "There's a craft there and perfection that he instills in writing songs. It's like a graduate class in songwriting."[1]

Counting Crows earned immediate recognition with the debut album *August and Everything After* (1993), a lyrically downbeat collection produced by Fort Worth, Texas, native T-Bone Burnett. (Burnett himself became particularly influential for his work on film soundtracks during the following decade, including *O Brother, Where Art Thou?* and *Crazy Heart*, among others.) *August and Everything After* infuses Duritz's somber storytelling into neighboring musical styles, including folk ("Omaha," "Anna Begins") and rock ("Rain King," "A Murder of One"). The album's idealistic and upbeat hit single "Mr. Jones," which outlines Duritz's desire to be a famous musician, turned a dream into reality and single-handedly launched the Berkeley, California, band to stardom.

Counting Crows went on to become one of the most commercially successful groups of the past two decades. *August and Everything After* has sold more than seven million copies, and the band has nearly tripled that number in total with albums such as *Recovering the Satellites* (1996), *This Desert Life* (1999), and the greatest hits collection *Films about Ghosts* (2003), which includes radio staples such as "A Long December," "Hanginaround," and "American Girls."[2] Counting Crows won a Grammy Award for the song "Accidentally in Love," from the soundtrack to the movie *Shrek* (2004).

Adam Duritz claims to struggle from a mental illness that influences his songwriting and impacts his personal life, which has included romances with actresses Jennifer Aniston, Courtney Cox, and Emmy Rossum. "I have a mental illness, and I am writing honest songs about it. They're just honest songs about my life," says the singer, who wears dreadlocked hair extensions and dresses flamboyantly onstage. "A dissociative disorder makes it impossible to attach to the world and relate to people."[3] Duritz says that coping with the illness might have been responsible for the six-year gap between Counting Crows albums *Hard Candy* (2002), which includes a popular rendition of Joni Mitchell's song "Big Yellow Taxi," and *Saturday Nights & Sunday Mornings* (2008).

Counting Crows split with Geffen Records in 2009 after eighteen years. Duritz suggests that the band might release future albums on its own record label and rely on online promotion.[4] "The Internet is the best thing that has ever happened to music in the history of music," he says. "It's just not necessarily the best thing that's happened to record companies."[5] The same year, Counting Crows began its ongoing Traveling Circus and Medicine Show tour with Michael Franti and Spearhead and Augustana. Similar to Joe Cocker's Mad Dogs and Englishmen tour in 1970, the Traveling Circus rotates its cast of performers throughout each concert. "We can do massive amounts of harmony," Duritz says. "To the fullest extent of the law, we prosecute the harmony."[6]

■ ■ ■

ADAM DURITZ

Counting Crows recorded Townes Van Zandt's "For the Sake of the Song" on the *Under the Covers* album. We did fourteen songs one weekend, and that was the album with the remixed acoustic hip-hop version of "Big Yellow Taxi." I love Townes, but there's something so special and unique about him. I don't know how to say it, really. Not that Willie Nelson and Merle Haggard didn't kill "Pancho and Lefty," because they did. It's a great version of that song. I like covering songs, but somehow I can't quite step in Townes's shoes—or it feels like I shouldn't. It's like there's only one guy who should step in those shoes, and maybe you make an exception for Willie and Merle.

I get "For the Sake of the Song," and I can feel what he's talking about. But me singing it isn't the same thing somehow. I'm good at putting myself in other people's shoes, and I think I'm good at making songs my own more than most people. There's something about Townes that's one

*Townes Van Zandt
on bed with guitar,
courtesy Harold F.
Eggers Jr.*

of a kind, which maybe is why life was so hard on him. Other than when we recorded "For the Sake of the Song" and have performed "Pancho and Lefty," I've hesitated to play more Townes. I'm not sure I could do justice to the songs, and I say that being a pretty egotistical person. We did those songs just because we wanted to do them so badly. I don't think that they're our best covers because I just can't inhabit them.

You hear "Flyin' Shoes" and listen to the arrangement—not just the song, the goddamn arrangement. I'll tell you, Nanci Griffith doing "Tecumseh Valley," that's a good cover. She does justice to it on the first *Other Rooms, Other Voices* CD. She nailed it. That's my favorite Townes Van Zandt song. I've heard Steve Earle sing Townes songs, and he's one of my two or three favorite songwriters. Steve really gets it, and I guess I can understand why. He took a life class in how to be Townes.[7]

KASEY CHAMBERS

Loop and Lil agree she's a sight to see
And a treasure for the poor to find
—TVZ, "If I Needed You," from *The Late, Great Townes Van Zandt*

Kasey Chambers's confessional lyrics typically favor dark recesses rather than rustic idylls. Chambers, born June 4, 1976, in Mount Gambier, South Australia, learned early lessons from kindred spirits under the freedom of an open sky. "Our family sang Hank Williams and Gram Parsons songs to each other," says the songwriter, who was raised on mobile campsites for her first nine years while her musician father earned a living as a foxhunter on Australia's desolate Nullarbor Plain.[1] Chambers later discovered Townes Van Zandt. "'Tecumseh Valley' is such a great song," she says, "and I knew 'Pancho and Lefty' from Emmylou [Harris] playing it."[2]

The Chambers family—parents Bill and Diane with Kasey and older brother Nash—formed The Dead Ringer Band in the early 1990s, and albums such as *Red Desert Sky* (1993), *Home Fires* (1995), and *Living in the Circle* (1997) closely reflected those early country influences. Moreover, Bill and Kasey's duet on Van Zandt's signature tune "If I Needed You" (from *Living in the Circle*) helped catch an influential ear. "It was like the first night I heard Townes in 1966," says Van Zandt's former manager John Lomax III, grandson of legendary folklorist John Lomax. "The Dead Ringers had . . . all the things Nashville has forgotten: honesty, purity, simplicity, and lovely harmonies."[3] Kasey's inspired delivery and engaging "ability to convey to contradictory emotions at once" proved the key.[4]

Kasey Chambers's solo debut *The Captain* (1999) launched her own highly successful career in Australia, and word swiftly spread throughout Americana circles and beyond. "Kasey Chambers is probably the best female hillbilly singer I've heard in a long, long time," Steve Earle said after listening to the album.[5] *The Captain* stuck relatively closely to The Dead Ringer Band's format, but Chambers became one of Australia's most popular radio stars of the new millennium with the increasingly pop- and rock-oriented albums *Barricades and Brickwalls* (2002), *Wayward Angel* (2004), and *Carnival* (2006).

Nevertheless, Americans continue to identify Chambers with her earlier alternative country sound. "My career in Australia is so different than it is in America," she says. "A lot of my success [in Australia] has come from outside of country music. I've had Number One pop singles, and it's a different audience. Here they want to hear me play what's on the radio, whereas I don't have that problem in America."[6]

Kasey Chambers and singer-songwriter husband Shane Nicholson's largely acoustic folk-based collaboration *Rattlin' Bones* (2008) earned two nominations at the Americana Music Association awards in 2009.[7] "We wanted to make a record that was like the music we listen to at home— Patty Griffin, Buddy and Julie [Miller] and Bob Dylan and Jimmy LaFave," Chambers says.[8] Songs such as "Sweetest Waste of Time," "Wildflower," and "One More Year," particularly channel their shared influences. In concert, Chambers occasionally indulges a request for "If I Needed You," which she recorded for the album *Storybook* (2011). "In Australia, it's not very often that you get asked to play Townes Van Zandt songs," she says. "So, when someone says, 'Can you play a Townes song?' you're like, 'Oh, cool, I'd much rather play that.'"[9]

■ ■ ■

KASEY CHAMBERS

I was actually a bit late with the whole Townes thing. I think just by being in Australia, we just didn't really hear that stuff very much. It was probably about ten years ago now that we first sort of started hearing his stuff. It was through my manager at the time, John Lomax, who lives in Nashville. He sent us some CDs, and we started listening to him just after the last time he toured to Australia.

The first time I'd ever heard Townes sing, or the first time I knew of Townes's writing, was "Pancho and Lefty." Lyrically, that song is amazing. My dad had a little 45 of him doing that song. It was just him and an acoustic guitar, and there wasn't a band or anything. He played that song, and I just fell in love with it. I listened to his version so much more than I listened to Emmylou's. Not to take anything away from her version—it's beautiful—but there was just something about this amazing voice that sounded so raw. There are some off notes on there, but it just sounded so cool. That's what I put on over and over and over again and cried and cried every time I heard it when I found out that Townes died.

As a songwriter, Townes had a way of putting words together that didn't always make sense. I'm sure it did to him when he was writing it, and it still rips out my heart and soul for some reason. I think just sitting down listening to a lot of Townes made me realize as a songwriter that sometimes it's okay that a line just sounds right and feels right, and it doesn't always have to make sense. John Prine is another songwriter who's one of my absolute heroes, and I just love him so much. I've read something about him where he says, "Some of my lines don't even make sense, but it rhymed so I put the line in." Sometimes you have to realize that being a songwriter isn't the most serious job in the whole world. You're not saving the world, you're just writing songs and expressing yourself, and it doesn't have to always be about something all the time. Some of it can just sound good.

The first time I ever came to Nashville, we went straight to Nashville to visit with John Lomax. We went to his house and had a little jam with Guy Clark and Susanna Clark, and Townes's wife [Jeanene] and their little son were there. Townes was alive, but he was in England at the time. We sat around and just had a jam with Guy and Susanna, and it was just amazing. This was maybe around 1993.

It was kind of overwhelming. Townes's wife—[she] was his ex-wife, but they were obviously still very good friends at the time—she knew we were big Townes fans. She said, "Do you know any Townes songs?" So, we sat there and played "Tecumseh Valley" to her and to Guy Clark, and that was a real buzz. We'd actually planned that the next time we'd come back to America that John was going to get us all together to jam with Townes, and then he died just after that. I actually haven't seen Guy or Susanna since, or anything like that, either.

We recorded "If I Needed You" a long time ago, and that's another song we knew before we knew of Townes because of Emmylou doing it with Don Williams. We used to sing that song years and years ago on the Nullarbor. I reckon we'd sit around and sing that song, and then we recorded it a little while later. We still do that song at every gig if all four of us are there. Every time we do it here in America, I never introduce it or anything and never say anything about it. But when we start, the whole crowd starts clapping every time. Everyone just loves it. It's just incredible.

That's one of those songs I reckon is a classic country song. That's what country music is—or was—all about. It's about just saying what you feel. That's a perfect example of how Townes can write such a simple song as well as writing something cryptic that I don't have a clue what he's talking about. The chorus of that song is just what you want to say to someone. He just says it, and he makes it sound like the most poetic thing you've ever heard. It'll go down as one of the most amazing songs ever written. You can tell he's just the kind of songwriter that just lets the songs come out. There's nothing forced about that song at all. It was supposed to be written like that.[10]

Kasey Chambers, Waterloo Records, Austin, TX, July 15, 2011

CHORUS
DARDEN SMITH

Be there tomorrow, now mama don't you cry
  I've got to kiss these lonesome Texas blues goodbye
  —TVZ, "Colorado Girl," from *Townes Van Zandt*

Darden Smith, born March 11, 1962, in Brenham, Texas, immediately divided his musical tastes when he first discovered Townes Van Zandt. "Everything else up to that time was put in one box," Smith says. "Townes was in another."[1] Albums such as *Trouble No More* (1990), *Circo* (2004), and *Field of Crows* (2006) have helped

Smith earn a reputation as an erudite easy-listening troubadour, and the current Austin resident earned brief mainstream recognition with the video for his single "Loving Arms," from the album *Little Victories* (1993). In 2003, Smith launched the Be an Artist program to encourage children in the creative arts.

"The first real awareness I had of Townes was in 1979," Smith says. "It was the old story of the kid lying in bed listening to the radio late at night when he was supposed to be sleeping. In Houston at that time, KLOL was a very cool radio station. On Sundays, there was a show called *Country Sundays*, of which I was an avid fan. Along with the usual radio stuff, they would also play songwriters, the kind of thing that was going on in Texas at that time—Guy Clark, B. W. Stevenson, Shake Russell, John Prine. This was my education. One night, very late, I woke up to this voice and guitar. It was 'Mr. Mudd and Mr. Gold,' then 'Loretta.' I remember thinking, 'Who the hell is that?'

"I devoured *Live at the Old Quarter*. Drove all my friends nuts, but couldn't take it off the turntable. As a writer, I learned by copying my heroes, and sadly, I wrote some very poor Townes songs. Eventually it got down to not writing like Townes. Once I started to do shows of my own, I did a few opening acts for Townes, both in Austin and Houston. I tried to hang around him a bit, but I always felt like the dumb kid in the room.

"The most memorable show I did with him was at Anderson Fair in Houston. My mother was there to see her son take over the world, and then out comes this guy that I had been raving about, this king of all songwriters, who was smashed out of his mind. He sang two songs, almost fell off his chair, and proceeded to tell bad jokes for the next ten minutes. I thought it was hilarious for many reasons, but my poor mother came up to me as they were leaving, shortly after Townes's third song, and said, 'Son, if that's who you're looking up to, I've made some terrible mistakes.'"[2]

KEVIN RUSSELL

It's cold down on the bayou, they say it's in your mind
  But the moccasins are treading ice and leaving strange designs
  —TVZ, "Two Girls," from *The Nashville Sessions*

Kevin Russell's colorful narratives (such as "El Paso" and "Lower 48") and nonlinear country blues ("Hooky Junk" and "Cranky Mulatto") accurately represent the mystique of Austin, Texas. After all, the capital city's unofficial motto is "Keep Austin Weird." While living in the heart of South Austin, one of the city's primary gathering points for bohemian craft and creativity, Russell and fellow songwriter Jimmy Smith formed The Gourds during the early 1990s. Neighborhood anchor Jovita's Mexican restaurant hosted several of the band's early concerts. "There was a lot of communal freedom there," says Russell, born May 21, 1967, in Beaumont, Texas. "People were always on their front porches, walking around and talking to each other."[1]

Album such as *Dem's Good Beeble* (1996), *Stadium Blitzer* (1998), *Gogitchyershinebox* (1998), and *Ghosts of Hallelujah* (1999) immediately displayed the band's knack for animated and surrealistic wordplay. Each pushes boundaries with adventurous instrumentation made even more diverse by multi-instrumentalist Max Johnston (formerly of Uncle Tupelo), who has aligned The Gourds since joining to record *Gogitchyershinebox*. By millennium's turn, The Gourds' "winning combination of fine musicianship, top-notch songwriting (by Russell and Smith) and glowing harmonies" earned the band a growing national following.[2]

Raucous live shows quickly became a trademark, with Gourds members swapping instruments in concert as frequently as Steve Earle digresses into politics. Russell, a flamboyant showman who often incorporates techniques such as Chuck Berry's signature "duck walk," remains the focal point throughout.[3] "When we moved to Austin in 1996, the first show we attended was a Gourds show with Kelly Willis and Toni Price at the old Waterloo Brewing Company," says Reckless Kelly's Cody Braun. "We were all blown away by the high energy. They are what Austin music is supposed to sound like—well-played original music that makes you want to drink and dance till the lights go out."[4]

Innovative interpretations both likely (including the Rolling Stones' "Miss You" and Doug Sahm's "Crossroads") and unforeseen (R. Kelly's "Feelin' on Yo Booty") typically prove high points. In fact, the band has made its most widespread impression with an acoustic bluegrass version of rapper Snoop Doggy Dogg's "Gin and Juice" from *Gogetchyershinebox*. Several online sources mistakenly attribute the song to Blues Traveler, Phish, and the Dave Matthews Band, unwittingly spreading Gourds music through the international jam-band community.

Especially when touring outside Texas, the song remains among the band's most requested in concert. "If you're in the mood for it and we're in the mood for it, it can be great," Russell says. "Sometimes we're not in the mood, and it's the wrong thing to do." Gourds keyboardist Claude Bernard acknowledges the band at times believes it to be an albatross: "We tried to drop ['Gin and Juice'] from our shows, but you really can't."[5]

Russell's songs on recent Gourds albums such as *Heavy Ornamentals* (2006), *Noble Creatures* (2007), and *Haymaker!* (2009) retain expected eccentricity (for instance, "How Will You Shine" and "Shreveport"), but lyrics are perhaps more aged with wisdom ("Our Patriarch" and "Steeple Full of Swallows").[6] Accordingly, his appreciation for Townes Van Zandt developed over time. "I first heard Townes in Jacksonville, Florida," Russell says, "but the only Van Zandt I was interested in those days was Ronnie Van Zandt."[7] Russell's side project Shinyribs recorded a ramshackle version of Townes Van Zandt's "Dollar Bill Blues" for the tribute album *More Townes Van Zandt by the Great Unknown* (For the Sake of the Song Records, 2010), a follow-up collection to *Introducing Townes Van Zandt Via the Great Unknown* (2009).

■ ■ ■

KEVIN RUSSELL

I didn't know nothin' about no Townes Van Zandt until after he was dead. My connection with Townes is purely as a fan. The Gourds have done some of his songs in the past; several we've done for weddings in Texas. We've played "Two Girls," "Pancho and Lefty," "If I Needed You." I was going to play one in Durango, Colorado, the other night, but I forgot. I was going to play "Two Girls," because this friend of ours just had twins. I was just out of it and didn't remember to do it. It's been a while since we've done any of those songs anyway. We'd have to go over them.

I never went to see Townes play, but I've heard some recordings of when he was older, and I was not impressed with his voice or his playing style. Everybody loved him, though, and said he was a great guy. I always thought he was just one of those hack Texas guys before that. I respect what they do, and I suppose in some respects I'm a hack as well, but when I heard *Live at the Old Quarter* that night in Jacksonville, I was like, "What the fuck is this?" My friend who played it for me was like, "This guy's from your state, don't you know him?" I said, "Well, yeah, I've heard of him, but I never heard this record." *Live at the Old Quarter* blew my mind, and I immediately went to get a copy of that. It's great, and I think it's all the Townes you really need. I haven't heard his whole catalogue, but I've heard some of the old records, and they're just produced really badly.

They just didn't know what to do with him. It's not Townes's fault; he was just writing songs and doing his thing.

I lived with *Live at the Old Quarter* for a long time. We all loved it. Everybody in the band loves that record. I remember we were on our way out to Amarillo, Texas, when we heard he died. It was the turn of the year, I guess, New Year's Day. And a couple days later I heard he died, but at the time I didn't really know who he was.

I think *Live at the Old Quarter* was his moment. He wrote these great songs, and that was it. I think that if he'd died after that, he would be Hank Williams redux. But he didn't. And if Hank Williams had lived, I think we would think the same about him—just focusing on that period of time when he wrote the great songs. You stick around long enough, and you're going to get really bad.

Townes wrote some incredible songs in the early '70s, and that's what I judge him on. I don't really judge him on anything he did with the Cowboy Junkies or anything like that. That's not interesting to me. I know a lot of people in Austin who put Townes in a god-like status, and think he's one of the greats of all time. I can't go there with that, but I'm not going to argue with anybody if they think that. As a songwriter, and that's the way you have to look at him because he wasn't much of a performer, I'd put Townes in the Top Twenty of all-time. He's maybe around Number Fifteen or Sixteen.

I don't think he's a better songwriter than Bob Dylan. I'd have to take issue with Mr. Earle on that one. He's not better than Bob Dylan, no way. He's not better than Ted Hawkins. I think Ted Hawkins is great. But Townes is up there; he's one of the greats, too. It's all from that one five-year period he had, and *Live at the Old Quarter* captures it all. If anybody ever asks me about Townes, I just say, "Go get *Live at the Old Quarter.*" Then forget about it. It's all there; it's brilliant. I wish I'd have been at that performance. Of course, if I was at that, I probably would have been crying and complaining to my parents that I wanted to leave because I was ten years old. But it was seven days of recording, and it produced a great piece of work.

I don't hear too many stories about Townes. It's just sort of people who worship him, who worship those songs. I'm sure he was hard to manage. I heard about this European tour where he was missing his girlfriend or something and not showing up for shows because he was on the phone with his girlfriend, crying and freaked out and unhappy. But, yeah, I've been in Europe and been like that, too. That's a human thing for someone like an American to feel.[8]

Terri Hendrix, Cactus Café, Austin, TX, July 31, 2010

TERRI HENDRIX

He got a green bottle from the freezing vaults
  My friend started doing backward somersaults
  Through the cottage cheese
  —TVZ, "Talking Thunderbird Blues," from *Live at the Old Quarter*

Terri Hendrix's album *Cry Till You Laugh* (2010) showcases the singer-songwriter's vast musical diversity. Bluesman Sonny Terry (on the song "Hula Mary"), country troubadour Rodney Crowell ("Slow Down"), and jazz icon Ella Fitzgerald ("Take Me Places") all haunt the collection Hendrix fashions as the "yin and yang of life."[1]

The broad scope keeps fresh her longtime musical partnership with Lloyd Maines, the legendary Grammy-winning instrumentalist and producer for Guy Clark, Ray Wylie Hubbard, Jerry Jeff Walker, the Dixie Chicks, and others.[2] "We're hungry for music," Hendrix says. "We're ruthless about digging for music. I'm into techno, drum loops, far out, weird, ethereal music. Lloyd isn't scared of that. He keeps me reaching artistically."[3]

Terri Hendrix, born February 13, 1968, in San Antonio, Texas, began performing at open mic nights at Cheatham Street Warehouse in San Marcos, Texas, in 1991. Today she regularly traces Townes Van Zandt's footsteps onstage at such Lone Star venues as Sons of Herman Hall in Dallas, the Mucky Duck in Houston, and Austin's Cactus Café. Many along the way share stories about a Van Zandt concert that was heartbreaking, hilarious, and sometimes both. "I once observed an entire club achieve a meltdown in his presence, people crying into their hands, a shared emotional participation I've never seen the likes of since," journalist Chris Dickinson recalls.[4] One of Van Zandt's several corny jokes to lighten such dark moments was, "What's white and runs up your leg? Uncle Ben's Perverted Rice."

"I think that it's wonderful that Townes could be funny and he could be serious, and you'd take him seriously," Hendrix says. "He'd have a ridiculously funny song, like this one on a Cactus Café recording that might be called 'Noah's Ark.' It was just silly, but yet he was taken seriously as a songwriter. That's had a really big impact on me."[5]

In her own way, Terri Hendrix's singularity shines as brightly as Townes Van Zandt's. Most notably, she designed a business model for other independent artists to follow by founding and managing her own Wilory Records, as well as publicity, publishing, and marketing ventures.[6] Hendrix established Wilory Records after failing to find a record label willing to release her debut album. "I was mad because I got three rejection letters for [1996's] *Two Dollar Shoes*," she says. "One of the rejection letters pretty much said 'No, and get a day job.' I put that record out on my own, and by the end of the summer not only had I paid back the record, I had paid off a student loan. I got satisfaction out of just flat not quitting."[7]

After a dozen albums, including popular collections earthy (2004's *The Art of Removing Wallpaper*) and ethereal (2007's *The Spiritual Kind*), supporters hail Terri Hendrix as one of Texas's premier independent musicians. The foresight helped earn Hendrix, who won a Grammy Award for cowriting the Dixie Chicks' instrumental "Lil' Jack Slade," a star on Corpus Christi's South Texas Walk of Fame in 2010.

Hendrix's participatory live performances have become legendary throughout Texas and folk festival circles nationwide. The songwriter captures the communal vibe she creates onstage on the albums *Live* (1999) and *Live in San Marcos* (2001). Her recent album *Cry Till You Laugh* is also notable for its song "Einstein's Brain," which directly addresses Hendrix's ongoing struggle with epilepsy and its effect on her career. "I've been dealing with epilepsy for twenty years," she says. "I use cheat sheets when I play, and nobody really knew why. But this record is about doing what I love to do—play music."[8]

■ ■ ■

TERRI HENDRIX

I never got the opportunity to meet Townes. At the time of his death, I was unaware of him. I came home from a gig, and my roommate was crying. She was crying because Townes Van Zandt had died. That's how I learned about him. I really started to get involved with trying to find out more about his music after his death. A friend of mine who was a club owner had a book that was full of Townes Van Zandt lyrics and sheet music. It was this old worn out book printed in San Antonio as a limited edition called *For the Sake of the Song*. So, I started to read these lyrics, and they blew me away.

It's his lyrics, but it's also his sense of humor. I thought he had a great, understated sense of humor. There's this light running through his songs, and I like his minimalist approach to writing. There's no fat in it. I love his train of thought, you know, "Ride the blue wind high and free, she'll lead you down through misery" [from "Rex's Blues"]. I love how he's talking about the wind, then "she'll lead you down through misery." I like the way he follows his train of thought, even though it's more abstract than story songs. He could do both. You have "Pancho and Lefty," which is obviously a story song. He was very versatile. I think it's pretty unique from a songwriting perspective. To me, Bob Dylan's more abstract. John Prine is more story song. Paul Simon is a poet, but he still leans more toward story songs. Townes is both a poet and a songwriter. That's what makes him such a giant.

Lloyd Maines has a great story about Townes. Jerry Jeff Walker can be a little, dare I say, cranky. I don't know him personally, but that's what I hear from people talking about him. It was Jerry Jeff's birthday, and Townes was supposed to open the show for Jerry Jeff. This was years and years and years ago. Townes was backstage, and somebody brought in a huge birthday cake for Jerry Jeff. They're struggling with the cake and Jerry Jeff got really grouchy about it, like, "Just put the cake over there," throwing his hands up in the air about the birthday cake. It just went on and on and on like this, moving the cake around, until finally they found a place that wouldn't be in the way for the darn birthday cake. As soon as the dust cleared, Townes goes, "Phew, that was a close one." Like the cake was gonna do something. Townes was watching the situation unfold and wasn't saying a word, then he says that at the end of it all.

Townes's reputation was as a respected songwriter, though he was somewhat reclusive. I know he drank. I hear that he was really admired, an unknown gem, pretty much. There's this famous song that I always think of when someone like Townes passes on, "Give Me My Flowers while I'm Living." It's to pay tribute to a person. Terry Allen recorded it. I think it's a Carter Family song, but I'm not sure who wrote it. I don't think Townes was recognized in his lifetime as such a remarkable songwriter.

Like when Johnny Cash was alive, sure, he was respected, but it took until he passed away that the CMA recognized him, I believe, for being what he was. When Johnny flipped off the people in that photo, wasn't that to the Country Music Association people for not nominating him?

Townes Van Zandt poster, beside stage door to the Cactus Café, Austin, TX, December 21, 2010

Townes falls into that same category. Why does it take until he dies for him to be somewhat revered? Why can't he have some of that respect while he's living? What kept it from being a reality? Why did I not, as an aspiring songwriter, know about Townes until he died? Maybe it was fear. Because the more successful you get, the more eyes are on what you do. Maybe he prevented himself and stood in the way of his own success. I got that *For the Sake of the Song* book down again recently, and my hope is to strive to have more of the yin and the yang of songwriting that Townes had—to be abstract, but also to be more realistic.

When you consider a list of the "best" songwriters of all time, I've never known what to think of that, because it's so subject to personal opinion. But if there is one, I would hope it's an alphabetical list, and that it's stated as such. I think Townes was one of the finest songwriters, even surpassing some of the people that we deem as being so great. I would say absolutely yes. Maybe he wasn't so prolific, but if you look at the quality as opposed to the quantity, I think it's pretty mind-boggling.

I would have loved to have the opportunity to have met him. I wish I had discovered him before his passing, because I think it could have had an earlier influence on me, but I'm just thankful that I did find out about his music. I'm thankful that I know it. I think that when they're teaching Walt Whitman in English classes, that they should teach Townes Van Zandt. I think he should have a place in our literacy courses. Songs are exactly what they teach us in school. Some of them are poetry, and I think that they should be included in our history. Think of all the aspiring writers that there are that should know about Townes Van Zandt, and that's it for me. I would have loved to have learned about him in high school. It would have had an impact on my life.[9]

BUTCH HANCOCK

Pour the sun upon the ground, stand to throw a shadow
  Watch it grow into a night, and fill the spinning sky
    —TVZ, "Highway Kind," from *High, Low and In Between*

Townes Van Zandt's poetry illuminates the Cactus Café at least once a year, thanks to Butch Hancock. "Townes's songs have a magic to them," says Hancock, who has hosted Van Zandt's birthday celebration at the venerable listening room every spring since the songwriter's death in 1997. "Sometimes a song or two gets repeated once or twice during the night. We talked about ending this show one time with the 'Snowin' on Raton' contest." When asked how Townes Van

Zandt might have celebrated his sixty-fifth birthday in 2009, Hancock replied, "I have no clue what he'd be doing. I couldn't figure out what he was doing in the first place."[1]

Hancock, born July 12, 1945, in Lubbock, Texas, long has served as a grassroots bullhorn for Van Zandt. Early on, The Flatlanders, Hancock's band with fellow Lone Star singer-songwriters Joe Ely and Jimmie Dale Gilmore, performed Van Zandt's "Waitin' Around to Die" and "Tecumseh Valley" on their album *Live at the One Knite, June 8th, 1972.* Today all three singers—together as The Flatlanders and separately as solo artists—often perform his popular "White Freightliner Blues" and others in concert.

The Flatlanders' introduction to Van Zandt and his immediate impact on the band has become part of Texas music folklore.[2] "I was living up in Lubbock then, just out driving around, and I see this long, tall, scarecrow-looking guy carrying a guitar, way out on the edge of town," Ely says. "He said he'd just come back from San Francisco, recording a record, and he was heading to Houston. I took him on the other side of Lubbock, out where I used to catch rides, by Pinky's liquor store. He said, 'Thanks a lot,' and reaches in his backpack.

"I kind of looked in the backpack, and there's not any clothes in there. It's nothing but albums. He reaches in and gives me one. He'd carried these all the way across the desert back to Houston. I was a little surprised. I'd never met anyone who'd actually recorded an album. I take the record back to Jimmie Gilmore, and we put the record on and we were just mesmerized by it. Ends up, we played that album over and over for weeks just rethinking what we're doing and what a song was all about."[3] "It was totally astounding," Hancock says. "Townes found a channel to float through."[4]

While Joe Ely and Jimmie Dale Gilmore followed The Flatlanders' *One More Road* (1980) with more prominent solo careers, Hancock arguably proved himself the more accomplished and prolific songwriter. In fact, Hancock composed many of the songs that made Ely and Gilmore more widely known. Ely included versions of Hancock's "She Never Spoke

Spanish to Me," "If You Were a Bluebird," "Boxcars," and "West Texas Waltz" on *The Best of Joe Ely* (2000), and Gilmore has recorded "Nothing of the Kind," "Just the Wave, Not the Water," "My Mind's Got a Mind of Its Own," and others. Notably, the popular jam-band Phish frequently has performed Hancock's "My Mind's Got a Mind of Its Own."

The Flatlanders, who took a quarter-century hiatus before recording the song "South Wind of Summer" for *The Horse Whisperer* soundtrack (1998), earned the moniker "more a legend than a band." By the time they regrouped in earnest with the albums *Now Again* (2002), *Wheels of Fortune* (2004), and *Hills and Valleys* (2009), Hancock had boosted his reputation as a songwriter with such albums as *Own & Own* (1989), *Own the Way Over Here* (1993), and *Eats Away the Night* (1994) for Sugar Hill Records. He is also an accomplished photographer, river rafting guide, and painter.[5]

Hancock's "epic" concerts at the Cactus Café in 1990, billed as "No Two Alike," in which Hancock and twenty-seven guests (including Ely and Gilmore) sang 140 of his songs over five nights without repeat, featured a legendary Townes Van Zandt appearance. As Hancock approached the "Pancho and Lefty" reference in his song "Split & Slide II," Van Zandt "almost magically appeared onstage, sang 'And all the *federales* said / We don't want them alive or dead,'" then slipped out the back door. "Nobody saw him for months after that," former Cactus Café manager Griff Luneburg says.[6]

In August 2010, "Hancock's Last Stand: The 20th Anniversary of No Two Alike" closed the original Cactus Café's "iconic years." Hancock and guests (again including Jimmie Dale Gilmore) performed several Townes Van Zandt tunes during the five nights, including "Pancho and Lefty" and the surrealistic "Billy, Boney, and Ma." Hancock ended the final night with a solo rendition of Van Zandt's "To Live's To Fly."[7] "I hate that [Townes] was such a tortured guy," Gilmore says. "He was an unhappy guy, but every now and then this light would come through. You knew that there was a really good, good soul in there."[8]

■ ■ ■

BUTCH HANCOCK

When Townes played the Cactus Café, the room was packed, and it didn't make any difference if he was on or off. He mesmerized everybody. It was sometimes painful, always melancholy, and it'd reach deep into the heart. He played out the drinking thing a little more than it actually was. He was known to act it out. It eventually caught up with him some, but he was a great prankster and a great spirit.

Our annual birthday tribute has remained about the same structurally. Griff keeps asking if I want to do anything differently, and I say, "Nah, let's just see what happens." There's not much real planning involved. Mickey White usually comes in to play, and we'd have a pretty good evening if it was just the two of us, but so many people who loved Townes and his songs come, and that variety makes it so special. I have a list of about twenty songs that I'm always revved up to do. I realize that some of the folks that come in to sing will pick those, but maybe not, too. Sometimes it's a totally obscure one that I don't know.

It'll just blow your mind sometimes when someone you don't expect goes over the top with one of his tunes. The songs are already up there at the top of the bar, but there are some great surprises. There's extra added attention and love because everyone loves the songs. You take the whole chain of songs, and I wish we could do all of them. There are the popular ones like "Pancho and Lefty" and "If I Needed You," of course, but there are so many other treasures that are more obscure. I guess most Townes fans are familiar with just about all of his songs.

If I knew what was most compelling about Townes's songs, I could make $1 million in the music business—if I started out with $2 million. I use the word "melancholy" a lot because his songs are so face-to-face with sorrow, but there's a light that you can see. The songs draw you in and take you beyond. That's a rare mark of any kind of art. It pulls you in and sends you out with more than you came in with—and more than you suspected was in there. They work like gateways to other parts of your psyche.

Townes once told me to worry more about a song's tone than its meaning. That's the nature of poetry and art. A lot of people forget that and get caught up in the subject or the craftsmanship of trying to make the words all just right. If you get the tone of the poetry or piece of art right, that's the inexplicable thing. It's either there or it's not. If it is, everything vibrates to that. You'd be amazed. Lyrics can come from anywhere and everywhere if they're matched up to the tone. That's not necessarily the musical tone; it's the atmosphere that sets the resonance. Everything has to come up to that.

People talk about a spiritual relationship with songwriting, but I think you have to be careful by what you mean by spiritual. I don't think songs come out of the air, but that refers to the nature of our minds. There is a deeper and wider and more all-encompassing part of our mind that sees the whole of existence as one big ball of wax. If a song is put together paying attention to that framework, you're going to have something that resonates. It may not do the same thing for everybody, but it plugs you into the rest of the universe. Townes's songs do that. They sound like a simple little love song at first and then all of a sudden—Zap!—he hits you with a line that makes you look death straight in the face.

Poetry jumps between concepts, one line right up against another. Some things don't seem right, up against each other, but you put them there. If the tone is right, then the jump does extraordinary things for your empathy with the work. Townes's songs have that tone that invites you in, and you get to experience that atmosphere.

I don't equate the drinking and that lifestyle with the songwriting. I won't say that didn't create the songwriting, and I won't say that it contributed to it, either. It's like, Have you got a spare tire or not? Well, yeah, I may or may not, but right now, my four good tires have air in them. I guess the question doesn't compute too much for me.[9]

(L-R) Jen Gunderman, Jack Ingram, Verlon Thompson, Blackbird Studios,
Nashville, TN, January 28, 2010

JACK INGRAM

I'll lie on my pillow and sleep if I must
  Too late to wish I'd been stronger
  —TVZ, "A Song For," from *No Deeper Blue*

As a student at Southern Methodist University, Jack Ingram,
born November 15, 1970, in The Woodlands, Texas, decided
he was "more interested in being Jerry Jeff Walker than Joe
College."[1] Accordingly, Ingram began performing at legendary Lone
Star honky-tonks such as John T. Floore's Country Store in Helotes
and Dallas's Adair's Saloon, where he recorded *Live at Adair's* (1995), a

buoyant blend of western swing and country music. Ingram discovered Townes Van Zandt during these formative years. "I first heard Townes the same way probably everyone else in the world heard his music," he says, "through Willie Nelson and Merle Haggard."[2]

An appearance with Van Zandt disciple and tour partner Robert Earl Keen on the Austin City Limits television series aligned Ingram with predecessors such as Guy Clark, Steve Earle, and Billy Joe Shaver.[3] His regional breakthrough Livin' Or Dyin' (1997), produced by Earle and Twang Trust partner Ray Kennedy, wore influences on its sleeve with covers of Clark's "Rita Ballou" and Jimmie Dale Gilmore's "Dallas," as well as a cowrite with friend and like-minded peer Todd Snider ("Airways Motel").[4]

Ingram's major-label debut Hey You (1999) increased his popularity throughout Texas, but it gained little traction nationally. The album blended sharp narrative storytelling (such as "Biloxi") with the confessional ballads that soon would boost his mainstream career ("Feel Like I'm Falling in Love"). "Jack Ingram packs them in at Billy Bob's [Texas in Fort Worth]," one writer said in 2003. "Ingram's big in Texas, but virtually unknown in the rest of the country."[5] Three years later, the current Austin resident earned commercial success with Billboard's Number One country single "Wherever You Are," from Live—Wherever You Are (2006), an album recorded at Gruene Hall. By This Is It (2007), Ingram suggested his potential worth as a politician: He counted both unrepentant outlaw Earle and mainstream country singer Toby Keith as supporters.[6]

Ingram earned the Academy of Country Music's Best New Male Vocalist award in 2008 after entering his following five singles into Billboard's Top Forty. His most successful hits covered songwriters such as Trent Sumner ("Love You," 2006), Hinder ("Lips of an Angel," 2006), and Rhett Atkins ("Barefoot and Crazy," 2009). Ingram made news headlines when he set a Guinness World Record on August 25, 2009, by participating in 215 radio interviews within a twenty-four-hour span to publicize Big Dreams and High Hopes. After performing the album's Top Ten single "Barefoot and Crazy" the following day on the Fox television network, Ingram claimed, "After the last twenty-four hours, I officially have nothing left to say."[7]

In late January 2010, Ingram returned to his roots with Rodney Crowell, Radney Foster, Kris Kristofferson, and others to record tracks for *This One's for Him: A Tribute to Guy Clark* at Nashville's Blackbird Studios. He cut his keeper version of "Stuff That Works" on the first take.[8]

■ ■ ■

JACK INGRAM

Townes was opening for Guy Clark at Rockefeller's in Houston. By the time Townes's set was over, he was just crying. He wasn't even playing music anymore. Guy had to come out and help him off the stage. It was just really sad.

That's what gets lost in translation in the mythical folklore about Townes, and especially in how much he's grown in mythical stature—the real harsh reality about alcoholism. The idea that someone as big as Townes Van Zandt gets reduced to being helped off the stage by an old friend takes some of the fun out of it. Having seen that, for me it's like the cold, hard light of day. It gets to the heart of the matter that drinking songs are about pain. That night I saw Townes was before I was playing music out, when I was young, like seventeen or nineteen.

Townes is a Christ-like figure in Texas. He's *the one*. I think that guys like Guy and others he ran with have lifted him up to that stature. They're still around to talk about him. For guys like me coming up, Guy Clark was probably better known around the scene. Townes was never a mainstream character in the whole Texas music scene, for my generation anyway. I heard more mainstream guys like Guy Clark and Jerry Jeff Walker and Willie Nelson always talking about Townes Van Zandt in these reverential tones. But, as they say, the music business is kind on the dead, but hard on the living. Couple that with these guys who are still alive and are legends in their own time talking about Townes in such reverential tones after his death. He's become *the* songwriter, the poet from Texas.

For me, Townes was one of those guys I'd always heard about but had never listened to very much. Somewhere along the line I heard Guy Clark or Jerry Jeff Walker mention his name in interviews and liner notes, and at some point I went out and got a record, his greatest hits maybe. I took a night, and put it on the headphones, but I listened to Townes Van Zandt for a long time before I got it, before I understood what everyone was talking about.

It wasn't until I was probably twenty-five years old, driving in a van after playing a gig that I got it. We were playing at the state fair in Oregon, and we had a thirty-three-hour drive to Minneapolis. I had the post-gig driving shift from 3:00 a.m. until daylight, and I put in Townes Van Zandt. It was the same kind of mind-altering moment as when I finally got Bob Dylan's stuff. Everybody's supposed to love Bob Dylan, so you get a Dylan record and you listen to an eight-minute song with all verses and somewhere you get lost. You just kind of pretend to get it, until you have a moment of clarity with that kind of music.

I was driving in Montana and put one of Townes's records in, and the sun was coming up and I was going eighty-five miles an hour, and a light bulb came on. It was like, "Okay, I get it. This is more than music, this is more than words and melody, this is the real stuff. This is as big a message as any writer can have." I don't know what it is. It isn't any single line that gets you. You just know that this guy has a connection with a deeper place. I don't put in Townes to listen to a song; I put it in to listen to him.

Did Townes have an effect on me as a songwriter? Fuck yeah. I don't pretend to understand to know exactly where he's coming from, but I do understand that he opened himself up to writing. He opened himself up to being led by something else to write the music. And that's what I got from him—to open up, and to write. To let things come out and say things in a poetic way. To not be afraid to use the language that I have.

I think a lot of people don't allow themselves to write in the kind of language that Townes allowed himself to write in. He didn't try to dumb down the language that he had the ability to use. That's part of what separates him. You can tell he's a poet. He's writing in this other structure, this other kind of poetry. He's melding poetry and folk music, which creates an interesting mix.

"Pancho and Lefty," that's easy to understand. I'm sure you can look at it and find the true poetry in it, but for me that's the simplest song that he has, language-wise. If the majority of his work was as simple and easy to hum along to and understand on a surface level, I bet Townes would be a lot better known. I'm a huge fan of music and I'm very open to all kinds of it, and it took me seven years of listening to him to finally feel like, at whatever level I can understand music and poetry, I can say, "Oh, my god, okay. I get it." Trying to understand it, trying to be a student of the music, it took me that long to get a grasp of what he was doing. That complexity and drinking all the time is probably what kept him from being better known during his lifetime.

I'm not a spokesperson for the evils of alcohol addiction, but I think people can have fantastic periods of inspiration doing whatever they have to do to get it. You do wonder what would happen with a guy like Townes if you'd get him in the studio with a clear mind to do more recording. What if he took himself more seriously as a recording artist? I'm sure the drinking was part of the creativity on one hand, but I'm also sure that he could have gotten over that. I don't believe for a second that a mind like his, an artist like that, needs anything to get to an artistic level that Townes had. And I think that anyone who would say that is just scared.

It's quite possible Townes was scared of success. There's nothing wrong with that. Looking at it that way, it maybe wasn't the alcohol that stunted his being more famous or well known or prolific; maybe alcohol was just a symptom of what was really behind it—being scared. I haven't had time with him on the couch, so I don't know. You can only speculate.

But guys like Townes influence the great songwriters. A guy like me

Townes Van Zandt (last concert), The Borderline, London, England, December 3, 1996.
Courtesy Harold F. Eggers Jr.

is going to listen to Townes and be influenced by him. A guy like Dylan and like Townes and like Kristofferson—they permeate the fabric of what happens years and years and years from now in the songwriting culture. So, it doesn't matter if his name is remembered and well-known 1,500 years from now. It's the fact that what he did is going to be a part of what happens later on. Townes Van Zandt has had a major influence on every songwriter that has picked up a guitar in Texas or Nashville for the last thirty years.

We all want to be remembered by name, but imagine if you could get past that and be remembered instead by deed. Maybe Townes was selfless about that, and that's why he didn't achieve the kind of success that other people look to as watermarks for that. Maybe he really, truly didn't care about that, and maybe that also goes into why he could write the way he did, why he wrote songs that people had to listen to hard to understand. He was writing on another plane. What if we could get over wanting to write a hit, and songwriters could write a song, as Townes said, for the sake of it, if they didn't give a shit about somebody knowing their name?

I see guys today that are great songwriters, but I don't see anyone else writing like Townes. Hayes Carll comes close, and he will get closer. I do think of Hayes as a guy who understands songwriting, understands where you should try to get to write about real, honest emotions. At least in my head, I didn't feel the kind of emotion Townes and Guy and the real songwriters—Randy Newman, Tom Waits, Kristofferson, Dylan—write about until I was turning thirty.

It's hard for me to say blanket statements about Townes. I have mixed emotions about him, his songwriting and his legacy. I know what his legacy is for me, and I think he's influenced the American culture. Think of bands like Wilco or Son Volt or guys like [Bright Eyes'] Connor Oberst, people who are songwriters' songwriters, they'll never mention Townes's name, but you know they've been influenced by him.

I think his legacy as a songwriter will be much bigger than anything I could ever talk about. On a human approach, I think it's sad that he died at such a young age, and basically by his own doing. I think that's a real tragedy. I don't know how you get his mythical status as a songwriter separated from his mythical status of this bullshit that alcoholism fueled his fire. I don't know how you separate those two with a broad stroke so people remember his legacy as this one thing. It's confusing for me, but he's one of the true ones. He's one that will last.[9]

Grace Potter, Austin City Limits Music Festival, Austin, TX, October 9, 2010

CODA

GRACE POTTER

The sun's upon a gambling day, his queen smiled low and blissfully
  Let's make some wretched fool to pay, plain it was she did agree
—TVZ, "Mr. Mudd and Mr. Gold," from *High, Low and In Between*

Grace Potter laughs righteously. She speaks jovially. Streams thoughts like an overfed water main. The youthful singer-songwriter, born June 20, 1983, in Waitsfield, Vermont, channels her buoyant traits into a modern musical hybrid that blends classic rock swagger and punk rock attitude with soul music's deep passion.[1] Grace Potter and the Nocturnals garnered critical acclaim and a significant jam-band following with early efforts such as *Nothing But the Water* (2005) and *This Is Somewhere* (2007), but did not earn commercial success until their self-titled third album entered into *Billboard*'s Top 20 in June 2010. By that point, Potter and the Nocturnals already had performed and toured with high-profile artists such as the Black Crowes, Dave Matthews Band, Gov't Mule, and My Morning Jacket's Jim James.[2]

Like James, Potter discovered the recently deceased Townes Van Zandt early on. His mournful spirit immediately transcended worldly binds. "I was sixteen years old and my parents were on a road trip," Potter says. "We had this house-sitter guy who was kind of a weirdo from Norway or Romania, and he played all this Townes Van Zandt. All I could think of was, 'This dude is crying with his voice.' Regardless of the lyrics, just the way he sounds in the background in another room sounds like somebody is moaning in a really haunting, beautiful, rich, soulful, completely unstylized way. It was completely his own thing, and I had never heard anything like it before. Townes and the way he played [were] singular.

"'Mr. Mudd and Mr. Gold' is my favorite. The thing that I love so much is that there's this whole double entendre of a card game, but really it's a true-life story. All those parallels he draws and all those things he describes and each card having its own character and its own spirit. Those are real people, and all that probably really happened. He just happened to fit it into a card game and made it into his own magic story. God, it's so good. I love the way he brings that song all the way back around like a fucking Rubik's Cube. He's telling a story, and it just happens to turn back around. It wasn't like he sat there and thought about it and went into his rhyming dictionary and picked over every single word. It really flows like complete stream-of-consciousness. It fell out of him. You're like, 'Holy shit, I just got mind-fucked by Townes Van Zandt.'"[3]

NOTES

The quote in the book epigraph is from Bill Flanagan, "Ragged Company," *Musician*, August 1995.

FOREWORD

1. "Cowboy" Jack Clement, interview with author, January 9, 2011.

PREFACE

1. Brian T. Atkinson, "Townes Van Zandt's Sixth Annual Wake, Old Quarter (Galveston, TX), January 1, 2003," *No Depression*, March-April 2003, 21; for more on Hayes Carll's dexterity as a live performer, see Brian T. Atkinson, "Hayes Carll, The Continental Club, Austin, TX, May 12," *Maverick Country*, August-September 2006, 25–26; and Brian T. Atkinson, "Role Models: Fred Eaglesmith," *American Songwriter*, November–December 2007, 114.

2. Hayes Carll, "I've Got a Gig," *Trouble in Mind*, Lost Highway Records, 2008.

3. Atkinson, "Townes Van Zandt's Sixth Annual Wake," *No Depression.*

4. Hayes Carll, interview with author, October 19, 2010; for more on Hayes Carll's development as a songwriter, see Brian T. Atkinson, "4 To Watch For," *Paste*, December–January 2004, 70; Brian T. Atkinson, "Hayes Carll: 'Everybody's Talkin',' " *No Depression*, March–April 2005, 28; Brian T. Atkinson, "Hayes Carll: *Little Rock,*" *American Songwriter*, March–April 2005, 61; Brian T. Atkinson, "Hayes Carll Q&A," *Texas Music*, Spring 2008, 22, 25–27; Brian T. Atkinson, "CD Review: Hayes Carll, Featured in iTunes This Week," www.austin360.com, March 28, 2008 (accessed February 13, 2011); and Brian T. Atkinson, "Everything Is Relative in Holiday Song," *Austin American-Statesman*, December 27, 2009, G2; Brian T. Atkinson, "Hayes Carll: KMAG YOYO Review," *Lone Star Music*, January–February 2011, 45.

5. Townes Van Zandt, "Tecumseh Valley," *For the Sake of the Song*, Poppy Records, 1968.

INTRODUCTION

1. Brian T. Atkinson, "*Be Here to Love Me* Review," *Relix*, February 2006.

2. Rodney Crowell, interview with author, June 19, 2004. "The last four or five times I saw him, he just wasn't that electric cowboy that he was before," Crowell said. "That always made me really sad"; Townes Van Zandt, "Still Lookin' for You," *At My Window*, Sugar Hill Records, 1987.

3. Brian T. Atkinson, "*To Live's To Fly: The Ballad of the Late, Great Townes Van Zandt* Review," *American Songwriter*, March–April 2007, 100; For a brief overview of Van Zandt's life and career, see John McVey, "John Townes Van Zandt," in Roy Barkley, ed., *The Handbook of Texas Music* (Texas State Historical Association, 2003), 338–40; For more detailed accounts of the singer-songwriter, see John Kruth, *To Live's To Fly: The Ballad of the Late, Great Townes Van Zandt* (New York: Da Capo Press, 2007) and Robert Earl Hardy, *A Deeper Blue: The Life and Music of Townes Van Zandt* (Denton: University of North Texas Press, 2008).

4. Billy Joe Shaver, interview with Richard Skanse, May 2001.

5. Stewart Francke, "Townes Van Zandt Interview," *Contemporary Musician*, December 7, 1992.

6. For critical praise of Townes Van Zandt, see William Hedgepeth, "Messages from the Outside," *Hittin' the Note*, May 1977; Roxy Gordon, "Townes Van Zandt Might Be Arriving," *Omaha Rainbow*, April 1977; Richard Wootton and Scott Giles, "Townes Van Zandt," *Omaha Rainbow*, December 1977; Robert Palmer, "A Hard Road, Seldom Taken," *New York Times*, June 7, 1987; Neil Strauss, "Townes Van Zandt, Singer and Influential Songwriter, 52," *New York Times*, January 3, 1997; Michael Corcoran, "Townes Van Zandt, a Songwriter's Songwriter, Dead at 52," *Austin American-Statesman*, January 4, 1997; Mark Brend, "The Late, Great Townes Van Zandt," *Record Collector*, February 2002, 48–53; Holly Gleason, "Legends: Townes Van Zandt," *American Songwriter*, January–February 2010; for a critical analysis of Townes Van Zandt's entire discography, see Brian T. Atkinson, "Mr. Record Man: Townes Van Zandt," *Lone Star Music*, January–February 2011, 58–60; Brian T. Atkinson, "Hank 3 Talks Towns and the Nashville Songwriters Hall of Fame," www .austin360.com, August 19, 2011 (accessed August 24, 2011).

7. Willie Nelson, interview with Richard Skanse, May 2001.

8. For more on the impact Townes Van Zandt's reclusive behavior had on his career, see Dorothy Palmer, "Recluse Ready to Share His Music with Arkansas," *Arkansas Gazette*, November 11, 1981, 28.

9. David Gritten, "Steve Earle Interview for the Album *Townes*," *Daily Telegraph*, June 2, 2009.

10. Jesse Dayton, interview with author, November 5, 2008.

11. Michelle Shocked, interview with author, October 19, 2009; for more on the Kerrville Folk Festival, see Barkley, *The Handbook of Texas Music*, 174–75; for more on Townes Van Zandt's final days, see Matt Hanks, "A Gentleman and a Shaman: The Last Days and Sad Death of Townes Van Zandt," *No Depression*, January/February 1999.

12. Mickey Newbury, from the packaging to Townes Van Zandt's debut album *For the Sake of the Song*, Poppy Records, 1968.

PRELUDE: VINCE BELL

1. Vince Bell, *One Man's Music: The Life and Times of Texas Songwriter Vince Bell* (Denton: University of North Texas Press, 2009), 66–68; for more on Vince Bell, see *Sixtyeight Twentyeight* (Santa Fe: vincebell.com, 2006).

2. Vince Bell, interview with author, July 2, 2010.

GUY CLARK

1. Brian T. Atkinson, "Songs Keep Finding Craftsman Clark," *Austin American-Statesman*, November 20, 2009, D2.

2. For more on the Houston folk club circuit in the 1960s, see Hobart Taylor III, "Music in Montrose," *Houston Chronicle*, February 5, 1977, Section 2, 1, 4.

3. For more on Guy Clark's early years, see Paul Kingsbury, *The Encyclopedia of Country Music* (New York: Oxford University Press, 1998), 94, and Paul Kingsbury, *Country: The Music and the Musicians*, Second Edition, (New York: Abbeville Press, 1994), 332; for more on Guy Clark and Townes Van Zandt's impact on Texas singer-songwriters, see Gary Hartman, *The History of Texas Music*, (College Station: TX A&M University Press, 2008), 186.

4. Guy Clark, interview with Tamara Saviano, April 1, 2000; Nick Evans and Jeff Horne, *Song Builder: The Life & Music of Guy Clark* (Maidstone: Heartland Publishing Limited, 1998), 82.

5. Evans and Horne, *Song Builder*, 82; Kruth, *To Live's To Fly*, 7.

6. Townes Van Zandt, "Pueblo Waltz," *The Nashville Sessions*, Tomato Records, 1993.

7. For more on the important role Guy Clark played in the progressive country movement, see Barry McCloud, *Definitive Country: The Ultimate Encyclopedia of Country Music and Its Performers* (New York: Berkley Publishing Company, 1995), 159–60; Rick Koster, *Texas Music* (New York: St. Martin's Press, 1998), 37; Richard Carlin, *Country Music: A Biographical Dictionary* (New York: Routledge Press,

2003), 65–66; Russell D. Barnard, *The Comprehensive Country Music Encyclopedia* (New York: Random House, 1994), 67; Waylon Jennings with Lenny Kaye, *Waylon: An Autobiography* (New York: Warner Books, 1996), 201, 362.

8. Guy Clark, "Desperados Waiting for a Train," *Keepers*, Sugar Hill Records, 1997.

9. Guy Clark, "L.A. Freeway," *Old No. 1*, RCA Records, 1975; for more on Jerry Jeff Walker's version of "L.A. Freeway," see Jan Reid, *The Improbable Rise of Redneck Rock* (Austin: University of Texas Press, 2004), 99–100.

10. Evans and Horne, *Song Builder*, 102–14; Lyle Lovett, interview with author, January 6, 2011.

11. David Cantwell and Bill Friskics-Warren, *Heartaches by the Number: Country Music's 500 Greatest Singles* (Nashville: Vanderbilt University Press, 2003), 136.

12. Evans and Horne, *Song Builder*, 76.

13. Ryan Bingham, interview with author, October 6, 2010.

14. For more on Guy Clark's approach to songwriting and overuse of the term "craftsman," see David Goodman, *Modern Twang: An Alternative Country Music Guide & Directory* (Nashville: Dowling Press, 1999), 64; Atkinson, "Songs Keep Finding Craftsman Clark"; Stuart Henderson, "Guy Clark: Somedays the Song Writes You," www.popmatters.com, September 23, 2009 (accessed February 13, 2011).

15. For critical praise of *Boats to Build* and *Dublin Blues*, see McCloud, *Definitive Country*, 160; Goodman, *Modern Twang*, 64; Billy Altman, "Boats to Build Review," www.ew.com, November 20, 1992 (accessed February 13, 2011); and Alanna Nash, "Dublin Blues Review," www.ew.com, February 3, 1995 (accessed February 13, 2011).

16. For more on Guy Clark's albums *Boats to Build*, *Dublin Blues*, and *Keepers—A Live Recording*, see Evans and Horne, *Song Builder*, 119–45.

17. Evans and Horne, *Song Builder*, 182–84.

18. Townes Van Zandt, "If I Needed You," *The Late, Great Townes Van Zandt*, Poppy Records, 1972.

19. Guy Clark, interview with author, November 12, 2009.

20. Guy Clark, interview with author, August 13, 2010.

21. Guy Clark, interview with Tamara Saviano, April 1, 2000.

22. Townes Van Zandt, "Two Girls," *The Nashville Sessions*, Tomato Records, 1993.

23. Guy Clark, interview with author, August 13, 2010.

24. Townes Van Zandt, "No Place to Fall," *Flyin' Shoes*, Tomato Records, 1978.

25. Guy Clark, interview with Tamara Saviano, April 1, 2000.

26. Guy Clark, interview with author, August 13, 2010.

27. Guy Clark, interview with Tamara Saviano, April 1, 2000.

28. Guy Clark, interview with author, August 13, 2010.

29. Guy Clark, interview with Tamara Saviano, April 1, 2000.

RAY WYLIE HUBBARD

1. Reid's *Improbable Rise of Redneck Rock* is still the most complete examination of the "progressive country" phenomenon, which is an eclectic mix of country, rock and roll, blues, and other elements that sprang from Austin's diverse and dynamic club scene of the 1970s; for further information on progressive country music, see Cory Lock, "Counterculture Cowboys: Progressive Texas Country of the 1970s and 1980s," *Journal of Texas Music History*, Volume 3, Number 1, Spring 2003, 14–23; for a discussion of the mythology surrounding progressive country and whether it can accurately be termed a "movement," see Jason Dean Mellard, "Home With the Armadillo: Public Memory and Performance in the 1970s Austin Music Scene," *Journal of Texas Music History*, Volume 10, Issue 1, 2010.

2. For more on Jerry Jeff Walker performing Ray Wylie Hubbard's "Up Against the Wall Redneck Mother," see Reid, *Improbable Rise of Redneck Rock*, 105–6, 358; for more on Ray Wylie Hubbard writing "Up Against the Wall Redneck Mother," see Kathleen Hudson, *Telling Stories, Writing Songs* (Austin: University of Texas Press, 2001), 234–35; See also Travis D. Stimeling, "¡Viva Terlingua! Jerry Jeff Walker, Live Recordings, and the Authenticity of Progressive Country Music," *Journal of Texas Music History*, Volume 8, Issue 1, 2008, 20–33 for a discussion of how studio recordings were sometimes made to sound like live performances, since live concerts were such an important part of the "spirit" of the progressive country scene of the 1970s.

3. Robert Earl Keen, "The Road Goes on Forever," *West Textures*, Sugar Hill Records, 1989.

4. For more on the important role Ray Wylie Hubbard played in the "Progressive Country" music movement of the 1970s, see Reid, *Improbable Rise of Redneck Rock*, 105–6, 358; for more on the impact of progressive country on the larger country music scene, see Hartman, *History of Texas Music*, 165–74.

5. Brian T. Atkinson, "Interview: Ray Wylie Hubbard," *Austin Music + Entertainment*, July–August 2006, 26; for more on Ray Wylie Hubbard achieving sobriety and his creative rebirth, see Grant Alden and Peter Blackstock, *The Best of No Depression: Writing about American Music*, (Austin: University of Texas Press, 2005), 60–63.

6. Ray Wylie Hubbard, interview with author, May 19, 2006.

7. Ray Wylie Hubbard, interview with author, June 19, 2004.

8. Brian T. Atkinson, "Hayes Carll Q&A," *Texas Music*, Spring 2008, 22, 25, 26–27.

9. Ray Wylie Hubbard, interview with author, June 19, 2004.

PETER ROWAN

1. Peter Rowan, interview with author, June 21, 2003; for more on Peter Rowan touring with Guy Clark and Townes Van Zandt, see Kruth, *To Live's To Fly*, 259–260; for more on Peter Rowan's formative years, see Kingsbury, *Encyclopedia of Country Music*, 461.

2. For more on Peter Rowan's involvement with Bill Monroe and His Blue Grass Boys, see Richard D. Smith, *Can't You Hear Me Callin': The Life of Bill Monroe* (Boston: Little, Brown and Company, 2000), 203–4, 206–9, 210, 233; Nicholas Dawidoff, *In the Country of Country: A Journey to the Roots of American Music* (New York: Pantheon Books, 1997), 103–4.

3. For more on the integral role that Peter Rowan played in modernizing bluegrass music, see Peter Doggett, *Are You Ready for the Country* (New York: Penguin Books, 2000), 38, 39, 118, 165, 182; for more on Peter Rowan's early years in Boston, see Carlin, *Country Music*, 354.

4. Doggett, *Are You Ready for the Country*, 98.

5. For more on "Old and In the Way," see Carlin, *Country Music*, 296.

6. For more on Peter Rowan's various musical groups, see Tony Byworth, *The Billboard Illustrated Encyclopedia of Country Music* (New York: Watson Guptill Publications, 2007), 298.

7. Paul Kerr, "Peter Rowan: Gather the Spirit," www.jambands.com, December 4, 2007 (accessed February 14, 2011).

8. Peter Rowan, interview with author, June 21, 2003.

RODNEY CROWELL

1. Brian T. Atkinson, "Art, Diamonds & Dirt," *American Songwriter*, July–August 2005, 38; for more on the Nashville Songwriters Hall of Fame, visit www.nashvillesongwritersfoundation.com (accessed February 14, 2011).

2. Rodney Crowell, interview with author, April 4, 2005.

3. For more on Rodney Crowell's early career and artists who have recorded his songs, see Carlin, *Country Music*, 89; for more on Rodney Crowell's role in the progressive country scene, see Kingsbury, *Will the Circle Be Unbroken*, 295; for more on Rodney Crowell's involvement with progressive

Nashville songwriters such as Steve Earle, Emmylou Harris, and Lucinda Williams, see Dawidoff, *In the Country of Country*, 278–79.

4. For more on Rodney Crowell's success as a commercial country singer, see Kingsbury, *Encyclopedia of Country Music*, 120.

5. Rodney Crowell, interview with author, April 4, 2005.

6. For more the Americana movement, see Kingsbury, *Will the Circle Be Unbroken*, 332; for more on Rodney Crowell's recording career, see Richard Carlin, *American Popular Music: Country* (New York: Infobase Publishing, 2006), 48.

7. Keith Urban, interview with author, April 7, 2005.

8. Rodney Crowell, interview with author, June 19, 2004.

KRIS KRISTOFFERSON

1. For more on Kris Kristofferson and his role in the outlaw country phenomenon, see Hartman, *History of Texas Music*, 175–76; Carlin, *Country Music*, 220–21.

2. Brian T. Atkinson, "Revering Friends," *Austin American-Statesman*, September 29, 2009, D1, D3; for more on Kris Kristofferson's groundbreaking role in Nashville's songwriting community, see McCloud, *Definitive Country*, 450–51.

3. Atkinson, "Revering Friends"; for more on Kris Kristofferson's involvement with members of the Highwaymen, see Hartman, *History of Texas Music*, 175–76; Reid, *Improbable Rise of Redneck Rock*, 256, 258–60.

4. Kris Kristofferson, "The Pilgrim, Chapter 33," *The Silver Tongued Devil and I*, Monument Records, 1971.

5. Kris Kristofferson, interview with author, February 2, 2006.

6. For more on Janis Joplin recording Kris Kristofferson's "Me and Bobby McGee" and Joplin's roots as a folksinger in Texas, see Alice Echols, *Scars of Sweet Paradise: The Life and Times of Janis Joplin* (New York: Henry Holt and Company, 1999), 281, 282; see also Jerry Rodnitzky, "Janis Joplin: The Hippie Blues Singer as Feminist Heroine," *Journal of Texas Music History*, Volume 2, Number 1, Spring 2002, 7–15, and Richard B. Hughes, "Janis Lyn Joplin," Barkley, ed., *Handbook of Texas Music*, 167–169.

7. See Cantwell and Friskics-Warren, *Heartaches by the Number*, 135–36, 177; for more on Ray Price's hit "For the Good Times," see Kingsbury, *Will the Circle Be Unbroken*, 247.

8. Don Was, e-mail interview with author, August 2009.

9. Kris Kristofferson, interview with author, February 9, 2006.

VERSE: CORY CHISEL

1. Cory Chisel, "Home in the Woods," *Cabin Ghosts*, Sony BMG, 2008; Brian T. Atkinson, "Interview: Cory Chisel," www.americansongwriter.com, December 10, 2008 (accessed February 13, 2011).

2. Cory Chisel, interview with author, November 7, 2008.

BILLY JOE SHAVER

1. Billy Joe Shaver, interview with author, February 10, 2010.

2. Billy Joe Shaver, interview with author, April 7, 2005; for more on the *Crazy Heart* soundtrack, see Michael Corcoran, "*Crazy Heart* soundtrack review," www.austin360.com, Jan. 17, 2010 (accessed February 13, 2011).

3. For more on Billy Joe Shaver's relationship with spirituality, see Billy Joe Shaver, assisted by Brad Reagan, *Honky Tonk Hero* (Austin: University of Texas Press, 2005), 69–70.

4. William Michael Smith, "Introducing . . . Lonesome, On'ry, and Mean," www.houstonpress.com, April 15, 2008 (accessed February 13, 2011).

5. Waylon Jennings discusses his creative partnership with Billy Joe Shaver in Jennings and Kaye, *Waylon*, 188–91, 196–98; Alden and Blackstock, ed., *No Depression*, 47–48; and Koster, *Texas Music*, 35–36.

6. For more on Billy Joe Shaver's heart attack and subsequent quadruple bypass surgery, see Shaver, *Honky Tonk Hero*, 67–69; and Patrick Caldwell, "Billy Joe Shaver Recovering from Minor Heart Surgery," www.austin360.com, July 13, 2010 (accessed February 13, 2011).

7. John T. Davis, "My Past Is Kickin' My Ass!," *Texas Music*, Summer 2010, 46.

8. Shaver, *Honky Tonk Hero*, 135.

9. Brian T. Atkinson, *Austin American-Statesman*, "The Gospel of Billy Joe," February 11, 2010, F7.

10. Steven Kreytak, www.statesman.com, "Jury Finds Billy Joe Shaver Not Guilty," April 6, 2010 (accessed February 13, 2011).

11. Billy Joe Shaver, interview with author, April 7, 2005.

CHIP TAYLOR

1. Chip Taylor discusses his background as a songwriter in Chip Taylor, *Songs from a Dutch Tour* (Amsterdam: Ambo/Anthos Publishers, 2008); see also www.trainwreckrecords.com (accessed February 14, 2011).

2. Chip Taylor, "Wild Thing," *From Nowhere—The Troggs*, Fontana Records, 1966.

3. Pete Clark, "How I Wrote Shaggy's No. 1," *The Evening Standard*, July 27, 2001; for more on Merrilee Rush and the Turnabouts' version of "Angel of the Morning," see Cantwell and Friskics-Warren, *Heartaches by the Number: Country Music's 500 Greatest Singles*, 176.

4. Chip Taylor, interview with author, April 14, 2004; Shore Fire Media press release, "Chip Taylor's Top 10 Best Duets of All Time," December 3, 2010; for more on the song "I'm Gonna Fly," see Kimmie Rhodes, *West Texas Heaven*, Sunbird Records, 1996.

5. For more on Chip Taylor's gambling years, see Derk Richardson, "Gamblin' Man: How 'Wild Thing' Writer Chip Taylor Got a Second Chance at Being a Singer/Songwriter," www.sfgate.com, August 10, 2006 (accessed February 13, 2011).

6. For more on Chip Taylor and Carrie Rodriguez's musical partnership, see Frank Goodman, "A Conversation with Chip Taylor & Carrie Rodriguez," www.puremusic.com, December 2003 (accessed February 13, 2011); and Brian T. Atkinson, "Chip Taylor & Carrie Rodriguez, *The Trouble with Humans*," *No Depression*, November–December, 2003, 139; for more on Carrie Rodriguez's solo career, see Brian T. Atkinson, "SXSW Interview: Carrie Rodriguez," *Austin American-Statesman*, March 18, 2010, F12, F17.

7. Brian T. Atkinson, "Interview: Carrie Rodriguez," *Austin Music*, September–October 2006, 32.

8. Chip Taylor, interview with author, November 18, 2010.

9. Chip Taylor, "Jesus Christ—Don't Let the Cactus Fall" single, Train Wreck Records, 2010; for more on the proposed Cactus Café closure, see Ralph K. M. Kaurwitz, "UT Defends Plan to Close Cactus Café," www.statesman.com, February 1, 2010 (accessed on February 13, 2011); Michael Corcoran, "No-Repeat Reprise: As He Did in 1990, Hancock Will Play 5 Distinct Sets," *Austin American-Statesman*, August 10, 2010, D1, D3.

10. Chip Taylor, interview with author, November 18, 2010.

11. Chip Taylor, "What Would Townes Say about That," *Unglorious Hallelujah*, Train Wreck Records, 2006.

12. Chip Taylor, interview with author, April 14, 2004.

TOM RUSSELL

1. Bradley Mason Hamlin, "Tom Russell: Tough Company Interview (2003)," www.mysteryisland.net, 2008 (accessed February 13, 2011).

2. For more on Tom Russell living in Austin and recording with Patricia Hardin, see Goodman, *Modern Twang*, 272.

3. Tom Russell, e-mail interview with author, March 27, 2006; For more about Tom Russell's worldview, see Monte Dutton, *True to the Roots: Americana Revealed* (Lincoln: University of Nebraska Press, 2006), 141–43; for more on Tom Russell's recording career, see Goodman, *Modern Twang*, 272–73.

4. Brian T. Atkinson, "A Musical Slice of Blue Collar Life," *Austin American-Statesman*, November 21, 2008, D2; for more on Tom Russell's approach to cowriting, see Dutton, *True to the Roots*, 139–40.

5. For more on Tom Russell's songwriting approach, see Rob Browning, "Tom Russell: Blood and Candle Smoke," www.popmatters.com, October 20, 2009 (accessed February 13, 2011); and Corey duBrowa, "Tom Russell: Blood and Candle Smoke," www.pastemagazine.com, September 15, 2009 (accessed February 13, 2011).

6. Atkinson, "A Musical Slice of Blue Collar Life," D2.

7. Tom Russell, "Stealing Electricity," *Love and Fear*, Hightone Records, 2006.

8. Ted Drozdowski, "Review: Tom Russell: Blood and Candle Smoke," www.thephoenix.com, September 22, 2009 (accessed February 13, 2011).

9. Tom Russell, e-mail interview with author, March 27, 2006.

GRAHAM LEADER AND HEARTWORN HIGHWAYS

1. For critical praise of *Heartworn Highways* and its soundtrack, see Raoul Hernandez, "Phases and Stages: *Heartworn Highways*," www.austinchronicle.com, August 29, 2003 (accessed February 13, 2011); Geoffrey Himes, "Van Zandt's Legend Enjoys Posthumous Fame," www.chicagotribune.com, September 21, 2003 (accessed February 13, 2011); Jim Caligiuri, "SXSW Records: *Heartworn Highways*," www.austinchronicle.com, March 17, 2006 (accessed February 13, 2011); Jeff Hinkle, "*Heartworn Highways* [DVD] Review," www.popmatters.com, September 30, 2003 (accessed February 13, 2011).

2. Wayne Bledsoe, "Guy Clark Still Has a Lone Star State of Mind," www.knoxville.com, July 8, 2010 (accessed February 13, 2011).

3. Hardy, *A Deeper Blue*, 144; for more on "Uncle" Seymour Washington and Townes Van Zandt, see Richard Dobson, *The Gulf Coast Boys* (Bryan, TX: Greater Texas Publishing Company, 1998), 50–52, 95–96.

4. For more on *Heartworn Highways*, see Graham Leader and James Szalapski, *Heartworn Highways*, Catfish Entertainment, 2003; Townes Van Zandt, "Waitin' Around to Die," *For the Sake of the Song*, Tomato Records, 1968.

5. Kruth, *To Live's To Fly*, 91.

6. Evans and Horne, *Song Builder*, 64.

7. Kruth, *To Live's To Fly*, 91.

8. Hardy, *A Deeper Blue*, 142–43, 146; for more on Townes Van Zandt's trouble with heroin abuse and its effect on his family, see Kruth, *To Live's To Fly*, 150–52.

9. Graham Leader, interview with author, August 7, 2003.

10. Graham Leader, interview with author, August 7, 2003.

STEVE YOUNG

1. For more on Steve Young's role in the evolution of the country-rock and outlaw country scenes, see Kingsbury, *The Encyclopedia of Country Music*, 608; Doggett, *Are You Ready for the Country*, 76, 106; and Dave Dawson, "Steve Young Interview," www.nucountry.com, December 14, 2006 (accessed February 12, 2011).

2. For more on the songs "Seven Bridges Road" and "Lonesome On'ry, and Mean," see author anonymous, "Interview: Steve Young," www.music-illuminati.com, January 25, 2010 (accessed February 13, 2011); for more on "Seven Bridges Road," see David Freeland, "Behind the Song: 'Seven Bridges Road,'" www.americansongwriter.com, November 1, 2007 (accessed February 13, 2011).

3. Kingsbury, *Encyclopedia of Country Music*, 608.

4. Steve Young, interview with author, July 23, 2010.

5. Goodman, *Modern Twang*, 334.

6. Steve Young, interview with author, July 23, 2010.

7. For more on Steve Young's career after he achieved sobriety, see Goodman, *Modern Twang*, 334–335.

8. Steve Young, interview with author, July 23, 2010.

VERSE: JAY FARRAR

1. For more on the important role Jay Farrar played in the alternative country movement with the bands Uncle Tupelo and Son Volt, see Kingsbury, *Encyclopedia of Country Music*, 560; Doggett, *Are You Ready for the Country*, 491, 492, 494–49, 496, 498; J. Douglas Waterman, *Song: The World's Best Songwriters on Creating the Music that Moves Us* (Cincinnati: Writer's Digest Books, 2007), 129–32; and David McGee, *Steve Earle: Fearless Heart, Outlaw Poet* (San Francisco: Backbeat Books, 2005), 205–6.

2. Will Levith and Eric R. Danton, "Jay Farrar: The List," *American Songwriter*, January–February 2011, 82.

3. Brian T. Atkinson, "Musicians' Ode to 'Big Sur,' with Love," *Austin American-Statesman*, January 27, 2010, D2.

4. Jay Farrar, e-mail interview with author, July 9, 2003; For more about Jay Farrar's role in the bands Uncle Tupelo and Son Volt and his career as a solo artist, see Alden and Blackstock, *The Best of No Depression*, 231–40; and Brian T. Atkinson, "Son Volt: Shifting Priorities," *Pop Culture Press*, Fall & Winter 2005, 20–22.

RAMBLIN' JACK ELLIOTT

1. Brian T. Atkinson, "Ramblin' Jack Elliott Stands Alone," *Country Standard Time*, July–August 2006, 7–8.

2. Ramblin' Jack Elliott, interview with author, July 23, 2010.

3. Atkinson, "Ramblin' Jack Elliott Stands Alone," 7–8; Aiyana Elliott, *The Ballad of Ramblin' Jack*, Winstar, 2001.

4. For more on Ramblin' Jack Elliott's friendship with Woody Guthrie and the Guthrie family, see Ed Cray, *Ramblin Man: The Life and Times of Woody Guthrie* (New York: W.W. Norton & Company, 2004), 341–42, 347, 349, 350, 362, 363; Amanda Petrusich, *It Still Moves: Lost Songs, Lost Highways, and the Search for the Next American Music* (New York: Faber & Faber, 2008), 224–27, 228–29.

5. Pete Seeger, *The Incompleat Folksinger* (Lincoln: University of Nebraska Press, 1972), 252–53.

6. For more on Ramblin' Jack Elliott's connection to Bob Dylan, see David Hajdu, *Positively 4th Street: The Lives and Times of Joan Baez, Bob Dylan, Mimi Baez Farina, and Richard Farina* (New York: Farrar, Straus and Giroux, 2001), 66, 74, 102, 105, 146; and Mike Marqusee, *Wicked Messenger: Bob Dylan and the 1960s* (New York: Seven Stories Press, 2005), 40–42, 260; for more on Elliott and Dylan and the Rolling Thunder Revue, see Bob Spitz, *Dylan: A Biography* (New York: McGraw-Hill Publishing, 1989), 472, 484, 485, 492; and Charles J. Fuss, *Joan Baez: A Bio-Bibliography* (Westport: Greenwood Press, 1996), 21, D73, D74.

7. Hardy, *A Deeper Blue*, 185.

8. Ramblin' Jack Elliott, interview with author, July 23, 2010.

9. Ramblin' Jack Elliott, interview with author, June 20, 2006.

10. Ramblin' Jack Elliott, interview with author, July 23, 2010.

DAVID OLNEY

1. Todd Snider, "From a Rooftop," *Peace, Love and Anarchy (Rarities, B-Sides and Demos, Vol. 1)*, Oh Boy Records, 2007.

2. Brian T. Atkinson, "Dave Olney: *One Tough Town* Review," *American Songwriter*, July–August 2007, 86.

3. Steve Earle, "'Saturday Night and Sunday Morning' at McCabe's Guitar Shop," www.youtube.com, December 18, 1987 (accessed February 13, 2011).

4. T. Wayne Waters, "David Olney: Literate, Rabble-Rousing Troubadour," www.americansongwriter.com, June 28, 2010 (accessed February 13, 2011).

5. David Olney, interview with author, October 28, 2010; for more on David Olney and Townes Van Zandt's friendship, see Vincent Wynne, "Q&A: David Olney Discusses Townes Van Zandt, His Songwriting Process, and His Favorite Gibson Guitars," www.gibson.com, May 26, 2010 (accessed February 13, 2011).

6. William Michael Smith, "Nashville Lifer Is Nobody's Dummy," *Houston Press*, January 10, 2008.

7. Atkinson, "Dave Olney: *One Tough Town* Review," 86; Townes Van Zandt, "Snake Song," *Flyin' Shoes*, Tomato Records, 1978.

8. David Olney, interview with author, October 28, 2010.

9. Edd Hurt, "Dutchman's Curve Review," *Nashville Scene*, April 1, 2010.

10. Waters, "David Olney: Literate, Rabble-Rousing Troubadour."

11. David Olney, e-mail interview with author, May 30, 2003.

12. David Olney, interview with author, October 28, 2010.

TODD SNIDER

1. Brian T. Atkinson, "ACL Live Interview: Todd Snider," www.austin360.com, October 3, 2009 (accessed February 13, 2011); For more about Todd Snider's sociopolitical songs, see Chris Willman, *Rednecks & Bluenecks: The Politics of Country Music*, (New York: The New Press, 2007), 233–36.

2. Brian T. Atkinson, "Snider and the Politics of Brevity," *Austin American-Statesman*, October 8, 2008, D2.

3. Todd Snider, interview with author, May 30, 2006.

4. For more on Todd Snider's connection to Townes Van Zandt and the Texas singer-songwriter community, see Hartman, *History of Texas Music*, 186–88.

5. Brian T. Atkinson, "Todd Snider's Return to Cheatham Street," *Austin American-Statesman*, November 29, 2007, 18.

6. Atkinson, "Todd Snider's Return to Cheatham Street."

7. Todd Snider, "Hello . . . Sorry," *Near Truths and Hotel Rooms*, Oh Boy, 2003.

8. Atkinson, "ACL Live Interview: Todd Snider."

9. For more about Todd Snider's connection to mainstream country music in Nashville, see Brian T. Atkinson, "Tirelessly Seeking, Helplessly Hoping," *American Songwriter*, September–October 2006, 24.

10. Atkinson, "Tirelessly Seeking, Helplessly Hoping."

11. Todd Snider, interview with author, June 28, 2003.

12. Todd Snider, interview with author, June 28, 2003.

SHAWN CAMP

1. For more on Shawn Camp's early years as a songwriter in Nashville, see Kingsbury, *The Encyclopedia of Country Music*, 75; and Vladimir Bogdanov, Chris Woodstra, and Stephen Thomas Erlewine, *All Music Guide to Country: The Definitive Guide to Country Music* (San Francisco: Backbeat Books, 2003), 112.

2. Shawn Camp, interview with author, August 20, 2010.

3. Shawn Camp, interview with author, August 20, 2010; for more on Shawn Camp collaborating with Guy Clark, see Michael Kosser, *How Nashville Became Music City, U.S.A.: 50 Years of Music Row* (Milwaukee: Hal Leonard Corporation, 2006), 290–91.

4. Brian T. Atkinson and Tamara Saviano, "Shawn Camp's Luminous '1994' Breaks Out of the Warner Music Nashville Vault on September 28," www.shawncamp.com, September 2, 2010 (accessed February 13, 2011).

5. For more on Shawn Camp's album *Lucky Silver Dollar*, see Jon Weisberger, "Shawn Camp: Lucky Silver Dollar," www.countrystandardtime.com, (accessed February 13, 2011); for more on Camp's album *Fireball*, see John Lupton, "Shawn Camp: Fireball," www.countrystandardtime.com, (accessed February 13, 2011).

6. John Esposito, interview with author, August 26, 2010.

7. For more on Shawn Camp's album *1994*, see Vernell Hackett, "Shawn Camp Finally Brings '1994' to Life, www.theboot.com, October 7, 2010 (accessed February 13, 2011); for more on the impact of *1994* on Warner Music Nashville, see Brody Vercher, "Shawn Camp Release to Lead to 'Lost Tapes' Series?," www.the9513.com, October 1, 2010 (accessed February 13, 2011).

8. Shawn Camp, "Stop, Look and Listen (Cow Catcher Blues)," *1994*, Reprise Records, 2010.

9. Atkinson and Saviano, "Shawn Camp's Luminous '1994.'"

10. Shawn Camp, interview with author, January 7, 2011.

11. Shawn Camp, interview with author, January 7, 2011.

CHORUS: BEN NICHOLS

1. Brian T. Atkinson, "Lucero, 1372 Overton Park Review," *American Songwriter*, November–December 2009.

2. Lucero, "Hey Darlin', Do You Gamble?," *1372 Overton Park*, Universal Republic Records, 2009.

3. Ben Nichols, interview with author, October 3, 2010.

JAMES McMURTRY

1. Franklin D. Roosevelt, radio address, October 26, 1939, www.quotationspage.com (accessed February 13, 2011).

2. Brian T. Atkinson, "*Just Us Kids* Review," *Relix*, June 2008.

3. For more on James McMurtry and his family's role in the Texas storytelling tradition, see Reid, *Improbable Rise of Redneck Rock*, 337–41, 339; and Monte Dutton, *True to the Roots*, 183–90.

4. Hardy, *A Deeper Blue*, 182.

5. For more on James McMurtry's early albums and his approach to songwriting, see Koster, *Texas Music*, 202; for more on McMurtry's role as a next-generation singer-songwriter in the Texas folk tradition, see Hartman, *History of Texas Music*, 189–91.

6. Hudson, *Telling Stories, Writing Songs*, 33.

7. James McMurtry, "Levelland," *Where'd You Hide the Body*, Columbia Records, 1995.

8. James McMurtry, interview with author, June 22, 2004.

LUCINDA WILLIAMS

1. Brian T. Atkinson, *Maverick Country*, "Lucinda Williams at Botanic Gardens, Denver," September 2005, 23.

2. For more on Lucinda Williams's early years, see Mary A. Bufwack and Robert K. Oermann, *Finding Her Voice: The Saga of Women in Country Music* (Nashville: Country Music Foundation Press and Vanderbilt University Press, 2003), 436, 490, 511; and Edward Lewine, "Domains: Lucinda Williams," www.nytimes.com, February 25, 2009 (accessed February 13, 2011).

3. For more on Lucinda Williams coming to terms with success after *Car Wheels on a Gravel Road*, see Alden and Blackstock, *The Best of No Depression*, 127–34.

4. Lucinda Williams, "Drunken Angel," *Car Wheels on a Gravel Road*, Mercury Records, 1998; for more on late Austin singer-songwriter Blaze Foley,

see Sybil Rosen, *Living in the Woods in a Tree: Remembering Blaze Foley* (Denton: University of North Texas Press, 2008); and Doug Freeman, "Faded Love: Blaze Foley's Long Lost Muse, Sybil Rosen," *Austin Chronicle*, October 31, 2008, 70; for more on Foley, his friendship with Townes Van Zandt, and evolution as a songwriter, see Joe Nick Patoski, "The Fall and Rise of Blaze Foley," *No Depression*, September–October 2006; and Kevin Triplett, *Duct Tape Messiah*, Abraxas Productions, 2011.

5. Melissa Etheridge, interview with author, July 19, 2010.

6. Emmylou Harris, "Songwriter: Lucinda Williams," *Time*, July 9, 2001; for more on Lucinda Williams's approach to performing and songwriting, see Brendan Vaughan, "What I've Learned: Lucinda Williams," www.esquire.com, March 31, 2002 (accessed February 13, 2011); and Michael D. Ayers, "Interview: Lucinda Williams on Getting Paid $250 for Her First Record, *Mad Men*, and Her Favorite Place in New York City," www.villagevoice.com, October 2, 2009 (accessed February 13, 2011).

7. Lucinda Williams, interview with author, February 2, 2011; for more on Lucinda Williams's album, *Blessed*, see Brian T. Atkinson, "A Blissful 'Blessed,'" *Austin American-Statesman*, March 1, 2011, D1, D3.

8. Brian T. Atkinson, *Austin American-Statesman*, "ACL Preview: Heartless Bastards," September 29, 2009, F11.

9. Lucinda Williams, interview with author, May 17, 2005.

LYLE LOVETT

1. For more on Lyle Lovett's 1998 album *Step Inside This House* and the role Lovett played in Nashville's songwriting community in the 1980s, see Doggett, *Are You Ready for the Country*, 470, 471–72, 477, 482, 483; Reid, *The Improbable Rise of Redneck Rock*, 329–30.

2. Brian T. Atkinson, "Gruene Hall Is the Envy of Other Venues," *Austin American-Statesman*, May 6, 2010, F10–11, F18.

3. For more about Lyle Lovett, Steve Earle, and Dwight Yoakam's emergence into mainstream country and later branching into "alternative country" and "insurgent country," see Byworth, *The Billboard Illustrated Encyclopedia of Country Music*, 276–78; for more on Lovett's early career, see Alan Cackett, *The Harmony Illustrated Encyclopedia of Country Music* (New York: Crown Publishers, 1994), 97.

4. Doggett, *Are You Ready for the Country*, 472.

5. For more on Lyle Lovett's musical diversity, see McCloud, *Definitive Country*, 487–88; and Hartman, *History of Texas Music*, 188.

6. Shelley Levitt, "Lovett First Sight," www.people.com, July 12, 1993 (accessed February 13, 2011); for more on Lyle Lovett's marriage to Julia Roberts and his 1998 album *Step Inside This House*, see Carlin, *Country Music*, 239.

7. Lyle Lovett, "All Downhill," *It's Not Big, It's Large*, Curb/Lost Highway Records, 2007; Lyle Lovett, interview with author, January 6, 2011; for more on Guy Clark, Joe Ely, John Hiatt, and Lyle Lovett's guitar pulls, see Brian T. Atkinson, "Telluride Bluegrass Festival, Telluride Colorado, June 17–20 Review," *Maverick Country*, September–October 2004, 23–24.

8. Michael Corcoran, "Lyle Lovett Setlist at 'ACL' taping 11/8," www.austin360.com, November 8, 2010 (accessed February 13, 2011).

9. Lyle Lovett, interview with author, April 30, 2010.

JOHN GORKA

1. John Gorka, interview with author, November 29, 2007.

2. For more on John Gorka's early years and the Razzy Dazzy Spasm Band, see John Gorka, *The Gypsy Life* (Collector's Edition), AIX Media Group, 2007; for more on Townes Van Zandt and the Kerrville Folk Festival, see Dobson, *The Gulf Coast Boys*, 174–175; for more on the Kerrville Folk Festival itself, see Rod Kennedy, *Music From the Heart: The Fifty-Year Chronicle of His Life in Music (With a Few Sidetrips!)*, (Austin: Eakin Press, 1998).

3. For more on John Gorka as leader in the "New Folk Movement," see Eliza Wing, *Rolling Stone*, August 8, 1991, p. 17; and Gregg Gillis, "John Gorka (Interview)," Popcorn Youth blog for *Ithaca Times*, November 2009 (accessed February 13, 2011).

4. For more on John Gorka in concert, see Brian T. Atkinson, "SXSW Review: Guy Davis and John Gorka at the Victorian Room at the Driskill Hotel," www.austin360.com, March 20, 2009 (accessed February 13, 2011).

5. Townes Van Zandt, "Snow Don't Fall," *The Late, Great Townes Van Zandt*, Tomato Records, 1972.

6. For more on Leslie Jo Richards and "Snow Don't Fall," see Kruth, *To Live's To Fly*, 126–29, 132–33; for more on how Richards's murder affected Townes Van Zandt, see Hardy, *A Deeper Blue*, 107–107.

7. John Gorka, interview with author, November 29, 2007.

BRIDGE: BIANCA DELEON

1. For more on Bianca DeLeon and her connection to Townes Van Zandt, see "Outlaws & Lovers: Bianca DeLeon and the Romance of the Borderlands," www.biancamusic.com (accessed February 13, 2011).

2. Bianca DeLeon, interview with author, June 27, 2007; For an alternate story on the inception of Van Zandt's song "If I Needed You," see Hardy, *A Deeper Blue*, 81. Guy Clark confirmed his version of the song's inception in a conversation with Tamara Saviano on June 12, 2011. For more on Townes Van Zandt's relationship with Bianca DeLeon, see Hardy, *A Deeper Blue*, 82.

MICHAEL TIMMINS

1. Michael Timmins, e-mail interview with author, June 25, 2003.

2. Hardy, *A Deeper Blue*, 214–17.

3. Michael Timmins, interview with author, December 20, 2010.

4. Townes Van Zandt, "Cowboy Junkies Lament," *No Deeper Blue*, Sugar Hill Records, 1994; for more on the recording of Townes Van Zandt's final studio album, *No Deeper Blue*, see Aretha Sills, "Townes Van Zandt Interview," *Maybelle*, Fall 1994, 1, 19.

5. For more on the Cowboy Junkies' early years and the band's connection to Townes Van Zandt, see Goodman, *Modern Twang*, 76.

6. Hardy, *A Deeper Blue*, 270.

7. Doug Heselgrave, "A Walk Through Renmin Park: A New Interview with Michael Timmins," www.nodepression.com, June 14, 2010 (accessed February 13, 2011).

8. Brian T. Atkinson, "'Nomad Series' Has Defined a Path," *Austin American-Statesman*, June 18, 2010, D2.

9. Michael Timmins, e-mail interview with author, June 25, 2003, and telephone interview with author, December 20, 2010.

KELLY JOE PHELPS

For more on the traditional song "Wabash Cannonball," see Elizabeth Schlappi, *Roy Acuff: The Smoky Mountain Boy* (Gretna, LA: Pelican Publishing, 1978), 28, 49, 199–121; The Carter Family, *The Very Best of*, Goldenlane, 2007; Roy Acuff and His Smoky Mountain Boys, *Wabash Cannonball*, Black Cat, 2008.

1. For more on the first time Townes Van Zandt and Steve Earle met, see Kruth, *To Live's To Fly*, 65.

2. From the liner notes, *Townes Van Zandt: Live at McCabe's*.

3. For more on Kelly Joe Phelps's approach to interpreting blues and spiritual songs, see author anonymous, "Kelly Joe Phelps," www.sixstringsoul.com, January 4, 2005 (accessed February 13, 2011).

4. Brian T. Atkinson, "Kelly Joe Phelps, Union Chapel (London, England), November 11, 2003," *No Depression*, January–February 2004, 18–19.

5. For more on Colin Firth and Kelly Joe Phelps, see Hermione Eyre, "The Q Interview," *The Independent*, January 11, 2004; for more on Kelly Joe Phelps's popularity in Europe, see Atkinson, "Kelly Joe Phelps, Union Chapel," 18–19.

6. Steve Earle, from the packaging to Kelly Joe Phelps's *Shine Eyed Mister Zen*, Rykodisc Records, 1999.

7. For more on Kelly Joe Phelps's evolution as a lyricist, see Andy Gill, "Album: Kelly Joe Phelps," www.independent.co.uk, January 21, 2005 (accessed February 13, 2011); and Robert R. Calder, "Kelly Joe Phelps: Tap the Red Cane Whirlwind," www.popmatters.com, June 1, 2005 (accessed February 13, 2011).

8. Billy Davis, "Interview: October 2001," www.kellyjoephelps.com (accessed February 13, 2011).

9. Kelly Joe Phelps, e-mail interview with author, May 29, 2003; Kelly Joe Phelps, conversation with author, November 12, 2010.

STEVE TURNER

1. Tony Engelhart, "Mudhoney: Grunge Grows Up," www.glidemagazine.com, April 4, 2006 (accessed February 13, 2011).

2. Greg Prato, *Grunge Is Dead: The Oral History of Seattle Rock Music* (Toronto: ECW Press, 2009), 471; for more on Mudhoney's important role in grunge music, see Prato, *Grunge Is Dead*, 174–186; for more on the origination of the term "grunge," see Scott Deveau, www.nationalpost.com, "NXNE 2010: Q&A with Mark Arm of Mudhoney," June 9, 2010 (accessed February 13, 2011).

3. Prato, *Grunge Is Dead*, 289; for more on Green River, see Prato, *Grunge Is Dead*, 93, 113–23.

4. Prato, *Grunge Is Dead*, 347; for more on Nirvana, Soundgarden, and other bands defining the grunge movement and their impact on popular music, see David Peisner, "Alive in the Super-Unknown," *Spin*, September 2010, 48–54.

5. For more on Mudhoney's early years, see Clinton Heylin, *Babylon's Burning: From Punk to Grunge*, (New York: Canongate Press, 2007), 602, 604–5, 607, 608–9.

6. Hardy, *A Deeper Blue*, 246; for more on Jimmie Dale Gilmore and Mudhoney's recording of Townes Van Zandt's "Buckskin Stallion Blues," see Sills, "Townes Van Zandt Interview," *Maybelle*, 21.

7. Steve Turner, e-mail interview with author, June 27, 2003.

8. For more on Townes Van Zandt's final recording session at Easley Studios, see Kruth, *To Live's To Fly*, 281–83, and Hardy, *A Deeper Blue*, 257–59.

9. Keith Cameron, "Bring It On Home," *Mojo*, September 2010, 85; and Stephen Rodrick, "Robert Plant's Mystical Mountain Hop," *Rolling Stone*, January 20, 2011, 55; for more on Robert Plant's recording of Townes Van Zandt's "Harm's Swift Way," see Will Hermes, "The Led Zep Golden God Is Reborn As a Rootsy Force of Nature," *Rolling Stone*, September 16, 2010, 75–76.

10. Steve Turner, e-mail interview with author, June 27, 2003.

DAVID BROZA

1. For more on David Broza's background, see *David Broza at Masada: The Sunrise Concert*, and the car accident that threatened Broza's career, see Greg Quill, "Israel's David Broza Is Incomparable," www.thestar.com, December 23, 2007 (accessed February 13, 2011); for more on David Broza's eclectic nature as a musician, see Andy Moskowitz, "David Broza Draws Inspiration from Diverse Sources," *The Johns Hopkins News-Letter*, November 15, 2002.

2. Linda Lowe, interview with author, December 9, 2010; for more on David Broza's colorful performances, see Suzan Berns, "Israeli Springsteen Wields Flamenco and Blues at Festival," www.jewishsf.com, May 31, 1996 (accessed at www.davidbroza.net/hp/press.aspx February 13, 2011); for more on Townes Van Zandt and David Broza performing at Linda Lowe's Writers in the Round series, see Marty Racine, "The New Troubadours," *Houston Chronicle*, May 8, 1996.

3. Brian T. Atkinson, "Van Zandt Still Has Something to Say," *Austin American-Statesman*, December 16, 2010, E10.

4. For critical acclaim and more on the making of David Broza's album *Night Dawn: The Unpublished Poetry of Townes Van Zandt*, see Andrew Dansby, "Dawn of a Tribute," www.chron.com, March 9, 2010 (accessed February 13, 2011); Gary Graff, "Six Questions with David Broza," *Billboard*, February 20, 2010; Ben Greenman, "Talk of the Townes," www.newyorker.com, December 18, 2009 (accessed February 13, 2011); Michael Corcoran, "Townes' Unseen Poems Set to Music," www.austin360.com, December 3, 2009 (accessed February 13, 2011); and J. Poet, "Album review: David Broza, *Night Dawn: The Unpublished Poetry of Townes Van Zandt*," www.crawdaddy.com, February 22, 2010 (accessed February 13, 2011).

5. David Broza, interview with author, December 8, 2010.

6. In David Broza's interview with the author on December 8, 2010, Broza noted that eight years passed between Townes Van Zandt's death and

his receipt of Van Zandt's unpublished poetry. "Linda Lowe said I should call Townes's wife, Jeanene, and ask about it," Broza said. "I called Jeanene and introduced myself and said that he left me some poetry. She said she'd come to New York and talk to me. Two weeks later, she came to a memorial service for Townes in New York. We met the night before that and had dinner, just the two of us. She told me that she really was in a dilemma because she didn't know who I was, but here she is, meeting me.

"She said would like to pass these poems on to Willie Nelson or Bob Dylan or any of those artists who have a great respect and love for Townes. I was humbled. I thought, Hey, I totally understand. I'm not gonna stand in your way. If you want to give it a shot with other artists who are bigger and better known and maybe have a better feel about it, go ahead with it.

"For the next eight years, I erased it from my memory and didn't want to deal with it. I knew there was something there that was perfect for me and yet I couldn't fight it. It wasn't like there was a written will saying this is for David Broza. This was hearsay. So, this went on for eight years until I played again in Houston and everything came back. I said, 'I've got to call Jeanene and see what happened with that poetry.' I asked her and she said, 'Like you said, nothing happened,' as if I already had told her that I doubted that something would happen. I don't remember saying that.

"I thought, Well, I'm in Houston, so I can come up to Nashville to pick up the shoebox. She mentioned a shoebox and said the poetry is all there. That was stuck in my memory because it was a strange thing to say. I said, 'I'm coming,' but she said, 'Don't bother, just give me your e-mail address.' I went back to Tel Aviv, and three days later I started receiving e-mails with poetry. I was so thrilled that I started writing music for it. 'Soul to Soul' came out like—Bang!—thunder on a summer day."

7. Van Zandt, "Harm's Swift Way."

8. David Broza, interview with author, December 8, 2010.

MICHAEL WESTON KING

1. For more on Townes Van Zandt's concert at Union Chapel on April 24, 1994, see liner notes by Harold F. Eggers Jr. and Michael Weston King in the packaging to *Townes Van Zandt Live at Union Chapel, London, England*, Tomato Records, 2005; and Atkinson, "Mr. Record Man: Townes Van Zandt," *Lone Star Music*. For more on Union Chapel itself, see Atkinson, "Kelly Joe Phelps, Union Chapel (London, England), November 11, 2003," *No Depression*.

2. Michael Weston King, interview with author, March 7, 2011.

3. For an extensive interview with Michael Weston King in which he talks about his early years as a songwriter, his band The Good Sons, the beginnings of his solo career, and inspiration drawn from Townes Van Zandt, see Steve Wilcock, "Michael Weston King: The Triste Interview," www.triste.co.uk, January 2002 (accessed March 8, 2011); for more on alternative country's impact on The Good Sons, see Anonymous, "Interview: Michael Weston King," www.americana-uk.com, September 17, 2008 (accessed March 8, 2011). According to this article, The Good Sons were the first band signed to Glitterhouse Records, which released the Townes Van Zandt tribute album *There's a Hole in Heaven Where Some Sin Slips Through* in 2007.

4. Michael Weston King, interview with author, March 7, 2011.

5. For more on Michael Weston King's album *I Didn't Raise My Boy to Be a Soldier*, see Naomi Koppel, "Michael Weston King Brings Back the Protest Song," www.backroadsmusic.co.uk, August 8, 2010 (accessed March 8, 2011), and Nick Dalton, "Music That's Always on the Move," www.morningstaronline.co.uk, August 30, 2010 (accessed March 8, 2011).

6. Michael Weston King, e-mail exchange with author, March 5, 2011.

7. Harold F. Eggers Jr., interview with author, March 8, 2011.

8. Michael Weston King, liner notes in the packaging to *Townes Van Zandt Live at Union Chapel, London, England*.

9. Townes Van Zandt, "Marie," *No Deeper Blue*, Sugar Hill, 1994.

10. Michael Weston King, interview with author, March 7, 2011.

VERSE: JEWEL

1. Brian T. Atkinson, "A Shining Jewel," *Austin American-Statesman*, November 12, 2009, F9.

2. Jewel, interview with author, September 23, 2009; for more on Jewel, see Nikki Tranter, "Wonderlands: An Interview with Jewel," www.popmatters.com, April 26, 2006 (accessed February 13, 2011).

DAVE ALVIN

1. Dave Alvin, "Abilene," *Blackjack David*, Hightone Records, 1998.

2. For more on The Blasters, see Goodman, *Modern Twang*, 29–30; and Jon Johnson, "Are The Blasters 'Trouble Bound,'" www.countrystandardtime.com, October 2002 (accessed February 13, 2011).

3. Dave Alvin, *King of California*, Hightone Records, 1994.

4. For more on Dave Alvin's solo career, see Robert Hilburn, "Dave Alvin

Finds Voice and Blasts Off Solo," *Los Angeles Times*, August 23, 1987; Peter Blackstock, "Dave Alvin: Welcome to the Working Week," *No Depression*, July–August, 1998; John Roos, "Dave Alvin: Strolling Into Folk With Just Plain Folks," *Los Angeles Times*, August 19, 1998.

5. Atkinson, "A Musical Slice of Blue-Collar Life."

6. Dave Alvin, "Ashgrove," *Ashgrove*, YepRoc Records, 2004; for more on Dave Alvin's concerts and his blues influences, see Brian T. Atkinson, "Dave Alvin & the Guilty Men: Tractor Tavern, Seattle," *Maverick Country*, March–April 2005.

7. Dave Alvin, interview with author, November 18, 2008; for links to Dave Alvin on social media, see www.davealvin.net (accessed February 13, 2011).

8. Dave Alvin, interview with author, November 18, 2008.

JOSH RITTER

1. Brian T. Atkinson, "Josh Ritter: Historical Conquests," www.glidemag azine.com, September 4, 2007 (accessed February 13, 2011).

2. Josh Ritter, "Me and Jiggs," *Golden Age of Radio*, Signature Sounds Recordings, 2001; for more on Josh Ritter's popularity in Ireland, see author anonymous, "Hot Press Launches Josh Ritter Week," www.hotpress.com, April 21, 2010 (accessed February 13, 2011).

3. Stephen King, "Stephen King's Top Music Picks of 2006," *Entertainment Weekly*, December 8, 2006; for more on Josh Ritter's breakthrough album *The Animal Years*, see Derk Richardson, "The Big Breakthrough? Josh Ritter's *The Animal Years* Is Earning Wider Recognition for the Folk-Pop Singer," www.sfgate.com, June 1, 2006 (accessed February 13, 2011).

4. Brian T. Atkinson, "Beauty in Uncertainty," *American Songwriter*, May–June 2006, 68–76.

5. For more on Josh Ritter's comparisons to Nick Drake and Bruce Springsteen, see Richardson, "The Big Breakthrough?"; for more on Josh Ritter performing Bruce Springsteen's "The River," see Mike Spinella, "Josh Goes Down to Springsteen's 'River,'" www.spinner.com, October 26, 2007 (accessed February 13, 2011).

6. Brian T. Atkinson, "Josh Ritter at the Parish Room 10/29/2007: Review," www.jambands.com, November 12, 2007 (accessed February 13, 2011).

7. Joan Baez, interview with author, February 14, 2006.

8. Atkinson, "Josh Ritter at the Parish Room."

9. Author anonymous, "Josh Ritter in Concert," www.npr.org, October 9, 2007 (accessed February 13, 2011).

10. Josh Ritter, interview with author, October 14, 2007.

11. Josh Ritter, interview with author, April 26, 2005.

SCOTT AVETT

1. The Avett Brothers, "Murder in the City," *The Second Gleam*, Ramseur Records, 2008.

2. Seth Avett, interview with author, January 7, 2009; for more on the Avett Brothers's influences and connection to Townes Van Zandt, see Scott Timberg, "Avett Brothers Heard Banjo's Siren Call," www.latimes.com, October 1, 2010 (accessed February 13, 2011).

3. Scott Avett, interview with author, January 8, 2009; Brian T. Atkinson, "The Avett Brothers: Life and Art, Ambition and Vision," *American Songwriter*, March–April 2009, 63–71.

4. Scott Avett, interview with author, January 8, 2009.

5. Brian T. Atkinson, "SXSW Interview: The Avett Brothers," *Austin American-Statesman*, March 26, 2009, F10; for more on the Avett Brothers's formative years, see Jedd Ferris, "Bro Interview with the Avett Brothers," www.blueridgeoutdoors.com, May 1, 2008 (accessed February 13, 2011).

6. Atkinson, "The Avett Brothers: Life and Art, Ambition and Vision."

7. Martha Waggoner, "Success Brings Distance From Fans," Associated Press, May 5, 2010; for more on the Avett Brothers's transition from relative obscurity to success, see Mario Tarradell, "Avett Brothers Build a Following," *Dallas Morning News*, January 2, 2010.

8. Derk Richardson, "Avett Brothers Honor North Carolina Roots but Look Forward," www.sfgate.com, August 8, 2009 (accessed February 13, 2011).

9. Seth Avett, interview with author, January 7, 2009.

10. Scott Avett, interview with author, January 8, 2009.

JIM JAMES

1. For more on Jim James and "My Morning Jacket," see J. Douglas Waterman, *Song: The World's Best Songwriters on Creating the Music that Moves Us* (Writer's Digest Books, 2007), 237–41; for more on Cowboy Jack Clement's production of Townes Van Zandt's early albums, see Gritten, "Steve Earle Interview for The Album *Townes*"; Author anonymous, "Was Townes Van Zandt Better Than Dylan?," www.guardian.co.uk/musicblog, February 26, 2008 (accessed February 13, 2011).

2. Hardy, *A Deeper Blue*, 77; "Cowboy" Jack Clement, interview with author, January 9, 2011.

3. Joe Tangari, "Album Review: My Morning Jacket, *It Still Moves*," www.pitchfork.com, September 17, 2003 (accessed February 13, 2011).

4. Patrick MacDonald, "My Morning Jacket: A Ton of Love, But Not A Lot of Sales—Yet," *Seattle Times*, September 26, 2008.

5. Steven Hyden, "Interview: Jim James of My Morning Jacket," www.avclub.com, June 10, 2008 (accessed February 13, 2001).

6. James Montgomery, "Monsters of Folk Are Serious About Supergroup Success," www.mtv.com, August 19, 2009 (accessed February 13, 2011); for more on Monsters of Folk in concert, see Betty Clarke, "Monsters of Folk: Troxy, London," www.guardian.co.uk, November 19, 2009 (accessed February 13, 2011).

7. Elizabeth Marcellino, "Jim James: Interview," www.malibumag.com, December 16, 2009 (accessed February 13, 2011).

8. Jim James, interview with author, May 16, 2004.

ADAM DURITZ

1. Adam Duritz, interview with author, July 31, 2009; for more on Adam Duritz's beginnings, evolution, and thematic focus as a songwriter, see Ryan Spaulding, "Adam Duritz Interview," www.rslblog.com, February 12, 2008 (accessed February 13, 2011).

2. For more on Counting Crows' early success and its affect on Adam Duritz, see Adrian Thrills, "Stone the Crows! As Counting Crows Tour UK, Frontman Adam Duritz Discusses Fame—And Coping with Kurt Cobain's Death," www.dailymail.co.uk, May 15, 2009 (accessed February 13, 2011).

3. For more on Adam Duritz's struggle with dissociative disorder and mental illness, see Paige Richmond, "Q&A: Counting Crows' Adam Duritz: 'It's Probably Time to Get a Life Now,'" www.seattleweekly.com, July 15, 2009 (accessed February 13, 2011).

4. For more on the Counting Crows' split with Geffen Records, see Clark Collis, "Adam Duritz Exclusive: Why Counting Crows Left Geffen," www.music-mix.ew.com, March 18, 2009 (accessed February 13, 2011).

5. For more on Counting Crows' approach to Internet marketing, see Josh Hathaway, "Introducing Saturday Nights & Sunday Mornings: Interview with Counting Crows' Adam Duritz," www.blogcritics.com, April 21, 2008 (accessed February 13, 2011); and Bill Palmer, "iProng Interview: Counting Crows Lead Singer Adam Duritz," www.beatweek.com, March 26, 2008 (accessed February 13, 2011).

6. For more on the Counting Crows' Traveling Circus and Medicine

Show, see Brian T. Atkinson, "Count on Collaboration at Crows' Show," *Austin American-Statesman*, August 3, 2009, D2; and Mike Ragogna, "Augustana & Beyond: A Conversation with Counting Crows' Adam Duritz," www.huffing tonpost.com, August 4, 2010 (accessed February 13, 2011).

7. Adam Duritz, interview with author, July 31, 2009.

KASEY CHAMBERS

1. Brian T. Atkinson, "Rocky Mountain Folks Festival Review," *Maverick Country*, November 2005; Kasey Chambers, interview with author, June 20, 2003.

2. Kasey Chambers, interview with author, June 20, 2003; for more on The Dead Ringer Band and Kasey Chambers' early years in music, see Alden and Blackstock, *The Best of No Depression*, 149–152.

3. Alden and Blackstock, *The Best of No Depression*, 152.

4. Alden and Blackstock, *The Best of No Depression*, 147; Brian T. Atkinson, "Carnival Review," *American Songwriter*, November–December 2006, 89.

5. Dave Dawson, "Interview with Steve Earle," www.nucountry.com.au/ articles/davesdiary.htm, February 5, 2004 (accessed February 13, 2011).

6. Kasey Chambers, interview with author, June 1, 2009.

7. For more on the Americana Music Association and past award winners, see www.americanamusic.org (accessed February 13, 2011).

8. Brian T. Atkinson, "Couple Takes Partnership into Studio," *Austin American-Statesman*, June 22, 2009, D2.

9. Kasey Chambers, interview with author, June 1, 2009.

10. Kasey Chambers, interview with author, June 20, 2003.

CHORUS: DARDEN SMITH

1. Darden Smith, e-mail interview with author, June 30, 2003.

2. Darden Smith, e-mail interview with author, June 30, 2003.

KEVIN RUSSELL

1. Brian T. Atkinson, "South Austin Roots Are No Masquerade," *Austin American-Statesman*, H2, December 28, 2008, H2.

2. Goodman, *Modern Twang*, 130; for more on The Gourds' early years and evolution as songwriters, see Hobart Rowland, Craig D. Lindsey and Brad Tyer, "In Gourds Country," www.houstonpress.com, October 24, 1996 (accessed February 13, 2011); and Nicole Barnett, "The Gourds Interview: SXSW 2010," www.spinner.com, March 16, 2010 (accessed February 13, 2011).

3. Brian T. Atkinson, "Gourds Review: Jovita's Austin, TX—12/29," www.jambands.com, January 5, 2008 (accessed February 13, 2011); Brian T. Atkinson, "The Gourds Fans Eat Them Up," www.countrystandardtime.com, January 13, 2007 (accessed February 13, 2011).

4. Brian T. Atkinson, "Hanging in the Ballads," *Austin Music*, July–August 2007, 18–21; for more on the Gourds' early years, see Goodman, *Modern Twang*, 130–31.

5. Atkinson, "Hanging in the Ballads," *Austin Music*, July–August 2007, 18–21; for more on the Gourds' innovative interpretations, see Chris Gray, "The Country Soul of R. Kelly's 'Feelin' On Yo' Booty," www.houstonpress.com, January 16, 2009 (accessed February 13, 2011).

6. For more on the Gourds' later albums, see William Michael Smith, "Lonesome On'ry, and Mean: The Gourds, Part 3," www.houstonpress.com, January 8, 2009 (accessed February 13, 2011).

7. Kevin Russell, interview with author, July 24, 2004.

8. Kevin Russell, interview with author, July 24, 2004.

TERRI HENDRIX

1. Terri Hendrix, interview with author, May 14, 2010.

2. For more on Terri Hendrix and Lloyd Maines's musical partnership, see Hartman, *History of Texas Music*, 191–92; for more on Terri Hendrix's overall career, see Kathleen Hudson, *Women in Texas Music* (Austin: University of Texas Press, 2007), 20–28.

3. Brian T. Atkinson, "Hendrix Puts Lively Mix in New Album," *Austin American-Statesman*, May 29, 2010, F2; for more on Terri Hendrix's approach to songwriting, see Nichole Wagner, "10 Questions: Terri Hendrix," www.uncommonmusic.org, August 3, 2009 (accessed February 13, 2011).

4. For more on Townes Van Zandt's legendary live performances, see Kruth, *To Live's To Fly*, 120–123.

5. Terri Hendrix, interview with author, September 28, 2004.

6. Hartman, *History of Texas Music*, 191; for more on Terri Hendrix's Wilory Records, see Goodman, *Modern Twang*, 152.

7. Terri Hendrix, interview with author, May 14, 2010.

8. Atkinson, "Hendrix Puts Lively Mix in New Album."

9. Terri Hendrix, interview with author, September 28, 2004.

BUTCH HANCOCK

1. Brian T. Atkinson, "A Cactus Café Legend Remembered," *Austin American-Statesman*, March 7, 2009, F2.

2. For more on The Flatlanders' Butch Hancock, see Kingsbury, *Encyclopedia of Country Music*, 226–27.

3. Margaret Brown, *Be Here to Love Me*, Palm Pictures, 2005; for more on Joe Ely meeting Townes Van Zandt and its effect on The Flatlanders, see Hardy, *A Deeper Blue*, 87, and Kruth, *To Live's To Fly*, 87–88.

4. Butch Hancock, interview with Richard Skanse, May 2001.

5. For more on Butch Hancock's solo work, see Goodman, *Modern Twang*, 142–43; for more on Butch Hancock and the Flatlanders, see Dawidoff, *In the Country of Country*, 291–307; Carlin, *Country Music*, 172–73; Alden and Blackstock, *The Best of No Depression*, 64–76.

6. For more on Butch Hancock's "No Two Alike" shows at the Cactus Café in 1990, see Goodman, *Modern Twang*, 142; for more on Hancock's reprisal of "No Two Alike" in 2010, see Michael Corcoran, "No-Repeat Reprise: As He Did in 1990, Hancock Will Play 5 Distinct Sets," www.austin360.com, August 9, 2010 (accessed February 13, 2011).

7. Patrick Caldwell, "No Two More Alike at the Cactus Café: Night Five," www.austin360.com, August 15, 2010 (accessed February 13, 2011); for more on Townes Van Zandt's connection to the Cactus Café, see Brad Buchholz, "Embracing the Cactus," www.austin360.com, January 29, 2004 (accessed February 13, 2011).

8. Jimmie Dale Gilmore, interview with Richard Skanse, May 2001.

9. Butch Hancock, interview with author, February 17, 2009.

JACK INGRAM

1. Koster, *Texas Music*, 73.

2. Jack Ingram, interview with author, October 9, 2004.

3. For more on Jack Ingram's early career, comparisons to Robert Earl Keen, and the pair's appearance on *Austin City Limits*, see Goodman, *Modern Twang*, 171–72.

4. For more on Jack Ingram, see Maddy Pumilia, "Interview Jack Ingram, Country Singer," www.blogcritics.com, Aug. 11, 2008 (accessed February 13, 2011), and Nancy Dunham, "Jack Ingram Checks Fans into Acoustic Motel Tour," www.theboot.com, March 26, 2010 (accessed February 13, 2011).

5. Dutton, *True to the Roots*, 1.

6. Brian T. Atkinson, "Jack Ingram: *This Is It* Review," *Austin Music*, March–April 2007, 44.

7. Stephen L. Betts, "Jack Ingram Sets Guinness World Record," www.theboot.com, August 26, 2009 (accessed February 13, 2011).

8. Jack Ingram, interview with author, January 29, 2010.

9. Jack Ingram, interview with author, October 9, 2004.

GRACE POTTER

1. Brian T. Atkinson, "Grace Potter and the Nocturnals: ACL Interview," www.austin360.com, September 24, 2010 (accessed February 13, 2011).

2. For critical praise of Grace Potter and the Nocturnals, see Stephen Holden, "The Sound of the '70s from a Singer in Her 20s," www.nytimes .com, February 25, 2008 (accessed February 13, 2011); Jon Dolan, "Grace Potter and the Nocturnals: *Grace Potter and the Nocturnals*," www.rolling stone.com, June 8, 2010 (accessed February 13, 2011); William Michael Smith, "Otis Redding, Jayhawks Help Us Overcome The Mailbox Cringe," www.houstonpress.com, May 12, 2010 (accessed February 13, 2011).

3. Grace Potter, interview with author, September 23, 2010.

DISCOGRAPHY

A SELECTED DISCOGRAPHY FOR TOWNES VAN ZANDT

1. *For the Sake of the Song*, Poppy Records, 1968.
2. *Our Mother the Mountain*, Poppy Records, 1969.
3. *Townes Van Zandt*, Poppy Records, 1970.
4. *Delta Momma Blues*, Poppy Records, 1971.
5. *High, Low and In Between*, Poppy Records, 1972.
6. *The Late, Great Townes Van Zandt*, Poppy Records, 1972.
7. *Live at the Old Quarter*, Tomato Records, 1977.
8. *Flyin' Shoes*, Tomato Records, 1978.
9. *At My Window*, Sugar Hill Records, 1987.
10. *Live and Obscure*, Sugar Hill Records, 1987.
11. *The Nashville Sessions*, Tomato Records, 1993.
12. *Rear View Mirror*, Sundown Records, 1993.
13. *Road Songs*, Sugar Hill Records, 1994.
14. *No Deeper Blue*, Sugar Hill Records, 1994.
15. *Townes Van Zandt: Live at McCabe's*, Varese Sarabande Records, 1996.
16. *In Pain*, Normal Records, 1996.
17. *Highway Kind*, Normal Records, 1997.
18. *The Highway Kind*, Sugar Hill Records, 1997.
19. *Last Rights*, Gregor Records, 1997.
20. *Townes Van Zandt: Anthology*, Charly Records, 1998.
21. *A Far Cry from Dead*, Arista Records, 1999.
22. *Steve Earle, Townes Van Zandt, Guy Clark: Together at the Bluebird Café*, American Originals Records, 2001.
23. *Texas Troubadour*, Charly Records, 2001.
24. *Texas Rain: The Texas Hill Country Recordings*, Tomato Records, 2001.
25. *Absolutely Nothing*, Normal Records, 2002.

26. *A Gentle Evening with Townes Van Zandt*, Dualtone Records, 2002.

27. *Legend: The Very Best of Townes Van Zandt*, Charly Records, 2003.

28. *Acoustic Blue*, Tomato Records, 2003.

29. *In the Beginning*, Compadre Records, 2003.

30. *Rear View Mirror: Volume Two*, Varese Sarabande, 2004.

31. *Live at the Jester Lounge, Houston, Texas, 1966*, Normal Records, 2004.

32. *Live at Union Chapel, London, England*, Tomato Records, 2005.

A SELECTED DISCOGRAPHY FOR TOWNES VAN ZANDT TRIBUTE ALBUMS

1. Jonell Mosser, *Around Townes*, Winter Harvest Entertainment, 1996.

2. Various Artists, *Poet: A Tribute to Townes Van Zandt*, Perdenales Records, 2001.

3. Various Artists, *There's a Hole in Heaven Where Some Sin Slips Trough*, Glitterhouse Records, 2007.

4. Various Artists, *Introducing Townes Van Zandt Via the Great Unknown*, For the Sake of the Song Records, 2009.

5. Steve Earle, *Townes*, New West Records, 2009.

6. Various Artists, *More Townes Van Zandt by the Great Unknown*, For the Sake of the Song Records, 2010.

7. Various artists, *Riding the Range: The Songs of Townes Van Zandt*, Righteous Records, 2010.

A SELECTED VIDEOGRAPHY FOR TOWNES VAN ZANDT

1. James Szalapski, *Heartworn Highways*, Catfish Entertainment, 1981.

2. Harold F. Eggers Jr., *Townes Van Zandt, Houston 1988: A Private Concert*, Varese Sarabande, 2004.

3. Margaret Brown, *Townes Van Zandt: Be Here to Love Me*, Palm Pictures, 2005.

4. *Townes Van Zandt: Live in Amsterdam*, TVZ Records, 2008.

There's no stronger wind than the one that blows down the

lonesome railroad line

No prettier sight than looking back on a town you left behind

—Townes Van Zandt, *"I'll Be Here in the Morning"*

In fond memory of Sharon Barr, my Arizona Star

INDEX

Other titles in the
JOHN AND ROBIN DICKSON SERIES IN TEXAS MUSIC:

The History of Texas Music   Gary Hartman
Texas Blues: The Rise of a Contemporary Sound   Alan Govenar